23.

24.

22.

The Entrées

GAIL MONAGHAN

The Entrées

REMEMBERED FAVORITES FROM THE PAST

Recipes from Legendary Chefs and Restaurants

Photographs by

ERIC BOMAN

Foreword by

GEORGE LANG

RIZZOLI
NEW YORK

For Tess, Kate, and Jeremiah

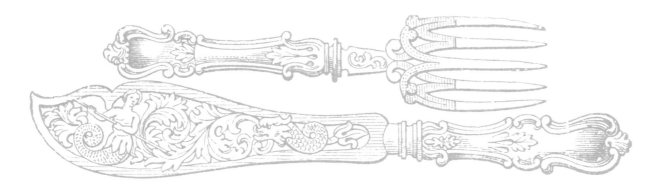

Contents

OMELETTES, MAIN COURSE SALADS, PASTA, and POLENTA

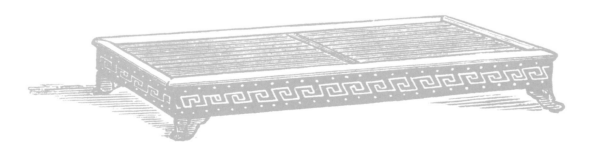

Foreword

BY GEORGE LANG

Forgive me if I am sounding a bit hazy as I write this paean to Gail Monaghan's new book. I feel as if I am recovering from jet lag, after consuming this magnificent tome in one sitting. You see, Gail has taken me on a very elaborate journey, to lovely places all over the world, in this century and in the past, and I didn't even have to leave home to get there.

Gail is a beautiful and sophisticated woman who is filled with charm and energy. She has elegant, stylish friends everywhere, and she wants you to enjoy them as much as she does. Sometimes these friends are alive and well today, and sometimes they are from days gone by, such as Diamond Jim Brady and Julia Child. They all have stories to tell, and—like all delicious tales—they involve food.

Isn't it delightful to know that the Duchess of Windsor, Wallis Simpson, who coined the phrase, "A woman can't be too rich or too thin," devoured cookbooks and set a magnificent table? She even wrote a cookbook and revealed that during her courtship with Edward, Prince of Wales, she cooked him a meal of southern American specialties from her childhood.

Gail has mined the past for the best classical recipes, ones with good stories, of course, but also recipes for food that tastes good, food with substance as well as sustenance.

My own culinary journey also began with classical, but music rather than recipes. When I came to the United States from Hungary in the late 1940s, I was a violinist. After working as a professional musician (under Serge Koussevitzky and in the Dallas Symphony Orchestra, among others), I put down the fiddle and switched professions: I got a job as a cook in the great Plaza Hotel in New York. This cavernous kitchen recalled the nineteenth century, blocks long and filled with classically trained European-born chefs. Their skill level was as daunting as that of the musical prodigies I had worked with.

One of the most memorable dishes I learned from the great *chef de cuisine* of the Plaza, Humbert Gatti, was pot-au-feu. This dish exists in some form in many countries: *tafelspitz, bollito misto*, New England boiled dinner. Gail offers us the French version—which has been called "the foundation of empires"—elaborate and delicious and just as I remember learning it.

When I opened my own restaurant, decades after working at the Plaza, I put pot-au-feu on the menu, of course. It was one of the only places in New York where it could be found at the time, and it remained on the menu for the entire thirty-four years that I owned the Café des Artistes, served in all its glory flanked by luscious marrow bones, coarse salt, toasted peasant bread, and cornichons.

After my stint as a *commis* at the Plaza, my professional progress led me to loftier jobs in the hospitality industry and many honors, but one of the most memorable was when I was asked to write the foreword to the formidable book *Le Répertoire de La Cuisine*, a compendium of classical dishes treasured by every culinarian for nearly one hundred years, providing *aides-mémoires* for all French-trained cooks.

Around the turn of the last century, French psychologist Émile Coué de Châtaigneraie developed a popular self-improvement method based on the hypnotic mantra: "Every day, in every way, I am getting better and better." I would call this a good description of Gail Monaghan and her culinary work. Her new book will give pleasure to so many people in so many ways: reading pleasure, cooking pleasure, eating pleasure, as well as the satisfaction of being benign voyeurs of a lost, luxurious world.

For me, professionalism can be reduced to a holy trinity, revealing the secret to success: Imagination—Craftsmanship—Enthusiasm! Gail embodies this definition beautifully, and her new book is the handbook for the good life, old- and new-style. Gail artfully shows how to keep tradition in the kitchen. Preserving these classics does not mean that living cooks are practicing a dead art, but that talented cooks are very much alive.

Introduction

As a child, I was passionate about food and therefore lucky to belong to a family that found even the slightest occasion an excuse to eat out. The Los Angeles of my childhood was a dining mecca with endless restaurants to choose from, many of them replete with period innocence, elegance, and glamour. I loved the Hobo Steak at Chasen's, Steak Diane at Perino's, Veal Oskar at Scandia, and for simpler evenings, planked steak surrounded by duchesse potatoes at Richlor's or roast beef at Lawry's. Later as a college student in Boston, we ate on campus during the week; but Friday and Saturday nights, Coq au Vin at both Henri IV and Chez Dreyfus in Cambridge made up for hum-drum weekday fare. Durgin-Park had portions of juicy prime rib that far exceeded the edges of the plates, and Anthony's Pier Four's oversize Maine lobsters were swimming in melted butter. I could not wait to graduate, have an apartment of my own, and cook fabulous dishes for myself. Julia Child's and Michael Field's cookbooks taught me to prepare the simple classics I was used to eating in Boston restaurants—perfect roast chicken, Duck à l'Orange, loins of pork and veal, shrimp and chicken curries, braised lamb shanks, and a whole range of stews, as well as the ubiquitous coq au vin.

My graduation coincided with the rise of nouvelle cuisine—created in France by the young Michel Guérard, Alain Chapel, Paul Bocuse, and Jean and Pierre Troisgrois—which soon marginalized the classic dishes I loved. Shorter menus and cooking times; simpler and lighter marinades, sauces, and preparations; and the freshest possible ingredients seduced diners and the press. For a number of years, it was hard to find "old-fashioned" food in popular upscale restaurants where the more precious, plated dishes had become the norm. By the mid-1980s, however, nouvelle cuisine became a hodge-podge, a parody of itself and a far cry from its original simplicity. As the fascination with nouvelle cuisine waned, chefs returned to a more classic repertoire, though one considerably edited and lightened as a result of the intervening revolution.

Once again, in this second decade of the twenty-first century, the re-worked classics are reappearing on restaurant menus as proprietors cater to a nostalgic clientele seeking the satisfaction of old favorites. But one needn't depend on restaurants. Lacking superfluous fuss and extra frills and garnishes, these dishes lend themselves to home-kitchen preparation. Make them to indulge and pamper family and special friends. What could be more welcome in winter than piping hot chicken à la king or a seafood pot pie? In fair weather, The Brown Derby's Cobb Salad is still one of the better meals on the planet. And guests will applaud an elegant table with succulent Beef Stroganoff, steaming Cioppino, crispy Hash à la Lübeck, or mustard-slathered leg of lamb in the center.

In a culture of speed, efficiency, and multitasking, the leisurely repast is getting harder to find. This book revisits past eras where hours, weeks, and even months drift by like the breezes of summer. Granted, a great dinner—or even a series of them—does not obliterate the world's woes, but taking time to celebrate the moment with carefully prepared food and a glass of wine is a good place to start. Lingering over a meal is one of the easiest ways to step back in time.

Beef Wellington, Coulibiac of Salmon, or Chicken Tetrazzini arriving at table, all crispy and golden—served up only after being ogled and admired—heralded a sense of festivity and occasion. Fragrant Beef Bourguignon, navarin of lamb, veal Marengo, and pot-au-feu, when served from communal pots or tureens, encouraged feelings of comaraderie and well-being. Sizzling crown roasts of pork and lamb as well as juicy and delectable chickens and ducks were carved tableside, filling dining rooms with a cozy yet glamorous intimacy. These historically relevant main courses—often having originated in palaces, grand homes, or famous restaurants—were beloved staples of generations past. In addition, contemporary chefs draw on these dishes in their attempt to make the tried-and-true once again new.

The majority of recipes in *The Entrées* are adapted from old cookbooks and from archival newspaper and magazine articles, but also included are several "heirloom" recipes passed on to me by friends and relatives. In certain cases, updating, reinvention, and reinterpretation seemed appropriate. Palates have changed from a time when ignorance was bliss, when butter, cream, and rich sauces existed solely to enhance a meal and a moment, their cholesterol and calorie content lacking in relevance.

As hundreds of wonderful old dishes culled from the heel of Italy's boot to the Bosporus and Havana deserve a place in the contemporary kitchen, reining in my selection was difficult. In the end, choices were personal and probably a bit idiosyncratic. Absolute criteria, however, were that each dish be delicious, not call for unduly expensive ingredients, and be easily reproducible at home in my kitchen. I am grateful that researching this book led me to discover Chicken à la Portugaise, Shad Roe Soufflé, Girardet's Monkfish Stew, Chicken Country Captain, and Chez Allard's Guinea Hens accompanied by the best lentil dish I have ever eaten. I hope these lesser-known dishes—as well as the more renowned classics in the book—will become part of your regular culinary repertoire, just as they've become part of mine.

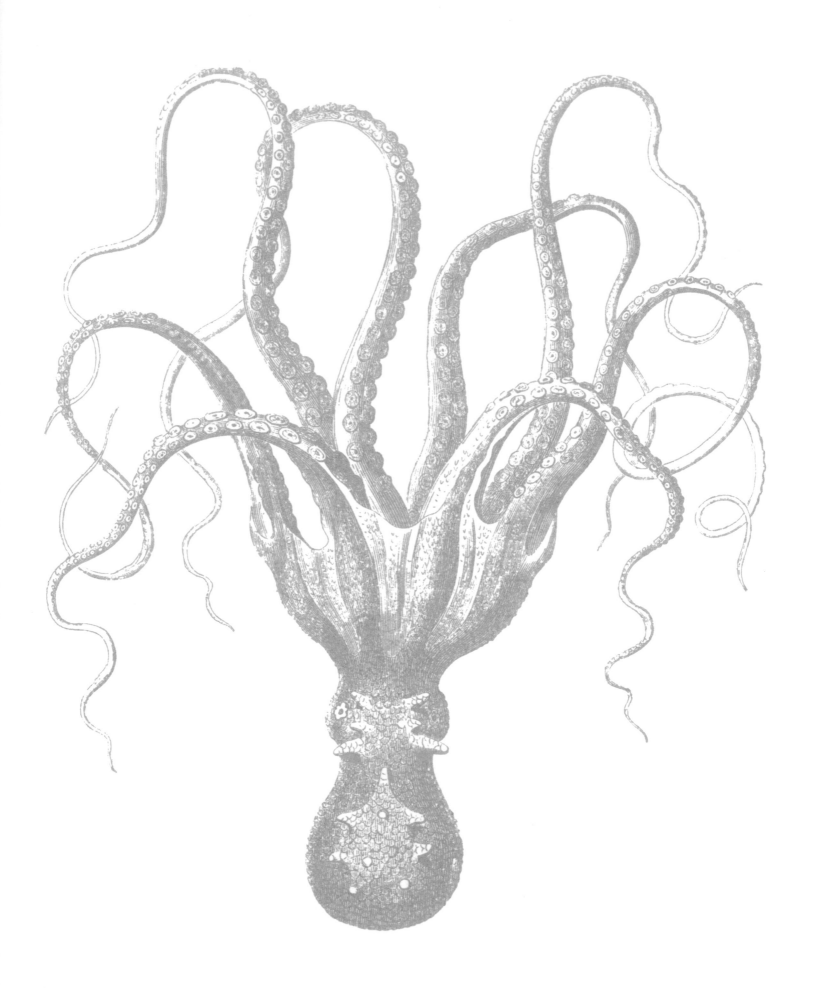

FISH and SHELLFISH

Diamond Jim Brady's Sole Marguery

Bass à la Dugléré

Roast Cod à la Dugléré with Tomato and Caper Vinaigrette

Fredy Girardet's Skate Wing with Mustard Butter and Dill

Le Grand Véfour's Coulibiac of Salmon Colette

Jeremiah Tower's Paillard of Tuna with Avocado, Lime, and Cilantro

Restaurant Dodin-Bouffant's Sautéed Soft-shell Crabs
with Sauce Choron and Cucumber-Hazelnut Slaw

Louis Fauchère's Lobster Newburg

Charleston Receipts' Frogmore Stew

Fisherman's Wharf Cioppino

Fredy Girardet's Monkfish and Salmon Stew with
Green Peas, Fava Beans, and Saffron

Vedat Basaran's Stuffed Squid

The Brown Derby's Seafood Pot Pie

Wallis Simpson's Shrimp and Corn Pie

Gene Hovis's Shad Roe Soufflé

Sole Marguery

In "G is for Gluttony," a chapter in *An Alphabet for Gourmets*, M.F.K. Fisher compares Diamond Jim Brady to an Olympic athlete based on his superhuman capacity for eating. Citing a well-worn anecdote in which Brady downed nine servings of Sole Marguery in one sitting, Fisher writes, "I myself would like to be able to eat that much of something I really delight in, and can recognize overtones of envy in the way lesser mortals so easily damned Brady as a glutton even in the days of excess when he flourished."

At his birth on August 12, 1856, in New York City, there were no indications that James Buchanan Brady would become the most flamboyant tycoon of the Gilded Age. The vast fortune he amassed while working his way up from bellboy to railroad magnate allowed him to indulge his two greatest passions—diamonds and food. Brady wore bigger diamonds and more at once than a dozen other robber barons combined, and his collected jewels were worth over two million dollars (approximately sixty million if adjusted for today's dollar). And the man's insatiable appetite and enormous girth were as legendary as his wealth. Diamond Jim ate from the moment he got up in the morning until he dropped into bed early the next. An avid theatergoer, most nights found him dining at Rector's, both before and after the play, polishing off enough for ten in one sitting, and always washed down with at least a gallon of orange juice. Breakfast included eggs, pancakes, cornbread, fried potatoes, hominy, muffins, pork chops, and steak. Lunch was no smaller and regularly ended with several whole pies. Large afternoon snacks were the norm, followed by dinner, which usually began with several dozen oysters, six crabs, and a few servings of green turtle soup. A typical main course consisted of two whole canvasback ducks, six or seven lobsters, a huge sirloin steak, two servings of terrapin, and mountains of vegetables. To end the meal, Brady selected eight to ten offerings from the dessert trolley, followed by a platter of pastries often supplemented by a two-pound box of candy.

His third passion—though a lesser one—was Lillian Russell, the famously voluptuous actress, singer, and great beauty of the era. *On the Town in New York* authors Michael and Ariane Batterberry call "Nell" his "natural-born soul and stomach mate," and go on to describe the two of them together as "one of the unnatural phenomena of the era—Lillian with her fabled figure and jewels, Brady with his fabled figure and jewels—as they sat down to a marathon banquet." For years, Diamond Jim defied the grim predictions of the medical community, until, at age fifty-six, he developed serious stomach problems. The fabled eating was over. When he died in 1917, five years later, the autopsy found his stomach had expanded to six times its normal size.

Nicolas Marguery, chef and proprietor of the internationally acclaimed Restaurant Marguery, died a few years earlier. His May 1, 1910, *New York Times* obituary read "Famous Restaurateur Dead, Marguery of Paris, Last of the Old-Time Gastronomes." This loyal, sympathetic, and modest officer of the French Legion of Honor was lovingly remembered for feeding his patrons free of charge during the difficult days of the Siege in 1870 while asking nothing in return. He was even more famous, however, for Sole Marguery—his special version of Sole à la Normande—than for all his personal qualities combined. This one dish was his staircase to both fame and fortune, and the normally generous man guarded the secret recipe with ferocity. It was safe until Diamond Jim—known for getting what he set out to get—decided that he wanted it.

On a trip to Paris, Brady dined at Restaurant Marguery, ordered the sole, and begged for the recipe. Denial led to obsession. Once back in New York and eating at Rector's, the ever-determined Brady told Charles Rector that unless he could provide the recipe, Diamond Jim would take his business elsewhere. Brady was probably joking, but Rector could not risk losing the business of his "best twenty-five customers." The next day, Rector's son George was pulled out of law school and sent off to Paris to hijack the elusive recipe. George, having spent summers in his father's kitchens, was already an accomplished cook and cleverly apprenticed himself to Nicolas Marguery under an assumed name. Beginning as a busboy, young Rector worked his way up the ladder to waiter and then sous-chef. But it took more than two years at Marguery before the would-be lawyer could return home, the coveted knowledge in hand. His father and Diamond Jim were waiting eagerly on the dock. Even before the gangplank was lowered, George heard Brady's big voice bellow out "Did you get the recipe?" George was immediately trundled off to Rector's and ordered to start cooking.

Thank goodness, the sole was as Brady remembered—the creamy, yet flavorful seafood sauce perfectly bringing together the various components of the dish. Brady ate his fabled nine helpings and proclaimed himself utterly satisfied. I don't suggest consuming nine portions, but this fish and shellfish medley is addictive, and you may be tempted to have more than one.

Serves 2

12 medium shrimp in the shell
1 cup dry white wine
2 cups best-quality fish stock
1 onion, peeled and thinly sliced
1 carrot, peeled and chopped
6 sprigs fresh flat-leaf parsley
24 mussels, debearded and well scrubbed
1 sole weighing approximately 2 pounds (have the fishmonger fillet the fish, and include the head, bones, and trimmings); flounder may be substituted

Sea salt and freshly ground (preferably white) pepper to taste
2 egg yolks, beaten in a medium bowl with ½ cup heavy cream
Large pinch of nutmeg, or to taste
12 oysters, shucked by your fishmonger, oyster liquor reserved

1. Place the shrimp in a medium saucepan along with the wine and fish stock. Bring to a boil over high heat and then simmer until the shrimp are done, about 5 minutes.

2. Drain and save both the shrimp and the liquid.

3. Put the liquid back into the saucepan. Add the onion, carrot, parsley, and then the mussels. Bring to a boil, then lower the heat to a simmer and cover. Cook until the mussels open, about 5 minutes. Remove them from the pan using tongs or a slotted spoon. When they are cool enough to handle, remove them from their shells and discard the shells. Set the mussels aside.

4. While the mussels are cooking, shell the cooked shrimp. Reserve the shrimp and the shells separately.

5. Once the mussels are removed from the pan, rinse the fish head, bones, and trimmings, and add them to the pan along with the shrimp shells. Bring to a boil, then reduce the heat to low and simmer for 30 minutes, then skim and strain through a fine sieve. Reserve the liquid and discard the contents of the sieve.

6. Place the sole in a pan just large enough to hold the fillets side by side. Pour the fish stock from Step 5 over, and season with salt and pepper. The liquid should barely cover the fish. If there is not enough to do so, add water. Place the pan over low heat and cook for about 8 minutes, until the fish is done. If using flounder, which is thicker, extend the cooking time by a few minutes.

7. Remove the fillets from the pan and set aside to keep warm. Preheat the broiler to high.

8. Reduce the fish-cooking liquid over high heat to approximately ¾ cup. Off heat, very slowly, while whisking, add the reduced liquid to the egg yolk mixture to make a smooth, thick sauce. Season with salt, pepper, and nutmeg. Pour the sauce back into the pan and cook over medium-low heat, stirring constantly, until the sauce thickens and can coat the back of a spoon. Be careful not to let the sauce come anywhere near a boil or it will curdle.

9. Arrange the fish on a buttered gratin dish or heatproof platter, and place the shrimp, mussels, and oysters over and around the fish. Pour the sauce over all, and glaze under the broiler until golden, 1 to 2 minutes. Watch carefully to prevent burning.

10. Serve with lots of white rice or buttered noodles.

Note: If desired, 8 very small white button mushrooms, stems removed, can be poached along with the fish. Arrange them in the gratin dish along with the fish and shellfish before pouring the sauce over all.

Bass à la Dugléré

Café Anglais opened in Paris in 1802 to a clientele of coachmen and domestic servants, but soon the eatery was discovered and frequented by actors and patrons of the Opera House nearby. In 1822, Paul Chevreuil bought and upgraded the restaurant, turning it into a place to see and be seen. However, it was not until 1866 with the arrival of Chef Adolphe Dugléré—a pupil of Antonin Carême and an ex-*chef de cuisine* of Rothschilds—that the café became a watering hole for the *crème de la crème* of Parisian society. Dugléré's culinary creations—Potage Germiny; sole, bass, and sea bream à la Dugléré; soufflé à l'anglaise; Tournedos Rossini; and Potatoes Anna, created for Anna Deslions, one of the most famous courtesans of the era—solidified its position as Paris's most famous Second Empire restaurant.

By adding diced tomatoes to his lightly sauced baked sole preparation, Chef Adolphe Dugléré claimed a prominent place for himself in the immortal annals of fish cookery. He went on to cook a variety of fish in this manner (called à la "dugléré"), most frequently bass or the original sole. The delicate sauce allows the subtle flavors of fresh fish and tomatoes to shine through. Don't even think of trying this recipe with insipid winter tomatoes or borderline fish. If flavorful summer tomatoes aren't available, substitute the canned San Marzano variety. The fish may be cooked up to three hours in advance and left at room temperature. In this case, pour the hot sauce over the fish just before serving. Either rice or mashed potatoes is a good partner for the extra sauce.

Serves 4

3 tablespoons unsalted butter, cut into small pieces, plus
   approximately 2 tablespoons to butter the baking dish
1 large onion, peeled and chopped
2 large shallots, peeled and chopped
1 cup diced white button or cremini mushrooms
1 cup diced fresh fennel, including some fennel fronds
4 cloves garlic, peeled and minced
4 large very ripe and flavorful tomatoes, peeled, seeded,
   and chopped (or substitute canned San Marzano
   tomatoes)
1¼ cups coarsely chopped fresh flat-leaf parsley
1 cup coarsely chopped fresh basil
½ bay leaf
3 sprigs fresh thyme, or ⅛ teaspoon dried thyme
½ teaspoon finely grated lemon zest
Sea salt and freshly ground pepper to taste
1 whole sea bass weighing 2 to 2½ pounds, scaled,
   cleaned, and boned, with head left on
¾ cup dry white wine, or good fish stock, or some
   of each
1 to 2 tablespoons *beurre manié*, made by blending
   equal amounts of butter and flour into a paste
1 teaspoon freshly squeezed lemon juice, or to taste

1. Preheat the oven to 425 degrees. Generously butter a shallow flameproof and ovenproof dish or pan.
2. Toss the chopped onion, shallots, mushrooms, fennel, garlic, tomatoes, half the parsley, and half the basil together in the pan. Add the bay leaf, thyme, lemon zest, salt, and pepper. Lay the bass on top of the vegetables. Season it inside and out with salt and pepper. Dot the fish with the butter and moisten with the wine and/or stock.
3. Cover tightly with foil, bring to a boil over high heat on the stovetop, then place in the oven and bake for 20 to 30 minutes, until the fish is cooked through and flaky.
4. Transfer the bass with a slotted spatula to a hot platter. Keep warm.
5. Remove the bay leaf and the thyme sprig, if used. Place the pan over high heat and reduce by about one third. The sauce should be a little thicker than heavy cream. This will take 10 to 15 minutes. While reducing, add the *beurre manié* and cook for at least 5 minutes more to cook the flour. When reduced, add most of the remaining parsley and basil. Adjust the seasonings with salt, pepper, and lemon juice.
6. Pour the sauce over the fish, sprinkle with the last of the basil and parsley, and serve.

Note: Striped bass or snapper may be substituted. If whole fish is hard to come by, use 2½ pounds of hake, cod, or halibut fillets. Cooking times may need adjusting.

Roast Cod à la Dugléré

WITH TOMATO AND CAPER VINAIGRETTE

For this recipe, I've retained Dugléré's concept of fish with a Mediterranean tomato sauce poured over. The basic ingredients are essentially the same as for the Bass à la Dugléré, but the addition of capers and orange and lemon juice and zest provides a more robust result. Make the easy raw summer sauce and the fish in advance, so there is no last-minute work in a hot kitchen. Multicolored tomatoes, green herbs, and paper-thin purple onion rings atop white fish create a stunning presentation piece. Served warm or at room temperature, the dish is perfect for entertaining when tomatoes are at their peak.

Serves 6 to 8

3 to 4 pounds cod fillets (halibut, haddock, or hake may be substituted)
¼ cup extra virgin olive oil mixed with 2 cloves minced garlic, the grated zest of 1 lemon, a few drops of Tabasco sauce, and pepper to taste
Sea salt to taste
Tomato and Caper Vinaigrette (recipe follows)

1. Marinate the fish in the oil mixture for at least 15 minutes, though ideally for 1 to 2 hours.
2. Preheat the oven to its hottest setting (500 or 525 degrees). Place a metal pan or baking sheet with low sides—large enough to hold the fish with plenty of room around each one, so the fish bakes and does not steam—in the oven for 10 minutes, or until very hot. Remove the pan from the oven, and quickly lay the fish pieces in the pan at least 2 inches apart. They should sizzle. Salt liberally.
3. Bake for 15 to 20 minutes, until the fish juices begin to ooze white and opaque rather than transparent (the juices will mix with the oil), and the fish is flaky.
4. Transfer the fish to a large platter. The fish may be served hot, warm, or at room temperature. When ready to eat it, spoon the vinaigrette over and serve.

Note: Large pieces of fish are preferable, but you can substitute several smaller pieces. If using pieces, buy or cut them to be more or less equal in size for even cooking.

TOMATO AND CAPER VINAIGRETTE

Makes approximately 6 cups

1 cup extra virgin olive oil
6 tablespoons freshly squeezed lemon juice
Finely grated zest of 2 lemons
Finely grated zest and freshly squeezed juice of 1 orange
¼ cup salted capers, soaked for 1 hour or more in several changes of cool water, or ¼ cup vinegar-packed capers (in either case, rinsed and well-drained)
2 large shallots or 1 medium red onion, peeled and sliced paper-thin
1 bulb fresh fennel, trimmed, halved vertically, and sliced paper-thin
3 cups quartered ripe cherry tomatoes
1 navel orange, peel removed with a knife so no pith remains, and cut into 10 segments
Sea salt and freshly ground black pepper to taste

1. Stir all the ingredients together in a medium bowl. This can be done up to 5 hours before serving. Do not refrigerate.
2. When ready to serve, adjust the salt and pepper.

Skate Wing

WITH MUSTARD BUTTER AND DILL

Joel Robuchon called Fredy Girardet *"le plus grand des grands chefs sur notre planete."* In his heyday, Girardet was considered by many to be the greatest living chef. From 1982 until 1996, when he sold the Michelin three-starred Girardet's, this master chef was always there behind the stove. His sole aim in life was to please his adoring customers. Everyone—from Richard Nixon to Johnny Weissmuller, Jacques Brel, and Salvador Dalí—made an appearance to enjoy the exquisite food and unpretentious atmosphere. The great man never left the premises during opening hours; it was said that if Girardet could not be in his kitchen, the restaurant would close for the day. In contrast to most other top French chefs, he spent no time or energy endorsing and consulting, nor did he seek celebrity or society status or appear on television. Everything was about the customer and the quality of the food.

Girardet's father had been the chef-proprietor of a bistro located in the Old Town Hall of Crissier, a suburb of Lausanne. When he died unexpectedly at age fifty-six, Fredy took over with a repertoire far beyond that of a simple bistro. His renditions of the classics were perfection, and fame and recognition grew. To keep himself amused, Girardet began experimenting. Like his counterparts in France—Bocuse, Outhier, and Vergé, and Robuchon a bit later—he focused on making food lighter and more contemporary. In a country known for cheese and chocolate, Girardet made a name for himself serving turbot pot-au-feu, tournedos of tuna, and sweetbreads wrapped in lettuce leaves. He did nothing, however, for shock value alone. Authenticity always won out, the cuisine being the extension of a man known for a quiet, meticulous manner and an integrity that informed everything he touched.

Fredy Girardet's inspired combination of grainy mustard and a barely cooked cucumber and tomato dice is the basis of the best skate dish I have ever tasted. I've simplified the recipe for the home cook, but none of the exquisite flavors are lost. Fresh dill perfectly complements the complex taste of the mustard sauce and adds a beautiful deep green to the pale green and red vegetables already on the plate. For optimal presentation, serve each person a skate wing with its garnishes on a large plain plate. If you and your guests are particularly hungry, serve a starchy first course—a mushroom or asparagus risotto or pasta would be a good choice. Or just follow the skate with cheese and a salad. Berries are a lovely dessert in summer, and a fruit tart is welcome any time of year.

This sauce and vegetable mix can be paired with other white fish—halibut, cod, flounder, sole, bass, snapper, or swordfish—or with chicken breast or turkey scaloppini (replace the fish stock with poultry stock). The mustard butter alone is delicious smeared over a hot steak just off the grill.

Serves 6

For the mustard butter:

9 tablespoons unsalted butter, softened

¼ cup whole-grain French mustard

Freshly squeezed juice of 1 small lemon

Cayenne pepper to taste

Sea salt and freshly ground black pepper to taste

For the skate:

Sea salt and freshly ground black pepper to taste

6 thick boneless skate wings weighing approximately
    7 ounces each

2 large shallots, peeled and finely minced

6 tablespoons unsalted butter

½ cup dry white wine

½ cup best-quality fish or shellfish stock

⅓ cup heavy cream

3 large cucumbers, peeled, seeded, and cut into
    small dice

2 large tomatoes, peeled, seeded, and the flesh cut into
    small dice

2 large stalks fresh dill, divided into small sprigs (with
    flower buds even better)

Cayenne pepper to taste

White wine vinegar to taste

1. For the mustard butter, mix together the softened butter, mustard, lemon juice, and cayenne. Add salt and pepper. This is easiest using an electric mixer or food processor.

2. Salt and pepper the skate wings on both sides and use a pastry brush to paint both sides with a bit more than one third of the mustard butter, reserving approximately two thirds for later use. Set aside.

3. For the sauce, cook the shallots with 1½ tablespoons of the butter in a small saucepan over medium heat until golden. Add the wine and fish stock and continue to cook until reduced by half. Add the cream. Boil for 30 seconds, stirring, then remove from the heat. Set aside. The recipe can be prepared a few hours ahead up until this point. The sauce can be refrigerated or left at room temperature. Refrigerate the diced cucumber, diced tomato, and dill sprigs in separate containers, covered and refrigerated until ready to use.

4. When ready to serve, melt 3 tablespoons of butter in a small skillet and cook the diced cucumber for 2 minutes, stirring. Add the diced tomato and half the dill and cook, stirring, until warmed through. Remove from the heat, season with salt and pepper, and set aside.

5. Reheat the sauce over low heat and whisk in the remaining mustard butter, little by little. Still over a very low heat, add cayenne, salt, and pepper, and then brighten with a splash of white wine vinegar. Leave over very low heat while you prepare the fish.

6. In a large nonstick skillet (or use two if necessary), heat the remaining 1½ tablespoons butter until very hot. Cook the skate wings for 30 to 60 seconds per side, until cooked through. If not done, cook a bit more.

7. Serve on warm dinner plates or a warm platter with the sauce spooned over. Garnish with the vegetable-dill sauté and the reserved fresh dill sprigs.

Coulibiac of Salmon Colette

In the 1950s and '60s, Raymond Oliver was Britain's most celebrated chef. The author of more than thirty cookbooks—including the famed *La Cuisine*—he also gave cooking lessons; led worldwide tours to promote French food; and was the star of a weekly television show, video cassettes, and records. In 1948, at age thirty-nine, Oliver bought Le Grand Véfour, an eighteenth-century restaurant in Paris's Palais Royal. Just six years after the purchase, it was awarded a prized Michelin third star. To quote Oliver's 1990 *New York Times* obituary, "Under the direction of its showman-chef, Le Grand Véfour was for more than two decades the place to be seen in Paris, offering magnificent and innovative food to a distinguished international clientele of serious and grateful eaters."

Often cited as one of the most beautiful and glamorous restaurants in the world, Le Grand Véfour has always been known for culinary brilliance as well as for opulent decor—a riot of gilt, crimson, plush black and white carpeting, sparkling chandeliers, and ornately painted scenes relating to food, women, and wine. The roster of famous patrons ran the gamut from Napoleon, Danton, Flaubert, Balzac, Turgenev, and Hugo to Camus, Sartre, and Simone de Beauvoir. Even now, when booking, you can request the table (marked with a little brass plaque) of your favorite historical regular, many of whom lived in the *quartier* and frequently popped in to check out the menu.

Twice in her life—from 1927 to 1930 and again from 1938 until her death sixteen years later—Colette lived at No. 9 rue de Beaujolais, less than a minute from Véfour. Late in life and crippled with rheumatism, the author of *Gigi* and *Cheri* was carried to her favorite corner table in winter, and in summer to a lovely spot under the arcade of the Palais Royal where she could eat, drink, and reign while commenting on the *haute monde* passersby. The aging Colette (she died in 1954) and Oliver were good friends as well as neighbors, and the chef named his spectacular version of the Russian classic after her, Coulibiac of Salmon Colette.

Coulibiac, an impressive Russian dish of unknown origin, entered the French culinary lexicon in the late 1890s. *Larousse Gastronomique* calls it "a Russian pie filled with fish, vegetables, rice, and hard-boiled eggs. The filling was topped with *vesiga* (dried spinal marrow of the sturgeon), a once indispensable finishing touch to the filling, which added an incomparably rich and pungent savory flavor to the dish." When Europeans adapted the recipe, they omitted the *vesiga* and turned the dish into a familiar *en croute*. Sturgeon, turbot, cabbage, or chicken are alternative fillings, but salmon is still deemed the most authentic. Rice, mushrooms, onions, parsley, dill, shallots, and eggs are mixed or layered with the fish and then enclosed in either a brioche or puff pastry crust. Now the (usually oblong) pie is cooked on a baking sheet, but traditionally it was baked in fish-shaped earthenware. Either way, coulibiac is impressive—festive during the holidays and on other special occasions. And it's user-friendly; most of the components can be readied a day or more in advance and refrigerated until time to assemble the dish. Or put the coulibiac together ahead of time, and then bake to serve. Since

this golden delight is not sliced until it reaches the table, it stays hot for at least thirty minutes once cooked. Coulibiac can also be eaten at room temperature, providing a gorgeous centerpiece for a summer buffet or elegant picnic.

With its crisp and buttery crust and beautiful layers of succulent salmon, rice pilaf, and juicy mushrooms, this dish is unforgettable. Green beans or peas make a fine side dish, though for me the coulibiac needs nothing more than a mixed green or cucumber salad, lemon wedges, and a sauce. Horseradish sauce is traditional, but I prefer a cucumber sour cream that I learned from Joel Kaye, whose parents owned the legendary Russian Tea Room in New York City (recipes follow). Historically, melted butter was poured over the piping hot coulibiac. In this loose adaptation of Oliver's recipe, I have already omitted a half pound of butter. I see no need to put any of it back in.

Serves 8

4 tablespoons (½ stick) unsalted butter
1½ pounds boneless salmon fillet, pin bones removed
    with a tweezer
½ cup Béchamel Sauce (recipe follows)
¼ cup finely grated Gruyère cheese
1 pound white button mushrooms, sliced, sautéed in
    butter, and seasoned with ½ tablespoon dried thyme,
    salt, and pepper (or if you prefer, like Raymond Oliver,
    use ½ pound diced cooked lobster meat instead of
    the mushrooms)
3 tablespoons minced chives
½ cup long-grain rice
1¾ cups fish or shellfish stock
¾ teaspoon chopped fresh thyme leaves, or ¼ teaspoon
    dried thyme
Several sprigs fresh flat-leaf parsley
1 bay leaf
⅛ teaspoon sea salt
Freshly ground black pepper to taste
3 hard-boiled eggs, peeled and minced
2 packages frozen puff pastry, thawed overnight in
    the refrigerator
6 tablespoons unsalted butter, melted
1 egg yolk whisked with 1 tablespoon heavy cream
Horseradish Sauce or Joel Kaye's Cucumber Sauce
    (recipes follow)
Lemon wedges for garnish (optional)

1. Over medium heat, melt the 4 tablespoons butter in a skillet large enough to hold the salmon. Alternatively, you can sauté the salmon in 2 or 3 pieces if that works better given the size of your pan. When the butter has melted, add the salmon to the pan and sauté for about 10 minutes, turning frequently, until the fish is just cooked through. Don't overcook, as it will be cooked a second time in the oven. Set aside the salmon and any pan juices for later use.

2. Heat the Béchamel Sauce to simmering, and off the heat, add the Gruyère. When the cheese has melted, cool to lukewarm and then stir in the sautéed mushrooms (or diced lobster) and chives. Adjust the seasonings and set aside.

3. To make the pilaf, put the rice, 1½ cups fish stock, thyme, parsley, bay leaf, salt, and pepper in a small saucepan. Cover tightly and bring to a boil. Reduce the heat to very low and simmer until the rice is tender, about 20 minutes. Uncover and cool, then fluff with a fork.

4. When the rice has cooled to lukewarm, add any salmon juices and the minced hard-boiled eggs. Adjust the seasonings and set aside.

5. Preheat the oven to 450 degrees. Roll a piece of thawed puff pastry into a rectangle approximately 17 by 12 inches. If this will not fit in your oven, you can make a square. It is easiest to roll the dough between sheets of parchment paper. If the dough gets too soft to work with (and it probably will), put it back in the refrigerator or freezer for a few minutes before continuing. Place the rolled dough on a large parchment-lined unrimmed baking sheet. Cover the rolled dough with a sheet of parchment paper. Prebake, weighted down with another baking sheet and some heavy pots or metal bowls, in the lower part of the oven until firm, about 15 minutes. Remove the weights, baking sheet, and top sheet of paper, and bake until pale gold and crisp, approximately 15 minutes more. Reduce the oven temperature to 400 degrees.

6. Leaving a 1-inch border free, spread the pilaf evenly over the baked crust. Flake the salmon over that, and

sprinkle lightly with salt and pepper. Top evenly with the mushroom or lobster mixture.

7. Mix the remaining ¼ cup fish stock with the 6 table-spoons melted butter and drizzle over the rice.

8. Roll out the other piece of pastry a bit larger than the first piece. Cover the pie and pinch the edges together to seal them. Be sure they are well sealed. Brush with the beaten egg yolk mixture, and use a sharp knife to make several slits in the pastry for steam to escape. Bake in the lower part of the oven until heated through and golden, about 30 minutes. Serve hot, warm, or at room temperature with Horseradish Sauce and lemon wedges or with Joel Kaye's Cucumber Sauce.

BÉCHAMEL SAUCE

Makes approximately 1½ cups

1¼ cups whole milk
1 small onion, peeled and chopped
1 clove garlic, peeled and sliced
A few sprigs fresh flat-leaf parsley
⅛ teaspoon celery seed
⅓ teaspoon whole fennel seed
½ bay leaf, crumbled
2 tablespoons unsalted butter
2 tablespoons all-purpose flour
Sea salt, freshly ground black pepper, and
    grated nutmeg to taste

1. Place the milk in a medium saucepan. Add the onion, garlic, parsley, celery seed, fennel seed, and bay leaf. Bring to a boil, then reduce the heat and simmer for 10 minutes. If not using right away, allow the steeping to continue.

2. To continue, melt the butter in a large saucepan set over medium heat. Add the flour and stir for about 5 minutes. Adjust the heat so the sauce does not color. Strain the milk into the pot and whisk hard so that no lumps form. Continue to whisk until the sauce comes to a simmer. Simmer for 5 to 8 minutes, stirring constantly with a wooden spoon. The sauce is ready when the taste of raw flour is gone and the sauce is thick enough to coat the spoon. Season with salt, pepper, and nutmeg. If not using right away, place a piece of plastic wrap on the surface to prevent a skin from forming and, once cool, refrigerate.

HORSERADISH SAUCE

Makes approximately 1½ cups

6 tablespoons freshly grated horseradish (if fresh horse-radish is unavailable, use bottled white horseradish, well drained)
6 tablespoons mayonnaise (homemade or Hellmann's)
¾ cup crème fraîche or sour cream, stiffly beaten
Sea salt and freshly ground black pepper to taste

1. In a small bowl, combine all the ingredients and serve. The sauce can be made up to 24 hours ahead and refrigerated. This sauce is also delicious on cold asparagus or with smoked fish.

JOEL KAYE'S CUCUMBER SAUCE

Makes approximately 2½ cups

1 small cucumber, peeled and coarsely grated
1 tablespoon sea salt
2¼ cups sour cream or crème fraîche
3 tablespoons finely minced fresh dill
3 tablespoons finely snipped fresh chives
Freshly squeezed lemon or lime juice to taste (or even
    better, a mixture, about 1 tablespoon total)
Freshly ground black or white pepper to taste

1. Mix the grated cucumber with the salt and set aside for at least an hour. Rinse and drain the cucumber in cool water, then squeeze it in a kitchen towel to dry.

2. In a medium bowl, mix the cucumber, sour cream, herbs, and seasonings to taste. Set aside for at least an hour to allow the flavors to combine. This sauce can be made up to 24 hours ahead—stir well before serving and adjust the seasonings.

JEREMIAH TOWER'S

Paillard of Tuna

WITH AVOCADO, LIME, AND CILANTRO

Jeremiah Tower's larger-than-life personal presence belies his poetic talent. In 2001, *Wine Spectator*, describing Tower's stint as co-owner and first chef of Berkeley's nascent Chez Panisse, called him "the father of American Cuisine," as he was largely responsible for the restaurant's early rise to fame, for its famous menu nights, and for initiating the now-common practice of replacing fancy culinary and menu nomenclature with plain English. When he outgrew "the Birkenstock Republic," he moved across the Bay to San Francisco, and in 1984 opened the now-legendary Stars. Downtown and minutes from the opera and city center, the restaurant attracted a star-studded cast of characters. Despite living on the East Coast, I ate at Stars several times in the eighties and was duly impressed with the food, the ambiance, and with Jeremiah, Mr. Charm, as he floated about the dining room, champagne glass in hand, jollying up the guests. Satellites followed, as did the Peak Café in Hong Kong. Tower was a featured "legend" in an early Dewar's ad, won a James Beard Award for his 1986 cookbook, *New American Classics,* and then in 1996 was named James Beard Outstanding Chef of the Year. In 2000, he moved to New York City and wrote several books, including *California Dish*, his page-turner of a memoir, and *Jeremiah Tower Cooks*. In 2007, in David Kamp's *The United States of Arugula*, the Chez Panisse chapter was devoted almost entirely to him. It was then excerpted in *Vanity Fair* with a double-page spread of Jeremiah sitting by his pool in Mexico where he now lives—writing and pursuing his passions for both scuba diving and architecture.

This conceptually brilliant dish is light and delicious and takes almost no time to prepare. Each portion consists of a tuna fillet pounded very thin—the same method as for Turkey Scaloppini (see recipe on page 95)—and cooked simply by placing it on a hot dinner plate. Jeremiah developed the recipe for the first Stars menu, wanting "to present at the opening of a restaurant, a fast, new, easily-cooked, foolproof, and easily understood dish." If you whisk the dressing together ahead of time, five minutes is all you'll need to chop the avocado and finish up.

In one form or another, this item never left the Stars menu; and over the years, Jeremiah successfully prepared it with many other fish, including salmon, sturgeon, halibut, and sea bass. The sauce and garnish changed according to season and whim. Lobster butter, fresh chiles, Chinese black beans, spiced crabmeat, green goddess mayonnaise, or an herb or ginger cream, to name just a few. Follow the recipe the first time, and then have fun experimenting.

Serves 6

Freshly squeezed juice of 1 lime
2 or 3 drops of Tabasco sauce or other hot sauce
2 teaspoons ground cumin
½ teaspoon minced garlic
2 teaspoons toasted sesame oil
1 large shallot, peeled, sliced paper-thin crosswise,
    and divided into rings
¼ cup minced cilantro
Sea salt and freshly ground black pepper to taste
Six 2-ounce slices fresh tuna, no thicker than ¼ inch
    (boneless, skinless filet of salmon, halibut, grouper,
    red snapper, sturgeon, sea bass, or albacore may be
    substituted)
Approximately 1 tablespoon unsalted butter, melted
2 avocados
1 tablespoon black sesame seeds or 1 tablespoon toasted
    white sesame seeds (or a mixture, ½ tablespoon
    of each)

1. Preheat the oven to 450 degrees. Make the dressing by stirring together the lime juice, Tabasco sauce, cumin, garlic, sesame oil, half the shallots, and half the cilantro. Season with salt and pepper. Set aside.

2. While the oven is heating, place each tuna fillet, one at a time, between 2 pieces of plastic wrap and pound with a kitchen mallet or rolling pin until evenly ⅛ inch thick. Season each fillet with salt and pepper.

3. Paint each of 6 heat-resistant dinner plates with ½ teaspoon of melted butter, and place in the oven until very hot, at least 5 minutes.

4. While the plates are heating, cut the avocado into a ½-inch dice, and toss with three quarters of the dressing. Set the remaining dressing aside.

5. Remove the plates from the oven, and immediately place one fillet in the center of each plate. Drizzle the remaining dressing over the fish.

6. Place one sixth of the dressed avocado on top of each piece of fish. Sprinkle with the reserved shallots, cilantro, and the sesame seeds, and serve. The fish will be perfectly cooked.

Sautéed Soft-shell Crabs

WITH SAUCE CHORON AND CUCUMBER-HAZELNUT SLAW

As Karen Pritsker told me with provocative precision, "It was Boston and the summer of '69. Dissenters raged about political boundaries and sang in protest. Man walked on the moon. And Bobby and I crossed into uncharted territory as we began our romance and a decades-long affair with everything culinary."

Bob Pritsker was from Rhode Island, had a business degree from Columbia, and was attending law school at night. Karen grew up in Westchester, the daughter of a Broadway impresario, and was working post-college in advertising. As their recreational cooking became an art, friends pushed them to turn professional. The idea held no immediate appeal, but then as Bob recalled, ". . . one day we went to Julia Child's butcher. There was a lot of fanaticism at that counter, a lot of intensity. I'd never seen anything like it." The zeal was contagious, and soon, gleaning recipes from Child, Raymond Oliver, Michel Guérard, Alain Chapel, and restaurants Lasserre and Taillevent, they taught themselves the tools of the trade. As Karen said, "Cooking was a romantic retreat from the harsh realities of the grown-up world . . . we wed and fed our culinary passions on a month-long honeymoon, crisscrossing the high temples of classic cuisine."

Now married to each other and to their love of food, the couple returned to Boston and created Epicuriosity, catering dinners for the Newton-Wellesley crowd. They were content making Riz

Impératrice, Coulibiac of Salmon, and Veal Prince Orloff for the locals, until a well-heeled client suggested they open their own restaurant and offered to foot the bill. They did not accept, but the incident made them see themselves as serious gastronomic entities. Bobby and Karen took out a loan and were prepared to show a stodgily provincial Boston what fine dining ought to be—black-tie service, crystal goblets, and fresh-grown herbs, along with the obligatory great sauces. In 1974, Dodin-Bouffant opened on Boylston Street. Bob went to market early each day, and he and Karen cooked together from morning until midnight. "Boston did not always suffer their ambition gently. A few critics felt patronized. Some found Karen arrogant. There was public name-calling, media scandal, a lawsuit, and finally . . . a separation. If the restaurant hadn't destroyed the marriage, the marriage would have destroyed the restaurant," commented *Boston Magazine* in 1977.

By the time the "insatiable gourmet" Gael Greene wrote her September 10, 1979, *New York Times* column, "Cuisine from a Marriage," Karen and Bob had opened the Boston Dodin-Bouffant, received rave reviews, separated from each other, closed the restaurant, reconciled, moved to New York, and opened a new restaurant of the same name in Manhattan's tony Sutton Place neighborhood.

In another article "Eight Wonderful Dinners: The Sensualist at Table," from March 10, 1980, Gael Greene stated, " . . . if I were free to go anywhere I pleased tonight, here's where you'd find me: Dodin-Bouffant . . . [which] is the most exciting French restaurant in town . . . the Pritskers are blossoming with great derring-do in their spare and elegant little Manhattan town house." In New York, a gradual change occurred. As Karen describes it, "Classic French cooking based on time-honored techniques remained, but the savor of the season was added and taken to a place which allowed the unfettered voice of each ingredient to speak." Sauces—based on intense stock reductions—were thick with flavor rather than with flour. And the critics ate it up, endlessly rhapsodic, using words such as "excellent," "exquisite," "discriminating," "heavenly," and "irresistible." But despite brilliance, dedication, passion, and perfection, the dream—which Karen says, "was all we thought it could and would be and more"—burned itself out. On December 31, 1982, Dodin-Bouffant closed its doors for good.

Pairing luscious soft-shell crabs in a *sauce Choron* (essentially a tomato béarnaise) with a vinegary cucumber slaw is a stroke of genius. Many customers returned to the restaurant again and again for the Pritskers' crabs—their flavor heightened by hours in an aromatic milk bath before being dredged in flour and sautéed. The culinary lily is further gilded by adding a soupçon of hazelnut oil to the vinaigrette and topping the slaw with a dusting of the chopped nuts just before serving. Aromatic jasmine rice is a perfect accompaniment.

Like a classic béarnaise, *sauce Choron* is ideally suited for grilled red meats, fish, chicken, and eggs. Try it on Eggs Benedict instead of Hollandaise sauce. To make classic béarnaise, just eliminate the tomato paste and cream. Other sauces Karen recommends for soft-shell crab are flavored mayonnaises such as aioli, or summer-fruit-based sauces including tomato-onion marmalade and peach or mango chutney. Sometimes she replaces the tarragon in the crab marinade with fresh dill, in which case the crabs are served with a dill-mustard-garlic mayonnaise brightened with lots of lemon zest.

Serves 6

For the marinade:
4 ½ cups whole milk
6 cloves garlic, peeled and crushed
⅛ teaspoon cayenne pepper
¼ cup chopped fresh tarragon leaves
2 tablespoons fresh thyme leaves
6 tablespoons snipped lemon verbena or lemon basil
   (if unavailable, substitute regular basil plus
    1 teaspoon finely grated lemon peel)
¾ cup minced shallots
½ teaspoon sea salt

12 to 18 cleaned soft-shell crabs (depending on size and
   the rest of the menu)
Approximately 2 ½ cups all-purpose flour for dredging
8 tablespoons (1 stick) unsalted butter
4 tablespoons extra virgin olive oil
Sauce Choron (recipe follows)
Cucumber-Hazelnut Slaw (see recipe page 34)

1. Combine the marinade ingredients in a container large
enough to hold them plus all the crabs. Add the cleaned
crabs to the milk marinade 3 to 6 hours prior to cooking.
Cover and refrigerate. When ready to cook, drain the
crabs and pat dry with paper towels.
2. Dredge each crab in flour, making certain to shake off
all excess flour.
3. In a very large sauté pan or skillet (or 2 or 3, depending on the number of crabs), heat the butter and olive oil
over high heat until the fats are hot but not browning.
4. Add the crabs and sauté until well-colored and crisp
on both sides and cooked through, approximately 6 to 8
minutes per side.
5. Serve on warmed plates with Sauce Choron and
Cucumber-Hazelnut Slaw.

Note: Your fishmonger can clean the crabs for you, but do
not purchase them until the day of cooking and refrigerate
on ice until ready to marinate.

SAUCE CHORON

Makes approximately 2 cups

½ cup white wine
⅓ cup white wine vinegar or cider vinegar
3 tablespoons minced shallots
¼ cup chopped fresh tarragon leaves
2 tablespoons minced fresh chervil (if available)
2 tablespoons finely minced fresh flat-leaf parsley
¼ bay leaf
⅓ teaspoon sea salt
½ teaspoon cracked peppercorns (preferably white)
4 egg yolks, at room temperature
1 cup (2 sticks) unsalted butter, melted, lukewarm
1 to 2 teaspoons freshly squeezed lemon juice
Large pinch of cayenne pepper
2 tablespoons best-quality tomato paste mixed with
    2 tablespoons heavy cream

1. Put the wine, vinegar, shallots, half the tarragon, half
the chervil, half the parsley, the bay leaf, salt, and pepper
in a medium saucepan. Cook over very low heat until all
but 5 to 6 teaspoons of liquid has evaporated.
2. Add the egg yolks and whisk constantly and energetically over low heat until the mixture is thick but still pale
yellow (a candy thermometer is useful; the temperature
should read about 160 degrees at this point).
3. Remove the pan from the heat, and add the lukewarm
butter drop by drop, whisking constantly. After about a
quarter of the butter has been added, you can add it by
the teaspoon rather than by the drop. Whisk energetically
and the sauce will slowly thicken. At this point, stir in the
lemon juice. Strain into a clean pan. Stir in the reserved
herbs, the cayenne, and tomato paste–cream mixture.
Adjust the salt and pepper. The sauce should be thick but
easily pourable. If too thick, whisk in boiling water, a teaspoon at a time, until the desired consistency is reached.
Adjust the seasoning.
4. Serve right away or hold by placing the saucepan in a
skillet filled with hot water and placed over very low heat.
The water should stay hot but not come to a simmer.
Ideally it should be around 155 degrees. Whisk occasionally. When ready to serve, if the sauce is too thick, whisk
in a teaspoon or two of boiling water.

Blender method: Place the infusion—still warm—from Step 1 in a blender along with the egg yolks and blend until foamy. Add the lukewarm butter in a slow, steady stream. If too thick, add a tablespoon or more hot water. Add the cayenne, tomato paste–cream mixture, salt, and pepper. Use a rubber spatula to scrape the sauce into a bowl if serving right away or a saucepan if holding as in the original recipe. Stir in the reserved herbs. Thin with boiling water if necessary and adjust the seasoning.

CUCUMBER-HAZELNUT SLAW

Serves 6

8 medium cucumbers, peeled, cut in half lengthwise, and seeded (scrape seeds out with a teaspoon)
5 teaspoons fine sea salt
1 cup white wine vinegar
2 teaspoons sugar
2 tablespoons minced fresh tarragon
¼ cup finely minced shallots or chives
1 teaspoon freshly ground white pepper (black pepper can be substituted), or to taste
3 tablespoons hazelnut oil
2 tablespoons toasted and chopped hazelnuts

1. Cut each halved, seeded cucumber into paper-thin, crosswise, half-moon slices. Put the slices in a large bowl, toss with the salt, and let sit for 1 hour.
2. Drain the cucumbers and rinse in several changes of cold water. Drain again and squeeze the cucumber slices dry in kitchen towels (a clean bath towel works even better).
3. Place the dried cucumbers in a nonreactive bowl, add the vinegar and sugar, and toss well. Add the tarragon, shallots, pepper, and hazelnut oil. The slaw can be prepared up to this point several hours in advance. When ready to serve, toss with toasted chopped hazelnuts.

Note: You can substitute 3 tablespoons olive oil and 2 tablespoons caraway seeds for the hazelnuts and hazelnut oil.

LOUIS FAUCHÈRE'S

Lobster Newburg

In 1823, Louis Fauchère was born in Vevey, Switzerland, very near the spot where the Delmonico brothers—owners of the first freestanding restaurant in the United States and his future employers—were born a few years later. Teenage Fauchère worked in Swiss hotel kitchens until 1851 when he immigrated to New York, immediately becoming Master Chef at Delmonico's, a position probably arranged in advance by mutual acquaintances. In summer, Fauchère followed his society clientele to elegant country hotels where he served up the delicious food they had become accustomed to in the city. The French Hotel, in Milford, Pennsylvania, owned by relatives of Fauchère's wife, was one of these. In 1867, this weekend and summer Poconos escape came up for sale; Fauchère bought it, changed the name, and moved to Milford full time. His kitchen histrionics earned him the sobriquet "The crazy Frenchman," but his innovative, stylish, and tasty food rendered the restaurant a raging success and such a cash cow that in the late 1870s he was able to add a marble foyer, a glassed-in dining room, and in the basement, the Chicken and the Snail, a gentlemen's oyster bar, all replete with Gilded Age opulence.

Even though Fauchère died in 1893, the hotel continued to thrive for many years. Frequented by politicians, statesmen, presidents, society figures, and stars of the silent Silver Screen—a favorite haunt of both Charlie Chaplin and Andrew Carnegie among others—the doors did not close until 1976. In 2006, the hotel reopened, and the new owners, Dick Snyder and Sean Strub, have returned both the inn and its restaurant to their former glory.

Lobster Newburg put Hotel Fauchère on the map. Pieces of lobster meat are removed from the shell and bathed in an egg-yolk-thickened, liquor-flavored cream sauce. The controversy is ongoing as to whether the dish was created in Milford or at Delmonico's Restaurant in Manhattan. Sean Strub said, "locally, to even suggest that Louis didn't whip it up on Broad Street in Milford is practically treason." But reality is hazier. Most plausibly, Fauchère was on his fall/winter shift at Delmonico's when regular customer—wealthy sea captain, vocational chef, and close friend of Charles Delmonico—Ben Wenberg arrived for dinner. Wenberg, who was engaged in the business of transporting tropical fruit between Cuba and New York City, requested a chafing dish with lobster, rum, cream, butter, and egg yolks brought tableside. He added hot chile peppers from the

West Indies and replicated a dish from his travels. Delmonico was delighted and immediately christened the creation Lobster à la Wenberg. Soon after, when Wenberg broke a house rule by engaging in a disruptive political argument—which turned into a fistfight—he was "blackballed" by the restaurant and his namesake dish struck from the menu. Wild about the exotic new lobster creation, outraged customers demanded it be reinstated. Delmonico acquiesced, but rearranged the letters, changing "Wen" to "New," and Lobster Newburg was born.

By 1894, in his book *The Epicurean*, Charles Ranhofer, executive chef at Delmonico's at the time, had tweaked the Newburg recipe, replacing the rum with Madeira. More recent versions use sherry or cognac, or the two together. I prefer cognac; but whichever liquor you decide on, and whether served over toast points or rice, this Caribbean extravaganza will impress even the most resistant. The elegant sauce is sublime, the true essence of lobster and the sea. Quite rich and intensely flavorful, a small amount goes a long way. Scaled down, Lobster Newburg is the perfect choice for a romantic "two's company" evening.

Serves 6

Six 1¼-pound cooked lobsters (the tail and claw meat carefully removed from the shells intact, both shells and meat reserved; refrigerate until needed)

6 tablespoons unsalted butter

1 cup peeled and diced carrots

1 cup peeled and diced onions

1 cup thinly sliced celery

1 cup diced white button mushrooms

¼ cup tomato paste

½ cup plus 2 tablespoons brandy

6 cups best-quality fish or shellfish stock

6 cups heavy cream

Sea salt and freshly ground black pepper to taste

½ cup peeled and minced shallots

⅛ teaspoon hot Caribbean pepper sauce or cayenne pepper, or to taste

⅛ teaspoon freshly grated nutmeg, or to taste

2 teaspoons freshly squeezed lemon juice, or to taste

⅓ cup minced chives and/or black or red caviar for garnish (optional)

Toast points, hot white rice, or buttered egg noodles as an accompaniment

1. Preheat the oven to 350 degrees.

2. Using a kitchen hammer and poultry shears, break up the empty lobster shells as best you can. The smaller the pieces, the more flavor will be imparted to the sauce.

3. Put the broken-up lobster shells in a roasting pan and place in the oven. Roast, stirring occasionally, until deeper in color and aromatic, about 15 minutes.

4. While the shells are roasting, heat 4 tablespoons of the butter in a large saucepan set over medium heat. Add the carrots, onions, celery, and mushrooms, and cook for 10 to 15 minutes, or until the vegetables are soft and light gold. Add the tomato paste, lobster shells, and the ½ cup of brandy. Cook, stirring, for 5 minutes. Then add the stock, raise the heat to high, and bring to a boil. Lower the heat to medium-high and reduce by two thirds. Add the cream, bring to a boil, then immediately lower the heat to a low simmer. Add salt and pepper, and cook, partially covered, stirring frequently until the thickness of heavy cream. Watch carefully to prevent scorching.

5. Remove the sauce from the heat and strain into a clean bowl. You should have approximately 4 cups of sauce. Press down on the solids with a ladle or spoon to extract as much flavor as possible. Doing this properly should take several minutes. Set the sauce aside. The sauce can be made up to 24 hours in advance and refrigerated once it is cool.

6. Slice the lobster tails crosswise into ½-inch pieces, and leave the claws whole.

7. Heat the remaining 2 tablespoons butter in a large sauté pan set over medium-low heat. Add the shallots, hot pepper sauce, and nutmeg. Cook, stirring constantly, for 2 to 3 minutes, until the shallots are translucent. Add the lobster meat and sauté until warmed through, about 3 minutes. Add the remaining 2 tablespoons brandy and stir to deglaze the pan. Add the reserved cream sauce. Raise the heat and bring to a gentle simmer. Simmer for a minute or two, until piping hot. Add the lemon juice and adjust the seasonings.

8. Using a slotted spoon, transfer 2 lobster claws and equal portions of tail meat to each of 6 soup plates.

9. Pour a sixth of the sauce over each portion of lobster. Sprinkle chives and/or caviar over, if using.

10. Serve right away, very hot with toast points, rice, or buttered egg noodles.

CHARLESTON RECEIPTS'

Frogmore Stew

Throughout this book as you will see,
We never mention recipe, —
The reason being that we felt,
(Though well aware how it is spelt!)
That it is modern and not meet
To use in place of old receipt
To designate time-honored dishes
According to ancestral wishes.

So begins *Charleston Receipts*, a treasure trove of 750 heirloom recipes and the oldest Junior League cookbook still in print. The book provides a window into history. Its title and evocative drawings from centuries past harken back to a time when recipes were "receipts," and a large percentage of South Carolina women spent their days behind the stove preparing "ancestral dishes." Some favorites included in the book are Breakfast Shrimp, Meeting Street Crab Meat, Red Rice, Huguenot Torte, and Benne Seed Wafers.

Gullah phrases add the distinctive flavor of old Charleston, conjure up lost eras, and have contributed to the book's reputation as a classic. The Gullah "language," in danger of extinction,

is not "Black English" nor a dialect of anything else, but rather one of the six languages known as "English-derived Atlantic Creoles" and the only one spoken on the U.S. mainland. Many of the dishes in the book—Champagne Punch, James Island Shrimp Pie, and Dah's Browning (a liquid caramel used as an ingredient in gravies), among others—were generally prepared and served by Low Country cooks and butlers. Gullah lines like these from *Charleston Receipts* "allow readers to meet these special people, share their humor, and 'hear' their language":

". . . gal fetch um one big plate pile' up wid baddle cake. Him pit two-t'ree 'pun 'e plate en' kibbuhr'um wid muhlassis, en' staa't fuh eat."

". . . w'en de preachuh cat to de 'ooman house, him fuh nyam de bes'! Nuttin' but de bes' fuh suit."

"Do chile! I ain' got time fuh mek fancy cooky. Teck dis penny en' go git uh horse-gunjuh."

Charleston Receipts has received several awards since its publication in 1950; and as of 2004, there were over three quarters of a million books in circulation. This success led to a sequel, *Charleston Receipts Repeats*—from which the Frogmore Stew recipe is adapted—and more recently to *Party Receipts*, providing recipes and myriad tips for entertaining.

The coastal hamlet of Frogmore, named after an ancestral English country estate nearby, is on the island of St. Helena, just off the coast between Charleston and Beaufort, South Carolina. The estate is gone but is commemorated by Frogmore Stew, a local dish served to this day during festivities. Also known as Beaufort Stew, this concoction is not actually a stew but rather an old-fashioned "boil" of shrimp, spicy sausage, and corn cooked in water to which a generous amount of "seafood boil" has been added. Potatoes and cleaned raw crab are optional inclusions, as are garlic, tomatoes, and onions, all of which further intensify the flavors introduced with the sausage. For many people, Frogmore stew epitomizes the simplicity of Low Country cuisine where—like the oyster roast, clambake, and crawfish boil elsewhere—this somewhat messy, finger-food favorite is traditionally served outdoors and eaten off paper plates on newspaper-covered picnic tables. Large napkins are a necessity, as are tangy lemonade and ice-cold beer.

The recipe that follows, loosely adapted from *Charleston Receipts,* serves eight but can be scaled up proportionately. With a large enough pot (or pots), making the dish for fifty is not much harder than making it for eight. Fluffy white rice and southern biscuits are perfect accompaniments. If you want something green, serve coleslaw, a salad of julienned romaine lettuce and scallions with lemon-dill vinaigrette, or a basket of crudités. Stay in the South, and offer spiced pecans, cheddar cheese coins, and/or ham salad sandwiches on tiny biscuits at cocktail hour, but avoid anything major, as the meal to follow is large. For dessert, however, go whole hog. Dessert buffets are great for large groups. Depending on the number of people, try a coconut or Lady Baltimore cake, a peach pie à la mode, something chocolate, and/or a fresh fruit salad.

Leftovers make a great soup. Slice the sausage; cut the corn off the cob; dice the potatoes, onions, and tomatoes if they have not fallen apart already; peel the shrimp; and remove the crabmeat from the shell. Stir all this into the reheated reserved broth, and garnish with chopped fresh parsley. If the broth is thinly flavored, reduce it or just add the ingredients to flavorful fish, shellfish, duck, or chicken stock instead. Pass Tabasco sauce, a pepper mill, and sea salt at the table.

5 tablespoons seafood seasoning such as Old Bay

2 tablespoons kosher salt

2 sweet onions, such as Vidalia or Walla Walla, peeled and quartered

1 head garlic, halved crosswise

16 new potatoes, halved

6 medium tomatoes, seeded and chopped

2 pounds andouille sausage, cut into 2-inch lengths (spicy smoked link sausage or kielbasa can be substituted)

4 live blue crabs, cleaned and halved (optional)

4 pounds unpeeled shrimp

12 ears freshly shucked corn on the cob, cut or broken into thirds

Fresh watercress or parsley sprigs and lemon wedges for garnishing the serving platter

1. In a large stockpot, combine the seafood seasoning, salt, onions, and garlic. Add 4 quarts of water and bring to a boil over high heat. Toss in the potatoes and tomatoes, reduce the heat to medium, and cook for 10 minutes.

2. Add the sausage and crabs and boil gently for 5 minutes.

3. Add the shrimp and corn and cook just until the shrimp curl, 3 or 4 more minutes. The secret to the recipe is not to overcook the shrimp.

4. Drain in a large colander and reserve the broth for another use. It makes a great base for soup or fish or shellfish stew. After cooling, it will keep for up to 3 days refrigerated and 3 months or more in the freezer.

5. Mound the stew on a warm serving platter and garnish with the watercress or parsley and lemon wedges. Serve right away.

FISHERMAN'S WHARF

Cioppino

When I was a child, San Francisco was famous for two things, the Golden Gate Bridge and Fisherman's Wharf. And "the Wharf"—where our family visits always began—was famous for the Ghirardelli Chocolate Factory and cioppino. The Chocolate Factory is gone, having moved to nearby San Leandro, but Ghirardelli Square still bustles, and cioppino—one of the world's great fish soups—remains a feature at a number of restaurants in the vicinity. However, this delicious fisherman's chowder, a local institution, is surprisingly unknown outside the Bay Area.

One in a large family of robust and flavorful seafood stews that flourish in ports around the world, cioppino originally came to the North Beach section of San Francisco from Italy—arriving with Genoese fisherman immigrating to America—sometime between the Gold Rush and the 1930s. Legend has it that a dockhand gathering ingredients for the communal meal from the moored fishing boats would cry out, "Chip in, chip in," which in a heavy Italian accent became "cioppino." More plausibly, the name and its ingredients reflect a Ligurian ancestor, the classic fisherman's chowder called Ciuppin, meaning "chopped" or "to chop." Most food historians agree that the stew originated on boats at sea—rather than in port—before refrigeration, when the crew had to make do with the basics on board: fish, canned tomatoes and vegetables, and wine. As Italian restaurants proliferated in San Francisco, the dish became a mainland staple.

Traditionally a catch-of-the-day affair, cioppino is now defined by freshness and a diversity of local ingredients, which in Northern California typically includes a variety of Pacific fish and seafood—Dungeness crab, local spiny lobster, clams, shrimp, scallops, squid, mussels, red snapper, halibut, and flounder—combined with lots of garlic, fresh tomatoes, and wine. The seafood is served in the shell, including the crab and lobster, which are often halved or quartered. The soup welcomes substitutions and additions. In California red wine is used as often as white, some feeling it provides greater depth and less acidity. And though not historically accurate, I've added saffron and orange zest and a garlic mayonnaise to stir into the soup or slather on toasts, and have roasted the tomatoes for a heartier flavor. Experiment with your local daily catch—when available, lobster or crab dresses the dish up and adds flavor. As long as your ingredients are fresh, it's hard to go wrong.

Though certainly not present on the rough-and-tumble fishing boats a hundred years ago, crab forks and lobster crackers come in handy for modern-day eaters. Bibs and plenty of napkins don't hurt either. Serve the soup with crusty bread—sourdough if you can get it—to sop up the juices. For an authentic City by the Bay meal, start with a big Caesar salad and finish with a fruit tart, cheesecake, or even brownies à la mode.

Serves 8 to 10

16 large tomatoes, cut into ½-inch slices
¼ cup plus 2 to 3 tablespoons extra virgin olive oil
Sea salt and freshly ground black pepper to taste
1 cup peeled and finely diced onions
¾ cup thinly sliced celery
¾ cup diced fresh fennel
¾ cup carrots, peeled and cut into small dice
8 cups rich fish stock
4 cloves garlic, peeled and minced
¼ cup Pernod or other anise-flavored liqueur
Finely grated zest of 1 orange
1 teaspoon saffron threads
40 mussels, debearded and well-scrubbed
40 cherrystone clams, rinsed
40 medium shrimp
2 pounds monkfish, cut into 1-inch squares
2 pounds cleaned squid bodies, cut into ¼-inch rings

¼ cup minced fresh flat-leaf parsley
¼ cup julienned fresh basil
Fennel leaves, if available
Tabasco sauce to taste
Garlic Mayonnaise (see recipe page 43)
Crusty peasant or French bread, toasted

1. Preheat the oven to 425 degrees. Lay the tomato slices on a greased baking sheet and drizzle with the 2 tablespoons olive oil. Sprinkle with salt and pepper. Roast until caramelized, 30 to 40 minutes. Cool and cut into medium dice. Set aside in a small bowl.
2. In a large casserole or stockpot over medium flame, heat the ¼ cup olive oil with the onions, celery, fennel, and carrots. Cook, stirring frequently, for 10 minutes. If the mixture becomes too dry or brown, add a bit of fish stock or water.

3. Add the garlic and cook until the vegetables are soft and beginning to color, adding water or stock again if necessary, approximately 10 to 15 minutes more.

4. Warm the Pernod in a small saucepan. Turn off both burners and flame the cooked vegetables with the Pernod, stirring until flames have completely subsided.

5. Return the pot to medium heat and add fish stock, zest, saffron, 1 teaspoon salt, pepper, and chopped tomatoes. Bring to a simmer, stir, reduce heat, and cook for 5 minutes. It can be prepared up to 48 hours ahead to this point, cooled and refrigerated.

6. When ready to serve, heat the broth over medium heat to a simmer, but do not boil. Add the mussels and clams and cover. Cook for 2 minutes, then add the shrimp and monkfish. Cover and cook for 2 more minutes. Add the squid and cook for a minute or so. Do not overcook, but make sure the clams and mussels are open and everything else is done.

7. Add the parsley, basil, and fennel leaves, if using, and season with salt, pepper, and Tabasco sauce.

8. Serve, divided into hot bowls, making sure to give everyone some of everything.

9. Pass the Garlic Mayonnaise and lots of toasted crusty French bread, sourdough or baguettes. Alternatively, place a piece of toast spread with garlic mayonnaise in the bottom of each bowl before adding the cioppino.

GARLIC MAYONNAISE

Makes approximately 1½ cups

All ingredients must be at room temperature.
1 egg
1 clove garlic, plus more to taste
1 to 1½ tablespoons freshly squeezed lemon juice, or
    to taste
¼ teaspoon sea salt, plus more to taste
A few drops of Tabasco sauce or a pinch of cayenne
    pepper
½ teaspoon Dijon mustard
⅛ teaspoon freshly ground black pepper, plus more
    to taste
¾ cup tasteless vegetable oil such as canola
½ cup extra virgin olive oil
More salt, pepper, garlic, and lemon juice, to taste

1. Put the egg, garlic, lemon juice, salt, Tabasco sauce, mustard, and black pepper in the bowl of a food processor and process until well blended.

2. Mix the two oils together and with the motor running, add the oil, initially drop by drop, and then in a very slow stream.

3. When the mayonnaise is thick and all the oil has been added, taste and adjust the seasonings.

Note: The Garlic Mayonnaise will have more flavor if made up to 2 days ahead, covered and refrigerated until ready to use.

Monkfish and Salmon Stew

WITH GREEN PEAS, FAVA BEANS, AND SAFFRON

There are many reasons that Fredy Girardet's restaurant in Crissier, Switzerland, ranked three Michelin stars year after year, and this sublime yet simple recipe adapted from Girardet is one of them. Monkfish, salmon, peas, and fava beans come brilliantly together, all bathed in a light and garlicky saffron cream. The bright green of the vegetables and the pinks and whites of the fish shine through the red-flecked, yellow sauce, beautiful to behold—even more so if you can find some purple basil to julienne and strew, confetti-style, on top. Serve with white rice or hot baguettes to absorb the sauce. A pan sauté of mixed mushrooms would make a good starter as would those same mushrooms atop a green salad. Either a chocolate or a fruit dessert would work well.

Serves 6 to 8

6 tablespoons extra virgin olive oil

9 cloves garlic, peeled and minced

10 pinches powdered saffron (or substitute ¼ teaspoon saffron threads, crushed)

¾ cup flavorful fish stock

1½ cups heavy cream

3 pinches of saffron threads

1 cup double-peeled fresh fava beans or 1 cup frozen lima beans, thawed

1 small lemon

1 cup frozen peas, thawed

2¼ pounds boneless monkfish, cut into 24 equal pieces

1 pound boneless salmon fillet, cut into ½-inch cubes

Sea salt and freshly ground black pepper to taste

20 leaves fresh basil (purple, if possible), julienned

Fresh herb flowers such as thyme, basil, or chive, if available (optional)

1. In a medium saucepan, heat 3 tablespoons of the olive oil over medium heat. Add the garlic and half the powdered saffron, and cook for 3 minutes, stirring frequently.

2. Add the stock, cream, saffron threads, and fresh favas or thawed lima beans, and simmer for 2 minutes. Adjust the seasonings and squeeze in lemon juice to taste, about 1½ tablespoons. Add the thawed peas. Keep warm over the lowest possible heat.

3. In a large nonstick skillet, heat the remaining 3 tablespoons olive oil over high heat. Season the monkfish and salmon with salt, pepper, and the remaining powdered saffron.

4. Sauté the monkfish for 3 minutes, or until almost done. Add the salmon and cook, stirring, for 1 minute. Transfer to warm plates or a warm platter. Nap with the sauce. Strew the basil julienne and optional herb flowers over all. Serve immediately, very hot.

VEDAT BASARAN'S

Stuffed Squid

In early October 2007, my daughter Tess and I set off for Istanbul to attend an Iftar feast at Engin Aiken's home on the Bosporus. Engin is a cookbook writer, cooking teacher, hostess extraordinaire, and often described as the "Julia Child of Turkey." Each year during the month of Ramadan, she hosts an Ottoman banquet—similar to our American Thanksgiving in sentiment, celebration, and feasting—for about thirty family members and close friends.

Iftar is a ceremonial "break the fast" meal that begins at sunset each evening during this holiday period when observing Muslims eat nothing all day beginning at sunrise. According to custom, Engin's special dinner began with Turkish breakfast foods set out family-style. Included were *pastirma*, the national pastrami, made from air-dried beef and flavored with fenugreek, garlic, cumin, and red pepper; *otlu börek*, a delicious baked pastry from her native Ula—thin, tender dough filled with whey cheese and either Swiss chard or a mixture of local wild greens; and *pide,* a bread similar to pita but softer inside and sprinkled with nigella seeds. A purslane and cucumber salad, various local cheeses, olives, and homemade jams complete the first course.

"Breakfast" was followed by a traditional chickpea soup and *keskek*, an Ottoman feast dish of lamb neck meat and husked wheat, slow-cooked together to a purée consistency, then drizzled with a hot pepper–spiked *beurre noisette* and strewn with toasted pine nuts. Highlights of the dessert buffet were a light baklava, fig pudding, pumpkins in syrup, baked quince with apples, and *alsa gullac*, a beautiful and delicate Ottoman dish of paper-thin pastry soaked in rose-scented milk, layered with chopped almonds, and topped with pomegranate seeds.

Speaking with Engin during dinner, I learned she was working on a cookbook, the gist of which is Ottoman cuisine—yesterday, today, and tomorrow. Culinary Istanbul is a small world, and it came up in conversation that she had shared the cooking of that night's Iftar dinner with Ottoman food authority Vedat Basaran. In 1987, with a master's degree in professional cookery, Basaran persuaded the management of Istanbul's toniest hotel, the Ciragan Palace, to let him switch the menu of their luxury restaurant Tugra from "continental" to Ottoman, a complex cuisine that he felt befitted a restaurant in one of the last royal palaces on the Bosporus. To guarantee authenticity, Vedat collected and taught himself to translate old Ottoman cookbooks written in Persian. Early to realize that the sophisticated traveler wants to eat food of the destination rather than the generic "continental," he started an international movement. Tugra was a brilliant success.

In 1995, Basaran left the Ciragan Palace to open his own—now famous—restaurant, Feriye Lokantasi, devoted solely to showcasing his updated Ottoman food, and just up the Bosporus from Tugra. Kitchen basics for the sultans included lamb, chicken, fish, rice, bulgur, eggplant, tomatoes, zucchini, yogurt, and both sweet and hot peppers. And lemon, garlic, onion, parsley, dill, mint, walnuts, pine nuts, currants, cinnamon, and paprika added interest and spiced things up back then, just as they do in modern-day Turkey. Vedat's combinations of these regional staples elevate Ottoman dishes to a level of refinement and perfection rarely seen since the Empire's fall in 1923.

Because Vedat was kind enough to share such a large number of his recipes with me, choosing one for this book was difficult. However, as so much of Turkey is coast or island, narrowing the choice to fish and seafood made sense. Squid is a national staple, and I settled on Vedat's version with a filling and a preparation similar to that of many Turkish stuffed vegetables. Served with Engin's purslane and cucumber salad, nothing but dessert is required. Smaller portions—with or without the salad—make a good appetizer before a Turkish lamb main course.

Serves 6 to 7

1 generous cup long-grain rice
⅓ cup currants
½ bunch fresh flat-leaf parsley
⅓ bunch fresh dill
Approximately 1 to 1¼ cups extra virgin olive oil
½ cup pine nuts
4 large onions, peeled and thinly sliced crosswise
½ teaspoon freshly ground black pepper
1 teaspoon mild paprika
1 teaspoon ground allspice
1 teaspoon ground cinnamon
3 tablespoons chopped fresh mint leaves
1 teaspoon sugar
1 teaspoon sea salt
24 cleaned squid bodies, each 3 to 4 inches long, total weight 1 to 1½ pounds
2 lemons

1. Soak the rice and currants separately in room-temperature water for 30 minutes.
2. Finely chop the parsley and dill. Reserve the stalks for later use.

3. Rinse and drain the rice and set aside in a bowl.
4. Drain the currants and set aside.
5. Put ½ cup of the olive oil into a medium saucepan over medium heat, and when the oil is hot, sauté the pine nuts until they begin to color. Add three quarters of the sliced onions, and sauté with the pine nuts until the onions turn light gold. Meanwhile, put 2 cups of water on to boil.
6. Add the drained rice to the onions and pine nuts and continue to sauté, stirring frequently, for about 10 minutes. Add the currants, stir, and then stir in the black pepper, paprika, allspice, cinnamon, mint, sugar, and salt.
7. Add the 2 cups boiling water and stir for 3 minutes over medium heat. Cover the pan and turn off the heat. Add the parsley and dill to the rice stuffing and mix well. Set aside.
8. Preheat the oven to 350 degrees. Strew the remaining sliced onions and the parsley and dill stalks in the bottom of a gratin or shallow lidded baking dish approximately 10 by 10 inches or 9 by 12 inches.
9. Use a small spoon to fill each of the 24 squid bodies about three quarters full. Do not overfill or the squid will burst when the rice swells during cooking.

10. Neatly arrange the stuffed squid in rows in the pan on top of the onions and herb stalks, sprinkle generously with salt, and pour over the rest of the olive oil. Add water to a level about ¼ inch below the bottom of the squid.

11. Peel the lemons, and cut them into very thin rounds. Arrange the lemon slices in one layer over the squid. Cover with a sheet of parchment paper or foil weighted down with an ovenproof plate. Cover the pan with the lid and cook for 40 minutes. Let the squid cool to lukewarm or completely before removing the lid. Remove the lid, plate, and paper.

12. The squid can be served whole or cut into halves or thirds diagonally. Place the squid on one side of large platter and drizzle with olive oil and chopped dill or parsley. Place the Purslane and Cucumber Salad (recipe follows) on the other side of the platter. Alternatively, serve the squid and salad side-by-side on individual dinner plates.

ENGIN AIKEN'S PURSLANE AND CUCUMBER SALAD

Serves 6 to 7

1 cup strained Greek yogurt
1 clove garlic, minced, or to taste
1 to 2 tablespoons milk or cream
1 tablespoon freshly squeezed lemon juice
Sea salt and freshly ground black pepper to taste
Small pinch of cayenne, Aleppo, or other hot pepper
3 medium cucumbers
8 cups purslane (mâche or lamb's lettuce can
    be substituted)
¼ cup coarsely chopped toasted walnuts
¼ cup coarsely chopped fresh mint leaves
¼ cup coarsely chopped fresh flat-leaf parsley
2 tablespoons minced fresh dill
3 tablespoons extra virgin olive oil

1. In a small bowl, mix the yogurt with the garlic, and thin with a little milk or cream to achieve a thick but pourable consistency.

2. Place the lemon juice in a small bowl and add salt, pepper, and hot pepper. Set aside while you prepare the other ingredients.

3. Peel the cucumbers and cut them in half lengthwise. Use a teaspoon to scrape away the seeds and slice the cucumber crosswise into very thin half-moons.

4. Toss the purslane, cucumbers, walnuts, mint, parsley, and dill in a large salad bowl.

5. Add the olive oil to the dressing, whisk, and adjust the seasoning. Toss enough of the dressing with the salad to coat and flavor. Transfer to a platter or individual dinner plates, dollop with the yogurt-garlic mixture, and serve right away.

Seafood Pot Pie

Who would have predicted that a restaurant inspired by the shape of a hat would become the talk of the town overnight? As described in *The Brown Derby Cookbook*, the whimsically designed Brown Derby Restaurant sprang up due to an off-the-cuff remark. One evening in 1925, Herbert K. Somborn was chatting with Abe Frank, then manager of the Los Angeles Ambassador Hotel, and Sid Grauman of Chinese Theatre fame. One of them, bemoaning the dearth of restaurants in the L.A. area, said things were so bad that ". . . you could open a restaurant in an alley and call it anything, and if the food and service were good, the patrons would come flocking." And come flocking they did when the original Brown Derby—for many years, the symbol of Los Angeles itself—opened a year later. Located on Wilshire Boulevard, smack across the street from the Ambassador, it quickly became the "in" spot for post-party bashes after closing time at The Coconut Grove, the hotel's famed nightclub.

The "Little Hat," as it was nicknamed, was such a success with the movie set that in 1929 Somborn opened a second Brown Derby near Hollywood and Vine. The local elite—including Mary Pickford, Loretta Young, Cecil B. DeMille, Clark Gable, and Carole Lombard—made this location a home away from home; celebrities still in costume would rush over from the studios at lunchtime to grant interviews and entertain friends. Many stars even received fan mail addressed to them merely "c/o The Brown Derby, Hollywood and Vine." With all of this hoopla plus the first tableside telephones, it is no wonder that legendary gossip columnists Hedda Hopper and Louella Parsons each used the Derby as a second office. Industry news was always heard there first.

The Brown Derby stayed open 24/7, attracting stars, playwrights, and composers from New York who shared lyricist Harry Ruby's sentiments about Hollywood that "no matter how hot it gets in the daytime, there is no place to go late at night." But now there was the Derby. And when Walter Winchell, Jimmy Durante, John Barrymore, and Will Rogers joined Somborn in booth 50, "some of the best stories in the world would get themselves told by some of the best storytellers of the land."

No one can resist pot pie, and this one—adapted from the Brown Derby's recipe and chock-full of seafood and mushrooms and bathed in a light saffron-and-curry-infused béchamel—is as good as it gets. The restaurant always had a pot pie on the menu—either this one or a chicken version containing green peas. I've included peas here also, as they provide extra flavor and are beautiful along with the bright red tomato dice, nestling like jewels among pink crustaceans and white scallops. And the already flaky and flavorful crust is even tastier with some of the white flour replaced by whole wheat.

Serves 8 to 10

¾ cup (1½ sticks) unsalted butter, divided into three
    ¼-cup portions
3 ribs celery, thinly sliced
1 large onion, peeled and chopped
4 cloves garlic, peeled and slivered
12 large white button mushrooms, cleaned and sliced
Sea salt and freshly ground black pepper to taste
2 cups frozen green peas, thawed (optional)
18 large raw shrimp, peeled, deveined, and split
    lengthwise
Six 2-ounce pieces halibut or other white fish
9 large sea scallops, halved horizontally
18 large fresh oysters, removed from their shells
2 cooked lobster tails, each cut into 6 equal pieces to
    produce 12 pieces in all
2 medium tomatoes, diced
¼ cup minced fresh chives
Freshly squeezed juice of 1 lemon, plus more to taste
4 tablespoons all-purpose flour
¾ cup light cream
Large pinch of saffron dissolved in 1 cup strong fish
    or shellfish stock
½ teaspoon dried thyme
A few drops of Tabasco sauce, to taste
The Brown Derby's Pastry for Covered Pies
    (recipe follows)

1. Preheat the oven to 200 degrees. Melt ¼ cup of the butter in a large skillet or sauté pan set over medium heat. Add the celery, onion, and the garlic and cook, stirring frequently, until softened, about 10 minutes.
2. Add the mushrooms and salt and pepper, and cook for about 10 more minutes, until all the vegetables are tender. Transfer the cooked vegetables to a large heatproof bowl. Place in the oven to keep warm.
3. Melt the second ¼ cup of butter in the same pan over high heat. When the butter foam begins to subside, add the shrimp and halibut and sauté, stirring, until the fish begins to color and the shrimp turn red. Add the scallops and salt to taste and cook, stirring, for 2 minutes. Then add the oysters and lobster pieces, and cook for 1 more minute. Make sure all the seafood is just cooked through.
4. Transfer the seafood mixture to the bowl containing the cooked vegetables and toss together with the tomato, chives, and lemon juice. Keep warm in the oven.
5. Place the pot pie tops and the six ramekins on a baking sheet and place in the oven to warm.
6. Melt the remaining ¼ cup butter in a medium saucepan. Whisk in the flour and cook, stirring, for 2 to 3 minutes, until the flour just begins to color. Whisk in the cream, saffron-infused stock, and thyme and cook, stirring, until thickened. If it gets too thick, add a bit more cream. If it's too thin, whisk in 1 or 2 egg yolks over low heat. If yolks are added, be careful not to let the mixture boil or the sauce will curdle. Off the heat, season with salt, pepper, Tabasco sauce, and lemon juice. Fold the sauce gently into the cooked seafood and vegetables. Adjust the seasoning.
7. Divide the seafood and vegetable mixture among ramekins or pot pie dishes. If the mixture is no longer hot, turn the oven up to 350 degrees and return the pot pies to the oven until they are heated through. Cover with the reheated prebaked pot pie tops. Serve very hot.

Note: You will need 8 to 10 ramekins or pot pie dishes that are 4 inches high and approximately 5 inches across. Or this seafood dish can be made as one large pot pie.

THE BROWN DERBY'S PASTRY FOR COVERED PIES

Makes enough pastry for 8 to 10 individual pot pies

3 cups flour (preferably 2½ cups all-purpose flour and
   ½ cup whole wheat flour)
1½ teaspoons sea salt
1 cup (2 sticks) unsalted butter, cold and cut into
   small pieces
4 to 6 tablespoons ice water
1 egg yolk whisked together with 1 tablespoon cream

1. Place the flour and salt in a food processor, and process 15 seconds to combine. Add the butter and pulse until the butter pieces are the size of small peas.
2. Add 4 tablespoons ice water all at once through the feed tube, and process until dough begins to come together. Do not let it form a ball. If dough is too dry to come together, add more ice water, 1 teaspoon at a time.

3. Form the dough into a ball and then press into a disk. Place the disk between two pieces of waxed or parchment paper and roll to about a ⅓-inch thickness. Refrigerate for at least an hour.
4. Using a 5-inch saucer or bowl rim as a template, cut dough into eight to ten 5-inch circles. Refrigerate cut circles for at least 30 minutes, preferably longer or overnight.
5. When ready to bake, preheat oven to 375 degrees. Place the circles on a parchment-lined baking sheet, paint with the egg yolk mixture, and bake until golden, about 20 minutes. Remove pastry from the oven and cool on a wire rack. Once cool, these pie tops will keep 2 to 3 days at room temperature or refrigerated if wrapped airtight in foil.

Note: The unbaked well-wrapped pastry tops may be frozen for up to 2 months. When baking right from the freezer, increase cook time by a few minutes.

WALLIS SIMPSON'S

Shrimp and Corn Pie

In 1936, for the first time ever, *Time* magazine's Man of the Year was a woman. That was the year Edward VIII of England abdicated the throne, finding it "impossible to carry the heavy burden of responsibility, and to discharge my duties as King as I would wish to do, without the help and support of the woman I love." Wallis Simpson, a twice-divorced American commoner, was the name on everyone's lips.

    Much of Wallis's story remains shrouded in mystery almost a century later. When she met Edward, Wallis, age thirty-five, was unquestionably a woman with a past. In addition to her marital history, a long list of affairs and dubious connections were attached to her name.

Ostracized by Buckingham Palace for their pro-Hitler leanings, the couple was sent to the Bahamas to get them out of the way. They were not happy there, and when the war ended, they wandered around a bit before settling in a beautiful house in the Bois de Boulogne where they were to establish the "Windsor style." The Duke was known for his trim physique, his flat stomach, and for having his suit jackets tailored on Savile Row, while the matching pants were made in New York. And Wallis's simple but elegant haute couture was designed specifically to showcase her legendary collection of jewels—Cartier, Van Cleef & Arpels, Seaman Schepps, Belperron, and more. The couple was a pleasure to behold, but unfortunately, they had nothing productive to do with themselves from the time Edward gave up the Crown until they died. They did their best to compensate, and like Gerald Murphy, felt that living well was the best revenge, but as the Duchess once said, "You can't abdicate and eat it."

Wallis had an unusual relationship to food. If she gained even a single pound, she began a strict regimen: for breakfast orange juice and coffee; lunch was two hundred grams of grilled meat, one hard-boiled egg, and tomatoes with lemon juice; dinner the same minus the egg. And despite coining the phrase "a woman can't be too rich or too thin," Wallis avidly read and reread her large collection of cookbooks and was renowned for her excellent table. Along with a certain cachet, an invitation to dine with the Duke and Duchess guaranteed imaginative dishes, good eating, and the promise of an exquisitely laid table. In her book *The Windsor Style*, Suzy Menkes quotes Jacqueline de Ribes as saying that instead of flowers, the table was "covered with things—little gold boxes, cigarette boxes, candelabra in *vermeil,* silver gilt—so much so that you could hardly see the tablecloth . . . and so much cutlery you never knew what to pick up." The Duke's magnificent old silver complemented his many sets of antique china. There were linens to match; Wallis had commissioned Porthault, the iconic French linen house, to embroider a tablecloth and napkins copying the detailed designs on each of the individual services of Sevres, Meissen, and Nymphenburg porcelain.

The first dinner Wallis cooked for her prince during courtship drew directly on her Baltimore roots—black bean soup, grilled lobster, fried chicken, and a raspberry soufflé. Initially her menus were informed by the rich and spicy Maryland and Carolinian recipes of her childhood. After the death of Wallis's father, her vivacious mother, an excellent cook, took paying dinner guests into their Baltimore apartment to make ends meet, feeding them squab, prime sirloin, and soft-shell crabs. Alice Montague Warfield passed this penchant for extravagance—as well as her sharp wit— on to her only child; and in 1942, to raise money for the British war effort, Wallis wrote her own cookbook, *Some Favorite Southern Recipes of the Duchess of Windsor,* based on what she had learned in her mother's kitchen. Her later repertoire expanded to include recipes from her days in China and the Bahamas and from famous chefs of the time. The first course at a Windsor dinner was rarely soup. "After all those cocktails, it's just another drink," said the Duchess. But everything else was fair game. Favorite dishes included roast beef slices alternating with those of foie gras; chicken with baby corn and bananas; grouse with bread crumbs; and Wallis's signature savory, Camembert ice cream, made by forming a concoction of Camembert, cream, and other cheeses into balls, then coating with bread crumbs and freezing. Next the ice cream was briefly heated and served—the recipe remaining enigmatic to this day—a savory Baked Alaska with a hot, crusty outside while icy cold within.

Shrimp Pie, once a Low Country staple, is a winning combination of cooked shrimp, milk, and eggs, thickened with bread crumbs or rice. Flavorings for authentic shrimp pies vary from quite bland to spicier versions that include Worcestershire sauce, red or green bell peppers, sherry, onions, mushrooms, tomatoes, nutmeg, curry powder, bacon, hot sauce, and/or mace. The Duchess placed raw biscuits on top and baked them along with the pie. In other variations, cooked biscuits are halved, toasted, buttered, and used to line the baking dish.

Serves 6 to 8

1½ pounds large shrimp, peeled and deveined
2 tablespoons dry sherry
2 tablespoons onion juice (made by pressing onion pieces through a garlic press)
2 large cloves garlic, passed through a garlic press
Sea salt and freshly ground black pepper to taste
4 tablespoons (½ stick) unsalted butter
½ cup thinly sliced scallions, white part only
½ cup thinly sliced celery
4 cups raw corn kernels, cut off the cob (or substitute frozen corn, thawed)
4 eggs, at room temperature and well-beaten
1 cup plus 2 tablespoons whole milk or half-and-half
Small pinch of cayenne pepper
¼ teaspoon ground nutmeg
2 teaspoons Worcestershire sauce
1 tablespoon Dijon mustard
Chive Biscuits (recipe follows)

1. Preheat the oven to 425 degrees.
2. Toss the shrimp with the sherry, half the onion juice, half the garlic, salt, and pepper, and set aside.
3. Over medium heat, melt the butter in a large heavy skillet. Add scallions, celery, and salt and pepper. Sauté until just beginning to color. Add the rest of the onion juice, garlic, and corn. Cook for 3 minutes more, stirring frequently.
4. Whisk together the eggs, milk, salt, pepper, cayenne, nutmeg, Worcestershire sauce, and mustard.
5. Spread the shrimp over the bottom of a heavy, 12-inch baking dish. Smooth the corn mixture over the shrimp, and pour the egg mixture on top.
6. Place the biscuits on top of the pie, at least an inch apart. Bake for 10 minutes. Reduce the heat to 325 degrees, and bake until biscuits are golden and pie is set, 35 to 45 minutes. Do not let the pie itself puff or brown.

CHIVE BISCUITS

Makes 12 biscuits

2 cups all-purpose flour
2½ teaspoons baking powder, sifted
¾ teaspoon sea salt
6 tablespoons unsalted butter, chilled and cut
    into 12 pieces
¼ cup chopped chives or watercress leaves
½ cup plus 2 tablespoons cold whole milk

1. Place the dry ingredients in a food processor and pulse until thoroughly blended.
2. Add the cold butter pieces and pulse until the largest butter pieces are the size of corn kernels and the rest resemble coarse bread crumbs. Turn off the motor and add the chives or watercress.
3. With the motor running, add all the milk at once through the hole in the lid, and then pulse until all the dry ingredients are almost moistened. Turn the dough out into a bowl, and knead a few times to finish blending the ingredients.
4. Form the dough into a ball and flatten the ball into a disk ¾ to 1 inch thick. Shape the disk into a rectangle as best you can. Cut the dough into 12 biscuits using a sharp knife. If you have time, let the unbaked biscuits rest in the refrigerator for several hours or overnight. They will be more tender this way than if you bake them right away.

GENE HOVIS'S

Shad Roe Soufflé

I first met Gene Hovis in the early 1980s at Brooke Hayward's, where Hovis was often a guest when not behind the stove cooking up batches of spareribs, cornbread, deviled crab, greens, black-eyed peas, and his famous oven-baked ham. Already Hovis was segueing seamlessly between his black, small-town roots in North Carolina and the New York City glitterati culture that embraced him once he moved north, bridging the racial divide along the way. His combination of social and culinary abilities was legendary, and whichever hat he happened to be wearing—guest, chef, or host at his own hot-ticket dinner parties—he was gracious, charming, funny, and beautifully dressed, manifesting an exceptional generosity of spirit in everything he did.

The title of his 1987 *Gene Hovis's Uptown Down Home Cookbook* says it all; he was known for down-home food—its southern roots almost always discernable—that transcended the genre and was in high demand for even the most ultra-uptown occasions. As he says in the book, "Fashions in food are as trendy and changeable as women's hemlines and men's lapels, but simple, delicious food will never go out of style."

Hovis grew up in a family focused on food. His father even smoked his own hams in a smokehouse he'd constructed himself. Each holiday and event was marked by a whirlwind of activity in the kitchen with Granny Dameron at the helm. Hovis speaks of her often and reverentially, as a tall, thin woman "with a quiet dignity and great elegance . . . a superb cook," a description that fits the grandson as well. Born in the mid-1800s, the daughter of slaves, Granny Dameron was the cook for a British-born family living in North Carolina. Hovis remembers her "food-heaped groaning board" from his childhood, marveling at its opulence—"fresh flowers in the center . . . [and] laden with watermelon pickles, chow-chow . . . pickled beets, stuffed baked chickens, an assortment of fresh cooked vegetables, hot yeast pocketbook rolls, a towering snowy coconut cake . . . and in the summer, delicious lemonade, rich creamy ice cream, and as much iced tea as we could hold." The home-grown bounty she served made a huge impact on the young Gene.

As an aspiring actor, Hovis moved to New York in the early sixties. However, he began selling chicken pot pies to his fellow actors and soon realized that his greatest talents lay behind the stove rather than onstage. Hovis took cooking classes with Dione Lucas and then the advice of Craig Claiborne, who encouraged him to follow in his own footsteps and attend L'Ecole Gastronomique in Lausanne. In addition to catering and food writing, Hovis became food editor for *HG*, for a time was spokesman for the Mississippi-based Catfish Institute, and served as creative director of Macy's East department stores in the early 1990s, during which time he oversaw the splashy renovation of the flagship store's food hall. Long a diabetic, he suffered a massive stroke in his early fifties, and in 2004, at age fifty-nine, died of cardiac arrest. Although gone and deeply missed by many, Hovis's wonderful soul food recipes are still with us, easy to make, and well worth recreating at home.

The arrival of shad and its roe each spring is one of the season's greatest gifts. "The shad is in" e-mail from my fishmonger fills me with anticipatory delight. When it's available, I cook both the fish and the roe as frequently as possible, usually sautéing the roe with bacon, onion, and garlic, and roasting the fillets with scallions, butter, and thinly sliced potatoes. And a useful tip: if broken, roe can be cooked, and combined with olive oil, garlic, and fresh herbs to create a unique pasta sauce. For a change and a real treat, however, I make my version of Gene Hovis's Shad Roe Soufflé. An unusual use of the roe, it provides a delicate brunch or lunch main course. Sometimes I make individual soufflés, served as their own course with nothing but toasted brioche alongside. Precede the soufflés with an interesting salad and follow with fruit—cherries on ice, fresh strawberries, or whatever's in season, along with shortbread cookies or *palmiers*. To make individual soufflés, use 10- or 12-ounce ramekins and reduce the cooking time to approximately 20 minutes.

Serves 6

2 to 3 tablespoons unsalted butter, softened, to grease the mold
3 tablespoons freshly grated Parmigiano-Reggiano cheese
½ cup water
½ cup dry white wine
1½ teaspoons freshly squeezed lemon juice
6 pairs very fresh shad roe (about 6 cups)
9 tablespoons unsalted butter
¾ cup chopped shallots
2 large cloves garlic, peeled and minced
9 tablespoons all-purpose flour
Sea salt and freshly ground black pepper to taste
2¼ cups milk
9 large eggs, separated
½ teaspoon cream of tartar
Lemon-Dill Butter (recipe follows)

1. Butter a 3-quart soufflé dish and sprinkle the bottom and sides with the grated cheese. Set aside.
2. Combine the water, wine, and lemon juice in a medium nonreactive saucepan and bring to a boil over high heat. Add the shad roe, cover the pan, and turn down the heat to medium-low. Steam until the roe loses its redness, about 5 minutes. When done, transfer the roe to a platter to cool and discard the liquid.
3. When the roe is cool enough to handle, peel off and discard the membranes, and set the peeled roe aside.
4. In another medium saucepan, melt the 9 tablespoons butter. Add the shallots and sauté over medium heat until soft. Add the garlic, and continue to cook until the shallots begin to turn gold.
5. Stir in flour, salt, and pepper, and whisk over medium heat until bubbly. Cook for 2 minutes, stirring, then add the milk and continue to cook over medium heat, whisking continually, until sauce is thickened and smooth. Stir in shad roe and mix well. Remove from the heat.
6. Preheat the oven to 400 degrees and place an oven rack in the lower third of the oven. Lightly beat the egg yolks and add them little by little to the roe mixture.

7. Preferably using an electric mixer, whisk the egg whites with the cream of tartar and a pinch of salt until soft peaks form. Lighten the shad roe mixture by stirring in one quarter of the beaten egg whites. Gently fold the base back into the rest of the beaten whites until no streaks remain.
8. Gently pour the mixture into the prepared soufflé dish. Place the soufflé in the middle of the oven, and immediately lower the heat to 350 degrees. Bake until the soufflé is puffed and golden and just set, 45 to 60 minutes. Serve at once, accompanied by the Lemon-Dill Butter.

Note: Alternatively, crumble cooked bacon over the finished soufflé and substitute a lemon-parsley butter (parsley and chives instead of dill and chives) for the lemon and dill mixture.

LEMON-DILL BUTTER

Makes approximately ½ cup

½ cup (1 stick) unsalted butter
1 tablespoon freshly squeezed lemon juice
1½ teaspoons grated lemon zest
1½ tablespoons snipped fresh chives
2 teaspoons chopped fresh dill
Sea salt and freshly ground black pepper to taste

1. Place the butter, lemon juice, and lemon zest in the container of a food processor. Pulse on and off until combined.
2. Transfer to a small saucepan and melt over low heat. Add the fresh herbs and salt and pepper, adjust the seasoning, and serve warm over the soufflé.

CHICKEN, DUCK, GUINEA HEN, PHEASANT, TURKEY, and RABBIT

Café Anglais's Chicken à la Portugaise

Il Convento's Pugliese Roast Chicken with Caper and Pecorino Stuffing

Richard Olney's Coq au Vin

The Russian Tea Room's Chicken Kiev

Chicken Country Captain

Chicken à la King

Alain Senderens's Duck à l'Apicius

Roast Duck with Raspberry Sauce

Alice B. Toklas's Duck à l'Orange

Chez Allard's Roast Guinea Hen with Lentils and Bacon

Jane Grigson's Pheasant with Apples, Cream, and Calvados

Gold and Fizdale's Turkey Fillets

El Verdugal's Braised Rabbit with Prunes, Fennel, and Orange

CAFÉ ANGLAIS'S

Chicken à la Portugaise

Paris's legendary Café Anglais (1802–1913) was the scene of a famous dinner that came to be called Le Diner des Trois Empereurs. Haunt of *la crème de la crème* of Parisian society, this sister-restaurant to Tour d'Argent was a favorite of William I of Prussia, who booked a table for himself, Tsar Alexander II of Russia, his son the tsarevich (who later became Tsar Alexander III), and Prince Otto von Bismarck—not an emperor but along for the ride—for June 7, 1867, to coincide with the "three emperors" trip to Paris to attend the Exposition Universelle.

William requested that Chef Adolphe Dugléré prepare a meal that would live in these royal minds forever—fabulous food accompanied by the greatest wines in the world. The chef's *plats* more than met expectations, as did the wines, which included—among many—a madère de retour des Indes (a Madeira that had been sent in a special boat to the East Indies and back just to help it age properly), a Roederer champagne so good that soon after the dinner Alexander II invested in the company, and a 1848 Château Lafite.

Although the scene of one sumptuous extravaganza after the next from the day the café opened in 1802, nothing compared with the eight-hour blowout, reputedly the most magnificent restaurant meal in history, organized by Dugléré for these out-of-town visitors. The diners entered a private room—mahogany-and-walnut-paneled—where chamber music played and row upon row of flickering candle flames were reflected in huge gilt-framed mirrors. The plush seats were red velvet, and much of the room was canopied to match. But the opulent decor was secondary, as the four discerning royals were there for the food.

Two soups were followed by *le premier plat*, which was composed of several dishes: a soufflé, fillet of sole, turbot au gratin, and a saddle of lamb. Next came the entrées: chicken *à la portugaise*, quail pâté, and a creamy lobster *à la parisienne*. That was just the beginning: grilled and roasted meats—the specialty of the house—followed in abundance along with a *canard à la rouennaise*, all

accompanied by asparagus, eggplant, and a *cassoulette princesse.* Next came the ortolans (small game birds—an endangered species no longer legal to eat—consumed whole with one's head hidden under a large napkin supposedly to better savor the experience, though probably to spare others having to watch the birds being chewed to bits, bones and all). Dessert was a *bombe glacée.*

Around one in the morning, the magical evening almost unraveled when Tsar Alexander II complained to Claude Burdel, owner of the restaurant, that there had been no foie gras. Quick-witted Burdel replied, "Sire, it is not the custom, in French gastronomy, to serve foie gras in the month of June. If you can wait until October, you will certainly not regret it." Luckily the Russian tsar chose patience over scene-making; the following October, each dinner guest received a terrine of truffled foie gras specially prepared for them by Dugléré. This terrine became known as Foie Gras des Trois Empereurs and is served to this day at Restaurant de la Tour d'Argent.

In classic French cuisine *à la portugaise* denotes an abundance of tomatoes. Dugléré's version for his three emperors was a whole chicken first stuffed with a tomato-rice pilaf, then cooked in a casserole, or as the French say, *en poele.* Braised—there is liquid in the bottom of the pot and a lid on the top—for most of the cooking, even tricky breast meat remains moist and succulent. The lid is removed for the last twenty minutes in the oven, allowing the bird to brown. Both chicken and rice are enhanced by the abundant sauce created by chunky tomatoes, red bell peppers, onion, garlic, spices, and wine simmering with the chicken as it cooks. As a chicken cavity is small, I prefer cooking the pilaf separately so there's plenty to go around. Its subtle and unusual flavor combination of tomatoes and lemons, however, remains the same as Dugléré's, and is perfect with the chicken. If making the pilaf is one step too many, serve the sauced chicken with plain rice or buttered noodles. The chicken can be prepared through Step 5 up to twenty-four hours ahead and refrigerated. Just bring to room temperature before continuing with the dish.

Serves 4 to 5

One 3½- to 4-pound roasting chicken, at room
    temperature
Sea salt and freshly ground black pepper to taste
1½ teaspoons dried thyme or savory (or a combination)
⅛ teaspoon cayenne pepper
1 bay leaf
1 large onion, peeled and chopped
1 large red bell pepper, seeded and diced
12 whole cloves garlic, peeled
Several sprigs fresh flat-leaf parsley and 3 tablespoons
    chopped parsley leaves for garnish
Several sprigs fresh marjoram, or ½ teaspoon
    dried marjoram
2 tablespoons extra virgin olive oil
1 teaspoon dark brown sugar

Two 28-ounce cans whole tomatoes, preferably
    San Marzano
Juice and freshly grated zest from 1 lemon
3 tablespoons cognac or fruity white wine
Tomato Rice Pilaf (recipe follows)

1. Preheat the oven to 350 degrees. Rub the chicken inside and out with the salt, pepper, dried thyme, and cayenne.
2. Crumble the bay leaf and place half inside the chicken along with about a quarter of the onion, red pepper, garlic cloves, and herbs.
3. Heat the olive oil in an ovenproof casserole just large enough to hold the chicken. Add the remaining onion, red pepper, bay leaf, garlic, and brown sugar. Sauté until the vegetables are soft and the onions turn gold.

4. Add the rest of the parsley and marjoram, the tomatoes, the juice and zest of the lemon, and salt and pepper to taste. Bring to a boil, then lower the heat and simmer for 2 minutes, stirring.

5. Place the chicken, breast-side up, in the casserole. Pour the cognac or wine over, and cover the casserole.

6. Place in the middle of the oven and roast for 1 hour.

7. Raise heat to 400 degrees, uncover casserole, and place it as close to the top of oven as possible. This is the time to begin the Tomato Rice Pilaf.

8. Continue roasting, basting occasionally, until browned and the chicken is done, about 20 more minutes. Test for doneness by piercing a drumstick with a fork. The juices should run clear rather than pink. Remove the chicken from the casserole and allow to rest for 15 minutes before carving.

9. While the chicken is resting, pour the tomato sauce from the casserole into a pitcher. The fat will rise to the top. When ready to serve, spoon off as much fat as possible.

10. Carve the chicken and arrange the pieces on a hot serving platter on top of the pilaf. Drizzle with sauce and sprinkle with chopped parsley. Pass the pitcher of extra sauce separately.

TOMATO RICE PILAF

Serves 4 to 5

1 medium onion, peeled and finely diced
2 tablespoons unsalted butter, melted
2 tablespoons olive oil
2 cups long-grain brown or white rice
1 very large tomato or 2 medium tomatoes, peeled and chopped
1 teaspoon finely grated lemon zest
1 tablespoon chopped fresh marjoram, or ½ teaspoon dried marjoram
4 cups boiling chicken stock or water
1¾ teaspoons sea salt, or to taste
Freshly ground black pepper to taste
2 tablespoons chopped fresh flat-leaf parsley

1. In a 2-quart casserole or saucepan, sauté over medium heat the onion in the butter and oil until golden, stirring frequently.

2. Add the rice and cook, stirring until glazed, about 1 minute. Stir in the chopped tomato, lemon zest, and marjoram, and cook for 1 minute. Add the boiling liquid and salt and boil for 1 minute.

3. Reduce the heat to low and simmer, covered, until the liquid has been absorbed, about 18 minutes for white rice, a bit longer for brown.

4. Turn off the heat. Place a folded paper towel or tea towel over the rice, cover the pot, and let it rest for 10 minutes before adding the pepper and parsley and fluffing with a fork.

IL CONVENTO'S

Pugliese Roast Chicken

WITH CAPER AND PECORINO STUFFING

Lord Alistair McAlpine of West Green is presently ensconced in Puglia leading yet another of his fairy-tale lives. Sexagenarian Alistair has reinvented himself once again and is living with his third wife, Athena—a charming and sophisticated Greek beauty—in a self-created paradise south of Lecce near the tip of the heel of Italy's boot. This scion of the McAlpine building dynasty, a sitting member of Parliament to this day, is remembered by many first as treasurer and then as deputy chairman of the Conservative Party under Margaret Thatcher. A compulsive and visionary collector since his teens, he's said to have compiled and then sold or given away more than forty major collections in his lifetime. I recall elegant "picnic" lunches brought around by Alistair in the 1980s to enhance the viewing and selling of his antiquities.

In addition, the many-faceted Alistair is a respected author, philanthropist, and international tastemaker as well as a publisher, gardener, zookeeper, and avid traveler; but to my mind, his current existence is by far the most enviable. After a prolonged honeymoon in India traveling and collecting, Lord and Lady McAlpine brought their newfound treasures to Italy. Overhauling a ruined fourteenth-century convent that Alistair had given to his young bride as a wedding present, they made a home for themselves, their Pugliese mutt Pompeiia, and their art. Athena, true to her name, does everything with seemingly no effort; she calls it "looking like a swan even if you are feeling like a duck." She has created a riotously colorful and rustically luxurious pleasure palace tucked away behind a somber gray stone façade.

In the spring of 2003, the McAlpines announced the opening of Il Convento di Santa Maria di Costantinopoli, an unusual bed-and-breakfast in the starkly beautiful southernmost tip of Italy. This long-talked-about renovation was going public. Ever since, celebrities of all types as well as curious adventurers have flocked to the tiny village of Marittima di Diso and fallen under the spell of the McAlpines with their over-the-top hospitality and willingness to graciously open their home to strangers, who often become friends. And one can't forget the wines freely offered from Alistair's incredible cellar and the spectacular food. Athena's passion for discovering and procuring the best local products and ingredients is evident every time you sit down to eat. At breakfast, a regional pastry filled with tomato, béchamel, and mozzarella is one of the best things I have ever eaten. Organic produce, super-fresh fish, lamb, pork, and sausages, plus mozzarella and *burrata* made daily nearby, are spun into delicious meals by adorable Emmanuele and Pierluigi. They are ever-cheerful and ever-present in the kitchen and always true to Athena's mantra—whether fava beans, artichokes, strawberries, peaches, or wild greens—"Always, always in season."

Stuffed with bread crumbs, capers, and pecorino, this roast chicken is an unusual Italian take on a universal favorite. Athena adapted the recipe from one in *Real Italian Food* by Paul Lay, who said it was often served at Easter and exemplified Puglia's less affluent past. As her neighbors in the Basso Salento, the southernmost and poorest section of Puglia, have no recollection of the dish, Athena suggests it may have come from farther north, nearer more affluent Bari, where people were better known for their cooking skills, and where meat and poultry were eaten more frequently.

In accordance with the "waste not, want not" *cucina povera* mentality of their poverty-stricken past, the Pugliese discard nothing. They dry their leftover bread—considered by many to be the best in Italy—in the sun to create bread crumbs for tossing into pasta, folding into cake batter, incorporating into meatballs, or stuffing into vegetables, fish, meat, and chicken. Inspired by the local custom, Pierluigi often turns Il Convento's stale loaves into bread sauce—one of the great British classics and a favorite of Athena—and, fusion-style, serves it to accompany the Pugliese chicken. I was skeptical, but the unexpected marriage of two very old recipes turned out to be a happy one. The Bread Sauce recipe that follows is adapted from Delia Smith. Its sweet creaminess and rich medieval spices are an interesting contrast to the chicken's piquant capers and pecorino. Athena, true to her British upbringing, serves a never-fail combination of roast potatoes, peas, and carrots alongside; but I prefer a local accompaniment, fava bean purée and sautéed chicories (see recipe page 170). But the chicken dish is a minor miracle, so you can't go wrong either way. If you serve the fava purée, however, do save the bread sauce for another time.

Serves 4 to 5

5 large chicken livers
2 tablespoons extra virgin olive oil
Sea salt and freshly ground black pepper to taste
1 medium onion, peeled and finely minced
4 cloves garlic, peeled and sliced paper-thin
Approximately 4 cups large, irregular bread crumbs, freshly made from a white French or Italian peasant loaf (The easiest way to make these is in a food processor, but tearing the bread into small pieces works fine as well. Leave the crust on the bread, as it makes for a less uniform, more interesting stuffing texture.)
2 heaping tablespoons capers, rinsed, drained, and chopped if large
3 tablespoons chopped fresh oregano
⅓ cup freshly grated pecorino cheese
1 extra-large egg, lightly beaten

One 3½- to 4-pound chicken
1 cup dry white wine or water
Bread Sauce (optional; recipe follows)

1. Preheat the oven to 400 degrees, and coarsely chop the chicken livers. Heat the olive oil in a small skillet, season the chopped livers with salt and pepper, and sauté over medium heat until browned. Transfer the cooked livers to a medium bowl and add the onion, garlic, bread crumbs, capers, oregano, and pecorino. Add the egg and mix well. The stuffing should be moist like wet sand. If it is too wet, add more bread crumbs. If it seems too dry, add a bit more egg. Season with salt and pepper.

2. Stuff the chicken. Place any extra stuffing in a small casserole, sprinkle with water or white wine, and cover tightly with foil.

3. Rub the chicken with salt, pepper, and a little olive oil. For an even more flavorful bird, mix olive oil with salt, pepper, chopped oregano, and garlic and rub the chicken inside and out before stuffing and then put some of the olive oil mixture under the skin.

4. Place the chicken on a rack in a roasting pan, breast-side down. Roast for 25 minutes. Turn the chicken breast-side up and roast for 20 more minutes. Pour the wine over the chicken and turn the heat down to 350 degrees. Place the casserole with extra stuffing in the oven.

5. Continue to roast until done—the thigh juices will run clear rather than pink when pierced with a sharp knife—approximately 20 to 30 more minutes, basting with the wine every 10 minutes. If the pan drippings dry up, add ¼ cup more wine or water. When done, let stand for 15 minutes before carving.

6. The stuffing can continue to cook, if necessary. When done, leave it in the turned-off oven until ready to serve.

7. Serve the roast chicken and piping hot stuffing. Pour the Bread Sauce (if using) in a sauceboat and pass separately.

BREAD SAUCE

Serves 8

1 large onion, peeled and cut in half
3¾ cups whole milk, plus more if necessary
⅛ teaspoon freshly grated nutmeg
Pinch of ground mace
1 bay leaf
1 large clove garlic, peeled and cut in half
8 whole black peppercorns
3 cups large irregular bread crumbs, freshly made from a
    high-quality white bread (see bread-crumb instruc-
    tions previous page)
5 tablespoons unsalted butter
Salt and freshly ground white pepper (black is a fine
    substitute) to taste

1. Place the onion halves in a large saucepan and add the milk, nutmeg, mace, bay leaf, garlic, and peppercorns. Bring to a boil, turn off the heat, and cover the pan. Let steep for at least 2 hours, preferably longer. You can even do this a day ahead of time and after several hours, cover and refrigerate until ready to use.

2. To make the sauce, remove the bay leaf, onion, garlic, and peppercorns and discard.

3. Stir the bread crumbs into the milk and add 3 table-spoons of the butter. Leave on very low heat, stirring occasionally, for 10 to 15 minutes, until the crumbs have "melted" into the sauce. Set aside until ready to eat.

4. Just before serving, reheat the sauce gently while stirring in the remaining 2 tablespoons butter. It should be the consistency of runny oatmeal. If it is too thick, add more milk, a bit at a time. If it is too thin, continue to cook. Adjust the seasoning and serve hot.

Coq au Vin

Like Escoffier before him with his "*Faites simple*," Richard Olney felt that food needn't be elaborate or complicated to be great; he believed, like Curnonsky, that "*la cuisine*" is when "things taste like themselves." Olney put his faith in the freshness and quality of ingredients rather than the intricacy of their preparation. In the preface to his 1974 classic, *Simple French Food,* he states, "Simple is the password to cooking today. If food is not simple, it is not good." He advocated preparing food "in a way least apt to modify its native qualities—poached, grilled, or roasted, accompanied by a sauce that though compounded of separately prepared essences strikes a single suave note, quietly enhancing the integrity of the basic product."

Beginning with his first trip to France after college, Olney became obsessed with French food. He worked his way through art school by waiting tables in New York's Greenwich Village, and once back in Paris, the culinary arts lured him away from his easel more and more insistently. Around the time he moved to Provence, his in-depth acquaintance with classic French food and wine landed him a job as a columnist writing "Un Américain (gourmand) à Paris" for the journal *Cuisine et Vins de France.* In 1970 *The French Menu Cookbook,* with its then-revolutionary seasonal menus based on French country cooking and careful wine pairings, gained him attention in both Britain and America. By the time *Simple French Food* was published four years later, Olney was one of the most important food writers of his generation with an impact on everything from nouvelle cuisine in France across oceans to Berkeley, where his friends Alice Waters and Jeremiah Tower were shaking things up at Chez Panisse.

Olney was the perfect choice to head the team creating the twenty-eight volume Time-Life book series *The Good Cook*. The immense endeavor began in 1977 and took five years. Hiring food experts including Jane Grigson, Jeremiah Tower, Richard Sax, Alan Davidson, and Julie Dannenbaum to write, edit, style, and oversee photography, he produced a magnum opus celebrated to this day.

His books went beyond the direct and precise recipes they contained. Olney was a serious writer and his literary voice a joy to read, even for those never intending to enter a kitchen. As an artist, he encouraged culinary improvisation and poetic license, but only once basic techniques were mastered: "By knowing and accepting rules, one frees oneself of rules." And he was a magician in the kitchen, able to spin the simplest vegetables, grains, and least expensive cuts of meat into culinary gold. Though he lived alone until his death in 1999 and was considered by some to be a recluse and a curmudgeon, Olney communicated regularly with friends and family in America

and frequently entertained both houseguests and dinner guests. In the introduction to *Ten Vineyard Lunches*, Olney explains, "There is nothing formal about my table—unless an array of wineglasses be considered formal—and, because I am most comfortable dressed in rags, that is the way I receive. My main concern is that everyone falls immediately into a relaxed atmosphere. As the kitchen is the largest room in the house and meals are served there, before the fireplace, when the weather does not permit eating on the terrace, it is also a combined center of cooking and social activity during the often extended aperitif hour . . . I don't much worry about timing—as long as the Champagne glasses are kept filled, no one minds lingering before going to the table . . ."

"Coq" is the French word for the cock or rooster that was originally used in slow-cooked chicken dishes. Cocks were good breeders and were kept on farms as long as they could fulfill their function. By the time they were slaughtered, they were old and tough and required long, slow cooking in a casserole. These days, *coq au vin* is usually made with chicken pieces or a hen and cooked for a considerably shorter time.

The dish used to appear on restaurant menus all over America. I remember delicious versions on both the Chez Dreyfus and the Henri IV menus in Cambridge in the seventies, although the eateries were only a block apart. But no longer. Trends, tastes, and times change; however, the pendulum may swing back. In the meantime, make and enjoy this delicious braise—redolent of red wine, vegetables, bacon, and the aromas of France—at home. It's even better made a day or two ahead and reheated for serving and is easily scaled up for a crowd. Leftovers freeze perfectly.

The additions of dried mushrooms and tomato paste are mine, as I like the increased depth of flavor they provide. To be true to the master, leave them out. Steamed potatoes or fresh egg noodles are the only accompaniment required.

Serves 6

2 tablespoons extra virgin olive oil, plus more if needed

¼ pound lean pancetta, cut into small dice, blanched for 1 minute in boiling water rinsed in cool water, drained, and dried

4 medium carrots, peeled and cut into rounds 1 inch thick

3 medium onions, peeled and coarsely chopped

3 ribs celery, cut crosswise into ¼-inch slices

5 cloves garlic, peeled and smashed

Approximately 6 pounds chicken legs—thighs attached to drumsticks

Sea salt and freshly ground black pepper to taste

3 tablespoons all-purpose flour

2 tablespoons cognac or brandy

1 bottle or more good red wine, preferably a Burgundy

3 tablespoons best-quality Italian tomato paste

1 ounce dried mushrooms, rinsed in cold water (optional)

Bouquet garni consisting of several sprigs fresh flat-leaf parsley and fresh thyme, 6 black peppercorns, and a bay leaf, wrapped in cheesecloth

Chicken stock, if necessary

1 pound white button mushrooms, trimmed, whole, halved, or quartered depending on size

8 tablespoons (1 stick) unsalted butter

30 small pearl onions, peeled (or use one 10-ounce box frozen pearl onions, thawed)

6 square slices firm-textured stale white bread (like *pain de mie*). If not stale, spread on a baking sheet and dry for a few minutes in a 350-degree oven. Cut into approximately ½-inch cubes.

¼ cup chopped fresh flat-leaf parsley

1. In a large sauté pan or casserole set over low heat, add approximately 2 tablespoons of olive oil and fry the pancetta cubes until golden. Using a slotted spoon, transfer them to paper towels to degrease.

2. Turn the heat to medium-low and add the carrots, onions, celery, and 4 of the cloves of smashed garlic. Cook in the same fat until soft and light gold, stirring frequently.

This will take 20 to 30 minutes. Add tablespoons of water if the mixture becomes too dry or to prevent burning.

3. When the vegetables are done, transfer them to a plate and set aside. Add more oil to the pan if necessary, season the chicken pieces with salt and pepper, and cook them over medium-high heat until nicely browned on all sides. Sprinkle them with the flour and continue to cook, turning frequently until the flour is lightly browned.

4. Return the vegetables to the pan. Stir in the cognac and then the bottle of wine and turn the heat to high. Use a wooden spoon to scrape up all the bits and pieces that are stuck to the bottom and sides of the pan (in other words, deglaze the pan). Stir in the tomato paste and dried mushrooms, if using. Tuck in the bouquet garni and if necessary add wine or chicken stock so that the chicken pieces are completely covered with liquid.

5. Bring to a boil, then cover and lower the heat so the liquid is barely simmering. Cook until the meat is tender but not falling off the bones. This will take 20 to 45 minutes depending on the age of the chicken and size of the pieces.

6. While the chicken is cooking, sauté the mushrooms— seasoned with salt and pepper—in a sauté pan in 4 tablespoons of butter over high heat, stirring frequently, until liquid is released and then evaporated and the mushrooms are lightly colored. Transfer them to a plate and set aside.

7. Add 3 tablespoons of the remaining butter to the pan along with the peeled onions. Add salt and pepper and cover. Cook over the lowest possible heat, shaking the pan from time to time, until they are tender but only slightly colored. This will take 20 to 30 minutes. If using thawed frozen onions, cook for only 5 minutes. Set aside.

8. When done, transfer the chicken pieces and carrots to a platter. Press juices from the bouquet garni and then discard it. Skim fat that has come to the surface of the sauce.

9. Strain the contents of the pan through a large sieve into a bowl. Press hard on the solids in the sieve to extract all the liquid. Let the sauce settle. If possible, put it in the refrigerator, which will hasten the fat rising to the surface.

10. Meanwhile, return the chicken and carrots to the pan. Scatter over the pearl onions, sautéed mushrooms, and the little pancetta lardons. Set aside. The recipe can be prepared up to this point a day ahead and refrigerated. When the sauce is really cold, you will be able to remove more of the fat.

11. To continue, remove all possible fat from the top of the cooking liquid and pour the liquid into a small saucepan. Place the saucepan over medium heat half off the burner. The fat will rise to the top. Keep skimming it off until the sauce is clean. At that point, reduce it over high heat, stirring constantly to bring it to a velvety, spoon-coating consistency. It should not be thick like gravy.

12. Correct seasoning and pour sauce over the chicken and vegetables in the pan, cover, and place over the lowest possible heat for 15 to 30 minutes, until piping hot.

13. While the chicken is reheating, place the 1 remaining clove of garlic with the bread cubes and last tablespoon of butter in a skillet and sauté over medium heat until the bread cubes are golden. This can be done ahead and reheated at serving time.

14. Arrange the chicken pieces on a hot platter. Spoon the sauce and vegetables over and then sprinkle with the bread cubes and parsley. Serve with steamed or boiled small potatoes or buttered noodles.

THE RUSSIAN TEA ROOM'S

Chicken Kiev

Classic Chicken Kiev—a chicken breast boned but leaving the first wing joint attached and then stuffed with chilled butter before breading and deep-frying—was a symbol of Russian haute cuisine in the late eighteenth and the nineteenth centuries. After cooking, the traditional dish resembles a fried chicken drumstick. Many people these days are adverse to deep-fried food. Thus I suggest a quick sauté finished in the oven, the assembly made easier by completely boning and then flattening the chicken breast before rolling it around a finger of frozen flavored butter. Properly made, the dish is identified by the spurt of hot butter—diners beware—at the first touch of a knife and fork. An absorbent white, brown, or wild rice or a pilaf, the ideal accompaniment, guarantees that none of the rich and flavorful liquid will go to waste.

Despite its name, the Kievian origins of this famous dish are obscure. Russian Empress Elizabeth Petrovna (1749–1762) was an obsessive Francophile, and by the late eighteenth century, all things French—including French food and French chefs—were the rage in wealthy Russian households. Most people agree that Chicken Kiev began life in France as a version of "cotelettes de volaille," or stuffed chicken breasts. In *The Russian Tea Room Cookbook,* Faith Stewart-Gordon credits the legendary chef Antonin Carême with inventing the dish during his tenure at the court of Tsar Alexander I, while others cite Nicolas Appert, a contemporary of Carême and known for his wizardry with confectionery, canning, and food preservation.

The name Kiev most likely did not attach itself to this dish until after the Russian Revolution, with New York restaurants trying to please the never-ending waves of Russian immigrants arriving at Ellis Island. The name then boomeranged back to Europe, and after World War II, Chicken Kiev was frequently seen on menus in Russia itself.

Serves 8 (1 cutlet each)

12 tablespoons (1½ sticks) unsalted butter, cold
4 tablespoons finely chopped fresh flat-leaf parsley, chives, dill, tarragon, or any mixture
1 clove garlic, put through a garlic press
1½ tablespoons freshly squeezed lemon juice
¾ teaspoon freshly ground pepper
4 whole small chicken breasts, approximately 3 pounds total (8 half breasts), cut into 8 halves, each half weighing approximately 5 to 6 ounces, boned and skinned, chilled
Sea salt to taste
Approximately 1 cup flour for dredging
2 large eggs, lightly beaten
Approximately 1 cup homemade fine dry bread crumbs
Approximately 6 tablespoons unsalted butter and 6 tablespoons tasteless vegetable oil for frying

1. Cream together the butter, herbs, garlic, lemon juice, and pepper. On a chilled plate, shape the butter into 8 rolls about 3 inches long and ¾ inch thick. Cover with plastic wrap and place in the freezer for at least 1 hour and up to several days.

2. Place each half chicken breast between sheets of waxed paper and pound with a kitchen mallet, a rolling pin, or the flat side of a cleaver, until approximately ⅛ inch thick. Try not to tear the meat. This will be easier to achieve if the chicken is cold, right out of the refrigerator.

3. Sprinkle each flattened chicken breast with salt, and lay 1 frozen butter finger lengthwise on each. Tuck in both ends and then roll the breast up, securing with a toothpick. Use more toothpicks to remedy any visible tears or openings in the meat so that the butter does not leak out during cooking.

4. Dip the rolls in flour, shaking off the excess. Then dip each floured roll in the beaten eggs and then in the bread crumbs. As finished, place each cutlet on a platter. When all the cutlets have been breaded, cover with plastic wrap and refrigerate for at least 4 hours.

5. When ready to cook, preheat the oven to 325 degrees. Melt 3 tablespoons of butter and 3 tablespoons of cooking oil in a large skillet or sauté pan. When very hot but not burning, brown the cutlets—in batches if necessary—on both sides until deep gold. As finished, place each cutlet on a baking sheet large enough to hold all the cutlets in a single layer. Add more butter and oil to the skillet as needed. Place the baking sheet with the 8 cutlets in the oven until the chicken is done, approximately 5 to 8 minutes. Serve immediately with or without sauce—the Georgian Sour Plum and Mushroom Sauces (see recipes on page 135) are both very good with this dish—but definitely with plain or wild rice or a pilaf to soak up the extra butter.

Note: If you prefer to deep-fry, heat tasteless vegetable oil in a deep fryer to 350 degrees, and fry until deep golden, about 8 minutes. Drain on paper towels and keep warm in a low oven until all the cutlets are cooked.

Chicken Country Captain

"Upscale plantation food, now totally gone with the wind" is how my friend Alex Hitz described this Low Country favorite from his Georgia childhood—a succulent, mild, and elegant version of chicken curry. Although an early recipe for Chicken Country Captain appears in Alessandro Filippini's 1906 cookbook *The International Cook Book* (see page 107), the first mention of the dish is in *Miss Leslie's New Cookery Book* from 1867. Miss Leslie claimed the dish had Indian origins and that "Country Captain" referred to a Sepoy or captain of native troops in the pay of the English. The recipe was probably brought to friends in Savannah by a British colonial officer who had eaten the curry when serving in Bengal, though some think the recipe arrived with a captain involved in the Caribbean spice trade. An even smaller contingent associates it with a "country capon."

Starting around 1875, Country Captain remained a dinner party mainstay of the Lowlands for many years, and by the 1940s, it appeared in every Junior League cookbook south of the Mason Dixon line. Mrs. W. L. Bullard from Warm Springs, Georgia, had made the dish for a banquet honoring F.D.R., who was taking spa treatments nearby for his paralysis. Once the Roosevelts built a home of their own in the neighborhood, they served the spicy chicken regularly to their own guests, including General Patton, who was such a fan that his name was soon associated with the dish. In 2000, the Pentagon chose to honor the legendary commander by making

Chicken Country Captain one of its packaged M.R.E.'s, or Meals Ready to Eat, given to soldiers in the field. It was a huge hit, but then a problem arose. In his July 7, 2006, article for the *New Republic*, Julian Barnes quotes an army source as saying "Country Captain Chicken got a reputation. During the initial invasion of Iraq, when I was embedded with the 101st Airborne Division, soldiers were fighting over the Hamburger Patty, but they left Country Captain for the reporters. 'Country Captain Chicken,' a young specialist told me, 'will make you gay.'" Whatever you may expect from this dish, these claims are entirely unsubstantiated. What is real, however, is the tastiness of Country Captain and its ability to conjure up the mystery of the old South.

This version of Country Captain is one of the most exuberant chicken dishes I know. It is rendered sweet, hot, and also salty by the unlikely incorporation of Eastern spices into a very Southern sauce. Bejeweled with currants, bacon, and pieces of multicolored local vegetables, it is then topped with tantalizing condiments—both homegrown and exotic. These extras are not mandatory; the basic recipe stands firmly on its own. However, I like using all of them, as their colors make a strong visual statement, and their textures add richness and complexity to a dish already hard to beat. And remember to serve a big bowl of fluffy South Carolina rice alongside.

The recipe can be made through Step 7 up to three days ahead, cooled, and refrigerated. Bring to room temperature and reheat in a moderate oven before proceeding.

Serves 8

Approximately ⅔ cup all-purpose flour

4 teaspoons sea salt or kosher salt

2 teaspoons freshly ground black pepper

1 tablespoon dried thyme

Approximately 6 pounds chicken thighs (breasts or mixed chicken pieces are also fine, but using all thighs results in a uniformly cooked and uniformly moist finished product), at room temperature

6 tablespoons unsalted butter

10 slices best-quality smoky bacon

3 large yellow onions, peeled and cut into medium dice

1 green bell pepper, cut into medium dice

1 red bell pepper, cut into medium dice

1 yellow bell pepper, cut into medium dice

5 ribs celery, thinly sliced

3 large carrots, peeled and very thinly sliced

4 tablespoons minced garlic

¼ teaspoon medium hot curry powder

1 teaspoon ground ginger

½ teaspoon ground cinnamon

½ teaspoon ground cloves

½ teaspoon freshly grated nutmeg

½ cup raisins or dried currants

Two 28-ounce cans whole or chopped tomatoes with their juice (preferably San Marzano)

2 tablespoons dark brown sugar or molasses

½ cup freshly squeezed lemon juice

Sea salt and freshly ground black pepper to taste

½ cup blanched almonds, toasted and roughly chopped

¼ cup coarsely chopped fresh flat-leaf parsley

10 to 16 cups hot cooked white rice

Optional condiments:

Toasted and coarsely chopped peanuts

Toasted coconut

Diced banana

Various chutneys

Chopped hard-boiled egg

Thinly sliced scallions

Diced fresh tomatoes

Diced mango

Diced Granny Smith apple

1. Preheat the oven to 325 degrees. Mix the flour together with salt, pepper, and dried thyme. Pat the chicken dry and dredge it in the seasoned flour. Shake off excess flour.

2. In a large skillet, melt the butter over medium-high heat. When the foam begins to subside, fry the chicken on both sides—in batches if necessary—until deep gold in color, about 8 minutes per side.

3. Transfer the chicken to a platter lined with paper towels and pat with more paper towels to absorb the extra grease.

4. When all the chicken has been browned, wipe out the pan with a paper towel and add the bacon slices. Fry the bacon over medium heat until crisp. Transfer the bacon to several thicknesses of paper towels and degrease. Crumble the bacon and set aside in a small bowl.

5. Add the onions, peppers, celery, carrots, garlic, all of the spices, and half of the raisins to the skillet and sauté over medium heat, stirring frequently, until the vegetables are soft and beginning to color, about 10 minutes.

6. Stir in tomatoes and their juices, dark brown sugar, and lemon juice. Bring to a boil, lower heat to medium-low and simmer for 15 minutes. Season with salt and pepper.

7. Place the chicken pieces in a very large casserole and pour the tomato sauce over the top. Bring to a simmer on top of the stove, cover tightly with foil and a lid, and place in the oven. Turn the chicken pieces every 15 minutes and bake (or simmer on top of the stove) until tender and the juices run clear when pierced with a fork. Add water or stock if the sauce is too thick. If too thin, remove the chicken and set aside, covered in foil, to keep warm and boil down the sauce—stirring often so it will not burn and skimming off accumulated fat and scum—until a proper sauce consistency is reached.

8. Serve from the casserole or transfer to a hot platter and sprinkle with the reserved crumbled bacon, the almonds, and parsley. Pass the rice and the optional condiments.

Chicken à la King

Charles Ranhofer is often given credit for inventing Chicken à la King in 1880 at Delmonico's. It is said that Foxhall P. Keene, son of James R. Keene, avid horse breeder and the "Silver Fox of Wall Street," asked the legendary chef to make him something in a pimento-studded cream sauce, and Chicken à la Keene—later renamed Chicken à la King—was born. But there is no evidence, and the fact that the recipe is not included in Ranhofer's magnum opus *The Epicurean* is probably proof that the dish was conceived elsewhere.

The theory with the most staying power gives credit to chef George Greenwald of the Brighton Beach Hotel in Brooklyn. It is likely that somewhere between 1898 and 1905, Greenwald—who enjoyed creating new recipes for people he liked—whipped up the chicken dish in question for the hotel's owners, Mr. and Mrs. Charles King. The next day—either at the request of the Kings or on a personal whim—the chef put Chicken à la King (at $1.25) on the menu, where it remained a perennial favorite for many years.

When made correctly, the moist chicken morsels and freshly cooked vegetables in a light béchamel sauce perfumed with onion, garlic, and thyme, taste divine. Because my mother called them chicken à la king pot pies, whenever I think of chicken à la king, my mind goes directly to the Swanson frozen chicken dishes of my childhood. There too were the peas, a bit of diced carrot, and a couple of pearl onions, but almost no chicken was apparent, and what was included was overcooked and drowning in glue-like yellow sauce.

For a variety of reasons, many Americans have similar gloppy "chicken à la king" associations. Made correctly at home, however, the meal represents comfort food at its best. Served over rice, buttered noodles, fluffy biscuits, in crêpes, or atop cut-open baked potatoes, this recipe aims to please. And bright green *petits pois* on the side (if you don't include them in the fricassee itself, which I am wont to do) provide color as well as extra flavor. And, of course, this recipe makes an excellent pot pie filling. Use it instead of the seafood filling on page 50. If making pot pie, definitely add 3 cups of thawed frozen green peas in Step 6 along with the sherry or brandy.

Serves 10 to 12 generously

For poaching the chicken:
3½ pounds boneless, skinless chicken breasts and/or
    thighs
4 to 6 cups chicken stock, preferably homemade
3 cloves garlic, peeled and smashed
Several sprigs fresh thyme, or ½ teaspoon dried thyme

For the mushrooms:
4 to 6 tablespoons unsalted butter
2 pounds white button mushrooms and/or cremini and/or
    mixed wild mushrooms, wiped clean and sliced
Sea salt and freshly ground black pepper to taste

For the vegetables:
4 tablespoons (½ stick) unsalted butter
3 large onions, peeled and diced
5 large cloves garlic, peeled and sliced
4 large carrots, peeled and cut into thin rounds
2 large red bell peppers, seeded, deveined, and cut into
    medium dice
3 ribs celery, trimmed and thinly sliced crosswise
Several sprigs fresh thyme, or ½ teaspoon dried thyme
Sea salt and freshly ground pepper to taste
One 10-ounce bag frozen pearl onions, thawed (optional)
One 10-ounce bag frozen green peas, thawed (optional)

For the béchamel sauce:
8 tablespoons (1 stick) unsalted butter
1 cup all-purpose flour
2 cups whole milk
4 tablespoons brandy

2 tablespoons medium sherry
⅛ teaspoon nutmeg, or to taste
Sea salt and freshly ground pepper to taste
Freshly squeezed lemon juice to taste
A few drops of Tabasco sauce
2 large eggs yolks, whisked together with ⅓ cup heavy
    cream (optional)
½ cup minced fresh flat-leaf parsley and/or minced
    fresh chives for garnish

1. Place the chicken pieces in a large saucepan. Pour the stock over. If it does not cover the chicken, add more until it does. Add the smashed garlic and thyme.
2. Bring to a boil. Cover, reduce the heat, and simmer until the chicken is done, about 8 minutes. Don't overcook.
3. Transfer the chicken and garlic to a platter to cool, and reserve 4 cups of the broth in the saucepan. Add or subtract broth so you have exactly 4 cups.
4. Put 4 tablespoons butter in a large skillet set over high heat. When it has melted, add the sliced mushrooms and salt and pepper. Add more butter if needed. Stir frequently until the mushrooms have given off their juice, the liquid has then cooked off, and the mushrooms are very tender, about 15 minutes. Then add to the chicken on the platter.
5. Wipe out the skillet and add 4 tablespoons butter. Set the pan over medium-high heat. When the butter melts, add the onions, sliced garlic, carrots, red pepper, celery, thyme, and salt and pepper. Sauté, stirring frequently, until the vegetables are soft and beginning to color, about

15 to 20 minutes. Add the pearl onions and peas, if using, and cook, stirring, for about 2 minutes or until heated through. Transfer the vegetables to the platter with the chicken and mushrooms.

6. While the vegetables are cooking, bring the reserved broth to a simmer. Place the remaining 1 stick of butter in a saucepan—large enough to hold the chicken, sauce, and all the vegetables—over medium heat. When the foaming subsides, add the flour and cook for 2 minutes, stirring. Whisk in the hot broth and whisk briskly to avoid lumps. Cook for 1 minute, then add the milk and any accumulated juices on the platter. Bring to a simmer and continue to cook, stirring, until the sauce fully thickens, about 3 minutes. Add the brandy and sherry and cook for 1 more minute. Season with the nutmeg, salt, pepper, lemon juice, and Tabasco sauce.

7. Add the chicken and vegetables on the platter and cook gently for a couple of minutes to heat through. Do not boil or the sauce may curdle. Adjust the seasonings.

8. For optional enrichment, stir in the cream and egg yolk mixture little by little (to avoid curdling) into the hot sauce.

9. Serve immediately over rice, noodles, biscuits, or crêpes, garnished with abundant chopped fresh parsley and/or chives.

ALAIN SENDERENS'S

Duck à l'Apicius

Renowned Parisian chef Alain Senderens—a founding father of nouvelle cuisine, and for twenty-eight years the proud possessor of three Michelin stars, first at L'Archestrate and then at Lucas Carton on elegant Place de la Madeleine—has always been both icon and iconoclast. Nonetheless, even in an unshockable post-9/11 world, Senderens created quite "le scandale," flabbergasting the French culinary establishment, when in 2005 he did the unthinkable and attempted to give back his three stars to *Le Guide Michelin. Le Guide* retorted with "... the stars are meant to inform the readers of the guide and can only belong to the guide that presents them. Restaurateurs just cannot return them like a gift." But return them he did; and at an age when most people retire, he relaunched the legendary Lucas Carton, renaming it Senderens and saying, "I want to simplify my cooking, allow myself more liberty, and reduce the average check at Alain Senderens to 100 Euros. I cannot do this with the level of effort required to maintain the three-star status." He updated both the menu and the dark, almost shrinelike, Belle Époque interior of Lucas Carton to create an establishment more in tune with modern life in terms of both food and ambiance, one that would attract the locals rather than catering primarily to American tourists.

My favorite Lucas Carton story comes from James Marlas, a close friend who long ago was a regular customer. Dining at the restaurant post-opera with his then wife—in a long gown, as back then certain people still "dressed" for certain things, Callas in *La Traviata* being one of them—

everything was going well. There were smiles, effusions, and little bows at the door; and then caviar to start followed by Senderens's signature Canard à l'Apicius. Things continued swimmingly until dessert, when a server managed to spill triple sec, meant for the crêpes suzettes, down the front of "Madame's" dress. She was soon ablaze. Terrified waiters headed for the door, leaving poor Jim to douse his wife with drinking water, barely managing to extinguish the fire before serious injury occurred. Needless to say, the couple was shaken, and both gown and dessert ruined, as were Jim's nerves. All this ruination did not stop Lucas Carton from charging full price for the meal—including the disastrous dessert—though it was suggested that the cleaning bill for the dress be forwarded to the restaurant, a moot point, as the devastated piece of clothing was destined for the trash heap.

Despite occasional missteps, perfectionist Senderens's inventive food was sublime. His approach to cooking was distinctly cerebral rather than intuitive, his inspirations coming primarily from the old and the older—often from the first-century writings of Roman merchant and pleasure-seeker Marcus Gavius Apicius, official gastronome at the court of Tiberius and credited with writing *De Re Coquinaria* (*On the Subject of Cooking*), the oldest cookbook in the Western world.

Duck à l'Apicius—capitalizing on the ancient flavor combination of sweet, spicy, hot, and tart—was the signature dish of Chef Senderens for many years at several different restaurants. The elaborate preparation included degreasing a Barbary duck in warm water and then roasting it with a basting glaze of honey, coriander, caraway, cumin, saffron, and white pepper. The meat was served with caramelized strips of the basting sauce on top and a second sauce made from rich duck drippings cut with red vinegar poured over and around. Turnips were served alongside as well as two purées—one of dates, ginger, and mint, the other of quince and apple. This dish represented restaurant cooking at its most exquisite and complicated. In simplifying the recipe for home cooks, I've retained the taste sensations that identify the dish but shortened the procedures and eliminated the purées, incorporating their flavors into the sauce itself. And to save time and effort, I've replaced whole ducks with magrets.

Serve with rice pilaf, buttered noodles, or mashed potatoes to absorb the rich and abundant sauce. Turnips, apples, and quince are part of the dish, so no other vegetable is needed, especially if you precede the duck with a composed salad. To add something green, consider string beans, peas, or sautéed spinach.

Serves 4 to 6

1⅔ pounds medium white turnips, peeled and cut into
    ¼-inch wedges
1 whole duck magret (two halves), approximately
    2 pounds total
Salt and freshly ground black pepper
2 Granny Smith apples, or 2 quince, or 1 of each, cored
    and cut into ¼-inch slices
2 cloves garlic, peeled and minced
¼ cup chopped onions or shallots
½ cup mild honey
6 tablespoons cider vinegar (white wine or champagne
    vinegar can be substituted)

2 to 3 pieces of star anise, coarsely ground
6 tablespoons whole coriander seeds, toasted and
    coarsely ground
2 tablespoons whole cumin seeds, toasted and coarsely
    ground
1 tablespoon caraway seeds, toasted and coarsely ground
¼ teaspoon saffron threads
1 cup white wine
2 cups duck or chicken stock
Approximately ¼ cup roughly chopped fresh dill,
    fresh mint, fresh cilantro, and/or fresh marjoram
    for garnish

1. Place the turnip wedges in boiling salted water and boil for 3 minutes. Drain and refresh in cold water. Set aside or refrigerate until needed.

2. Deeply score the duck fat in a ½-inch grid, and rub the magrets all over with salt and pepper.

3. Over medium-high flame, heat a skillet just large enough to fit the magrets. Place the magrets skin-side down in the hot skillet. Cook for 6 minutes, or until the skin is quite brown and most of the fat has been rendered. Turn down the heat and cook the other side for 1 minute. Keep removing the rendered fat, and reserve it for a later use. The breasts should be removed from the heat when cooked to almost the desired doneness. Rare is recommended.

4. Set the breasts on a platter and pour all but 2 tablespoons of fat from the pan. Reserve with the other saved fat. Sauté the turnip wedges and apples and/or quince for 2 minutes in the same fat, stirring. Remove to the platter with the duck.

5. Add 2 to 3 tablespoons fat back to the pan and sauté the garlic and onion for 2 to 3 minutes. Add the honey and vinegar and cook for several minutes, stirring constantly, until syrupy and a bit caramelized. Add the spices and cook another minute. Off the heat, add the duck breasts and coat both sides with the honey-spice mixture. Return the duck to the platter.

6. Dissolve the saffron in the wine, add it to the pan, and boil for 1 to 2 minutes. Add the stock and reduce until the sauce is syrupy. The recipe can be completed to this point several hours ahead and set aside, or 24 hours ahead and cooled, covered, and refrigerated. Bring to room temperature before continuing.

7. To complete the recipe and serve, reheat the sauce over medium heat. Reheat the duck in the sauce. Remove the duck and keep warm. Add the reserved sliced apples or quince and the turnips to the pan and heat through. Adjust the seasoning. Arrange on a platter or individual plates, sprinkled with the fresh herb garnish.

Roast Duck

WITH RASPBERRY SAUCE

I first tasted the winning combination of duck and raspberries in Brittany more than twenty years ago. My friend Dan Wolfe was on a summer pilgrimage to visit the wonderfully eccentric American Field Service family he'd lived with junior year of high school. My then-husband Willy and I were tagging along to experience life in a mint-condition (virtually untouched for four hundred years) seventeenth-century French château. It was July, and the days were long, especially that far North. Although we didn't arrive until late afternoon, there were several hours of daylight left to explore.

The sweeping lawn in front of the old stone mansion was just-mown and fragrant. At first glance the stately silhouette of the mansard roof kept us from noticing it was riddled with holes. The entire edifice, in fact, was in utter disrepair. Dan had neglected to mention that the charming vicomte and vicomtesse—his "parents" during the AFS stay—lived a hand-to-mouth existence, as did generations of château inhabitants before them. Despite having lost an arm in the war, the cheerful vicomte was gainfully employed repairing televisions. Against major odds—there was no indoor plumbing and no heat except that generated by wood-burning stoves scattered throughout the house—his wife turned out one delicious meal after another. Her only assistance came from their daughter, ten-year-old Agnes, who was more interested in playing house in the 10-foot-high fireplace.

Dinner was not until nine, so Willy and I opted for a short walk around the property. Ambling through woods along overgrown paths, we came upon a rusty iron gate, set in a tall, crumbling stone wall. Upon entering, we discovered—despite the weeds and wildly entangled disarray—that some of the plants were still recognizable: climbing roses and wisteria twisted their way up the old walls, and the occasional ripening apricot or pear hung from gnarled branches. Aha . . . an abandoned garden. Perhaps it was skipping lunch that drew us to the raspberry bushes and made us greedily pick and eat every berry in sight. We were pleased with our find—enough fruit to stave off hunger until dinner.

Returning to the château, we found the vicomtesse in the kitchen preparing dinner while chatting with Dan. We joined them and hung about trying to be useful. Soon Agnes was given a basket and sent to *chercher les framboises.* Once the implications of the situation sunk in, Willy and I looked at each other in mutual panic. The child returned empty-handed and befuddled. Luckily, there were raspberries for sale in the village, and Dan trotted off to buy some. Nonetheless, I can't prepare this duck and raspberry dish without thinking of our "secret," and, despite the intervening years, I find myself discomforted by small pangs of guilt—but fewer and fewer as the years pass.

It is fitting that I first ate this dish in an ancient château, as the recipe too is very old; its combination of rich duck balanced by tartly acidic fruit harks back to the Middle Ages. Sauced and sprinkled with fresh raspberries and minced parsley or chives, it is visually appealing as well as delicious.

American home cooks are often reticent to prepare duck, but they shouldn't be. Because the bird is all dark meat and exceptionally fatty (though the fat is concentrated in the skin so the meat is particularly lean), it is virtually impossible to ruin, in contrast to pheasant or the white meat of chicken, which can dry out with just a few extra minutes in the oven. The abundant fat given off during cooking does present a potential mess, but is well worth it, as the fat can easily be removed and saved to use instead of butter to flavor and sauté vegetables and poultry.

Ideal dinner party fare, the piquant sauce can be made up to three days ahead, refrigerated, and then warmed up when needed; and even the duck reheats perfectly. Buttered noodles and creamed or sautéed spinach or a rough mash of parsnips and potatoes are perfect alongside. The raspberry sauce is also delicious with duck confit, sautéed magret, goose, and pork roast or chops.

Serves 6

For the ducks:
2 whole ducks, each weighing 5 to 6 pounds
Sea salt and freshly ground pepper to taste
4 cloves garlic, peeled and crushed
1 large onion, peeled and quartered
8 sprigs fresh thyme, or 2 teaspoons dried thyme
Approximately 3 tablespoons chopped fresh chives and/or
    parsley for garnish (optional)

1. Preheat the oven to 475 degrees.
2. Prick the ducks all over as much as possible—more than you think possible—with a fork and rub them with salt and pepper inside and out. Put half of the garlic, onion, and thyme inside each duck cavity.
3. Place the ducks on a rack, breast-side down, in a roasting pan large enough to hold them without crowding. Put a little water in the bottom of the pan and roast until done, 1 to 1½ hours, turning halfway through and continuing to prick and baste with the water every 15 to 20 minutes. When the ducks are done, set them aside to rest for at least 10 minutes while you finish the sauce.

For the sauce:
1 large carrot, peeled
1 rib celery
1 onion, peeled
2 cloves garlic, peeled
Several mushrooms (mixed wild mushrooms are ideal,
    but white button mushrooms or cremini are also
    delicious) (optional)
One 10- to 12-ounce bag frozen raspberries, or 4 cups
    fresh raspberries
½ cup ruby port
3 tablespoons Armagnac or cognac
1 tablespoon balsamic vinegar
1 teaspoon dried thyme or several sprigs fresh thyme
½ cup duck or chicken stock
Sea salt, freshly ground black pepper, Tabasco sauce,
    sugar, and more vinegar and/or lemon juice to taste
1 cup fresh raspberries

1. Using a food processor or a knife, finely chop the carrot, celery, onion, garlic, and mushrooms, if using. While the ducks are roasting, combine the frozen berries, port, Armagnac, vinegar, chopped vegetables, and thyme, and simmer until the mixture is reduced by half. Strain and reserve. The sauce may be prepared to this point a day or two ahead.
2. Once the ducks are cooked, pour the extra fat out of the roasting pan and, with the pan set over medium heat, deglaze the pan with the stock, stirring and scraping up coagulated bits from the bottom of the pan. Add the reserved sauce and reduce until the desired thickness is reached. Season with salt, pepper, Tabasco sauce, sugar, and vinegar and/or lemon juice.
3. Carve the duck and keep warm. When ready to serve, reheat the sauce. Off the heat, stir in the fresh raspberries. Arrange the duck pieces on a hot serving platter, top with the sauce, and sprinkle with a few minced fresh herbs if desired.

Note: The duck can be made up to 2 days ahead and cooled. Cut each duck into quarters or eighths. If the duck pieces are to wait longer than 5 hours to be served, cover and refrigerate. When ready to serve, place the cut duck on a sheet pan. Flash in a 475-degree oven for 5 minutes, or until hot. Reheat the sauce adding the fresh raspberries at the last minute.

ALICE B. TOKLAS'S

Duck à l'Orange

In *A Happy Publisher's Note to the New Edition* [1984], Simon Michael Bessie explains how the now legendary *Alice B. Toklas Cookbook* came into being thirty years before. After Gertrude Stein's death, the young New York publisher tried to persuade Alice to write a book about the life, people, and adventures she and Gertrude had shared. Alice demurred, saying it had already been done—referring to Stein's 1933 *Autobiography of Alice B. Toklas*. Bessie could think of no response but looked so sad that Alice, in "her cigarette-rough and sensuous voice," thought a moment before capitulating: "'What I could do,' she said as tentatively as she was able, which was not very, 'is a cook book.' And then, 'It would of course, be full of memories.' She kept her promise."

Alice Babette Toklas was born in San Francisco to middle-class Jewish parents in 1877. She briefly studied music at the University of Washington before moving to Paris in 1907 where she met Stein the day she arrived. As stated in her "autobiography," Stein knew from that first moment that the two would be "married for life." In 1908, Toklas began typing manuscripts for Stein, and by 1909 was acting as Stein's confidante, lover, cook, secretary, muse, editor, critic, and general organizer. Alice referred to Gertrude as her "strong-strong husband," while for Stein, her "secretary-companion" was always "Wifey" or "Pussy." They were inseparable companions until Stein died in 1946. Toklas lived another twenty-one years, writing two cookbooks and a memoir while continuing to have adventures. Unfortunately, however, poor health and financial problems—aggravated by the fact that Stein's heirs claimed and took possession of the priceless art collection left to her by Gertrude—made those later years difficult. Stein remained the center of Alice's life even in death, and Toklas spent much of her time dealing with Stein's writings, papers, and estate. In losing the great love and raison d'être of her life, Alice also lost a large piece of herself, even becoming a Catholic before she died when a priest suggested conversion as a way to reconnect with Gertrude in the afterlife.

Much of what both Stein and Toklas accomplished could not have been done without the other. At times the two were virtually one and the same, this merging exemplified by Stein's brilliant conceit of writing her own memoir as though it were Alice's autobiography. During their thirty-nine years together, it is said that Gertrude wrote, talked, and ate, and that Alice cooked, talked, and ate, as they navigated their way through two world wars and many complex friendships. From their apartment on the rue de Fleurus, they presided over the most famous salon of the

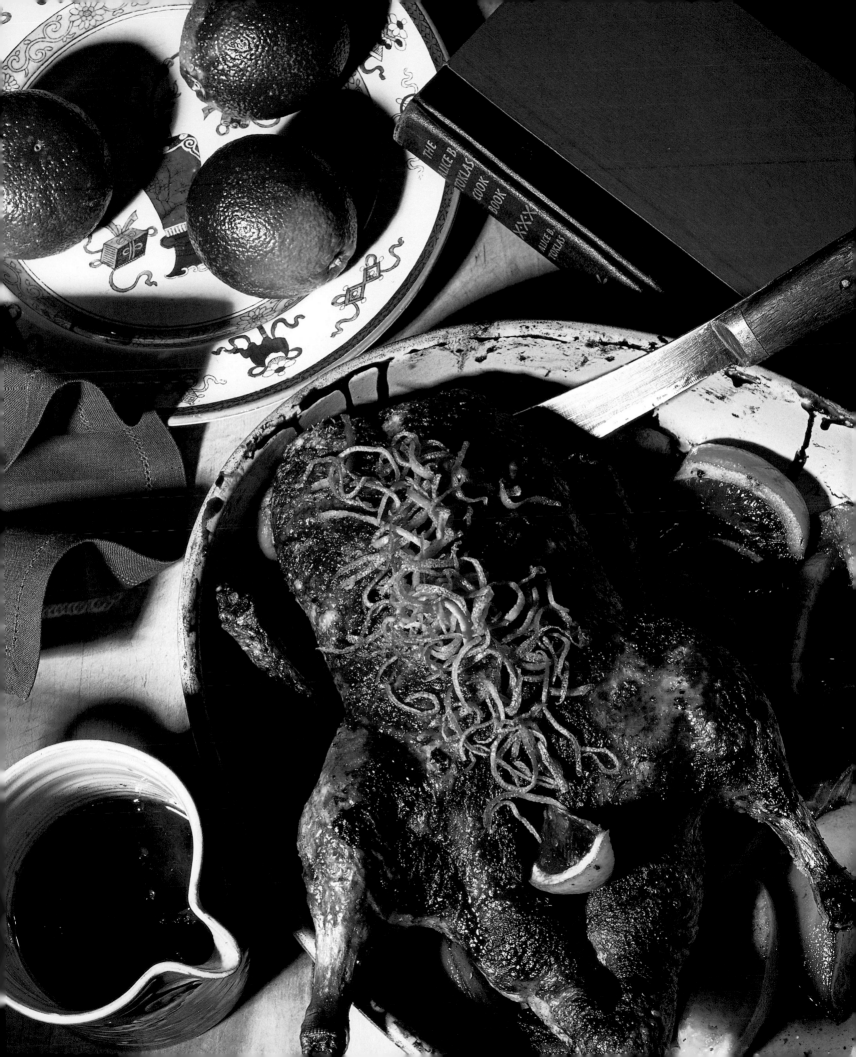

twentieth century. American ex-patriot writers Ernest Hemingway, F. Scott Fitzgerald, and Thornton Wilder, as well as avant-garde painters Picasso, Matisse, and Braque, are just a few of those who showed up for provocative conversation and culinary offerings.

The Alice B. Toklas Cookbook was published when Toklas was seventy-seven. Although the book is large, its initial fame was due to a recipe, given by a friend, for Haschisch Fudge. The recipe was omitted from the first American edition, but when included in the British caused a sensation. The headnote stated, "This is the food of . . . Baudelaire's Artificial Paradise: it might provide an entertaining refreshment for a Ladies' Bridge Club or a chapter meeting of the DAR. In Morocco it is thought to be good for warding off the common cold in damp winter weather . . . Euphoria and brilliant storms of laughter; ecstatic reveries and extensions of one's personality on several simultaneous planes are to be complacently expected. Almost anything Saint Theresa did, you can do better if you can bear to be ravished by '*un evanouissement reveille.*'" Close friends attested to the fact that poor Alice, nearing eighty, had not tried the recipe nor did she even understand the nature of the ingredients. Nonetheless, her name was later associated with a variety of different marijuana concoctions under the heading of Alice B. Toklas brownies. Some even believe that the slang term "toke," meaning to inhale the drug, derives from her name.

The book's later celebrity, however, reflected its genuine merit. As well as presenting recipes, Toklas tells wonderful stories and gives sound opinions on gastronomy, politics, and art. In addition, she recounts the splendid pair's comings and goings and the marvelous meals they shared throughout it all in ancient farmhouses, army mess halls, royal hunting lodges, modest homes of painters, and châteaux of the super-rich and famous. This brilliant mix of recipes and reminiscences has never gone out of print and has been translated into numerous languages.

Though nineteenth-century French recipes often specify wild birds, Duck à l'Orange probably originated in Rouen, the center of French duck domestication. The practice of pairing citrus fruits with fatty meat is thousands of years old and ubiquitous, most likely originating in the Middle East. The sweetness of the fruit balances the fatty duck tastewise, and its acidity aids digestion. Jane Grigson (see page 90)—who certainly should know, as her *Fruit Book* is considered by many to be the definitive book on the subject—tells us, "Of all the meats enhanced by fruit, duck is the best."

The Duck à l'Orange recipe and story appear in chapter four of Toklas's book, tantalizingly entitled "Murder in the Kitchen" along with other mini tales of crime, death, and depravity involving carp, pigeons, and Frederich, the two women's beloved Austrian cook. In brief, Blanchette, the couple's Barbary duck, was so maimed by a neighbor's bird-dog that Frederich felt the need to put it out of its misery—but not before sedating it with three tablespoons of eau de vie, which substantially improved its taste at table.

Plain roast duck with veggies and potatoes makes an easy and delicious family supper. For guests, however, I prefer to fancy it up. The classic preparations of duck with fruit—berries, apples, cherries, or orange as in the recipe that follows—are perfect for special occasions. And an added perk: This delicious, moist, and meltingly tender bird can be roasted in advance and reheated at mealtime without losing its just-cooked flavor (see recipe note page 83).

Serves 6 generously

For the duck stock (or substitute 1 cup of duck or
    chicken stock):
Giblets, neck, and wing tips from the duck
1 teaspoon sea salt
Freshly ground black pepper to taste
1 small onion, halved with a clove stuck in one half
¼ teaspoon dried thyme or 1 sprig fresh thyme
1 small blade mace or 1 pinch of ground mace
½ bay leaf

1. Put all ingredients in a medium saucepan with 3 cups
of water, and simmer, covered, for 1 hour. Remove the
lid, strain, and discard the solids, then reduce the liquid
to 1 cup. Set aside.

For the duck:
1 duck, weighing 5 to 6 pounds, rinsed and dried
2 tablespoons freshly squeezed lemon juice
2 tablespoons Grand Marnier or other orange liqueur
Sea salt and freshly ground black pepper to taste
2 large cloves garlic, peeled and cut in half
1 navel orange, peel left on, cut in 6 wedges
1 onion, peeled and sliced
1 bay leaf
Several celery leaves

For the sauce and finishing the dish:
3 tablespoons sugar mixed with 3 tablespoons water
Freshly squeezed juice of 2 oranges and 1 lemon
2 tablespoons Grand Marnier, other orange liqueur,
    or brandy
Zest of 2 oranges (bitter oranges if possible), cut into very
    thin strips
1 cup Duck Stock (see recipe above)
Watercress for garnish (optional)
Segments from freshly peeled oranges for garnish
    (optional)

1. Preheat the oven to 475 degrees.

2. Rub the duck cavity with lemon juice and Grand
Marnier.

3. Prick the duck all over—much more than seems
possible—with a fork and rub it—inside and out—with
salt and pepper and cut garlic, then put the garlic in
the cavity along with the orange, onion, bay leaf, and
celery leaves.

4. Place the duck breast-side down on a rack in a roasting pan, put a little water in the bottom of the pan, and
roast for 1 to 1½ hours, until done, turning halfway
through and continuing to prick and baste with pan drippings every 15 to 20 minutes. Add boiling water to pan
if drippings dry up.

5. While the duck is roasting, start the sauce. Caramelize
the sugar with the water in a small saucepan set over
medium heat. When a dark caramel is reached, remove
from the heat, immediately add the citrus juices and
liqueur, and set aside.

6. Place the thinly sliced orange peel in a medium saucepan with cold water to cover. Bring to a boil and simmer
for 10 minutes. Drain, rinse, and set aside.

7. When the duck is done, transfer to a cutting board
and keep warm. Pour the pan drippings into a cup and
degrease. Return the degreased juices to the roasting
pan. Place over medium heat, add the cup of chicken or
duck stock, and stir, scraping up all the crusty bits from
the bottom and sides of the pan.

8. Add the reserved caramelized sugar mixture, and simmer until reduced by approximately one half and a sauce
consistency is reached.

9. Carve the rested duck and place on a heated platter.
Pour some of the sauce over. Sprinkle with the blanched
orange zest and garnish with watercress and orange segments. Pass the remaining sauce separately.

Roast Guinea Hen

WITH LENTILS AND BACON

Young Marcel and Marthe Allard moved to Paris from their native Burgundy with nothing but a notebook of family recipes and baby André in tow. Needing to earn a living, they tried their luck with several ventures before taking on the proprietorship of a "bistrot à vins" in the thirteenth, serving wine and snacks to a local clientele right out of Zola. Pushed by these heavy-drinking men who needed real food rather than tidbits, Marthe got out her mother's recipes and began experimenting with simple peasant fare—pâté en croûte, cassoulet, braised beef with carrots, chicken in red wine, and pheasant with chestnuts.

Her efforts met with huge success, as did Marcel's wines, and the small bistro soon attracted diners from outside the neighborhood. A wine distributor friend knew of a spacious restaurant for sale near the Sorbonne. Unchanged from the previous century, À la Halte d'Eperon was ungraceful and almost severe with dark wood paneling and lack of ornamentation, but it was ideally located and could accommodate a crowd. In 1934, the Allards persuaded its owner Vincent Candré to sell them the restaurant. After six months in the kitchen working alongside Candré's chef, Marthe went solo. A bit reticent at first—as at this time very few French restaurant kitchens were staffed by women—she soon found her stride. She was known for her special *beurre blanc* served over scallops as well as for grouse, pheasant, rabbit, and other game—an ever-growing repertoire of Burgundian dishes transcribed and adapted from that invaluable *cahier des recettes*—and for the *plats du jour*. The bistro—renamed Chez Allard—soon became a gastronomic landmark, serving generous portions of classic bourgeois dishes and wines from its extensive "cave" to both locals and wealthy tourists forsaking their luxury hotels on the right bank to "slum it" Chez Allard.

The restaurant survived two wars and two generations of women in the kitchen. Marthe, considered by many to be one of the great women chefs of France, was joined and then eventually replaced by her daughter-in-law, Fernande. Known as Les Mères Allards (Les Mères de France was an affectionate name given to an elite group of exceptional female chefs—primarily in the area of Lyon from the late 1800s until roughly the 1940s), they received their first Michelin star in 1954 and achieved a second before the restaurant was sold out of the family in 1985.

This irresistible bistro combination of crisp-roasted guinea hen and smoky, bacony lentils was for many years my favorite item on Chez Allard's winter menu. The caramelized sweetness and beautiful colors of roasted beets and carrots, though unnecessary, would be a nice addition to the plate. And consider making extra lentils. They keep for several days in the refrigerator, and reheated with a salad on the side, provide a hearty lunch or Sunday supper. I've given a Rock Cornish hen option, as guinea hen is often hard to find. The lentils are also delicious paired with roast chicken.

Serves 4 to 6, depending on the size of the birds

For the guinea hens:

5 tablespoons unsalted butter

4 tablespoons chicken fat or extra virgin olive oil

2 guinea hens, 2 to 3 pounds each, or 6 Rock Cornish
   hens, each weighing about 1¼ pounds

Sea salt and freshly ground black pepper to taste

½ cup chicken stock

For the lentils:

1 pound lentils, rinsed

2 large onions, peeled and cut into wedges

2 cloves garlic, peeled

1 bouquet garni (several fresh thyme and flat-leaf parsley
   sprigs and a bay leaf tied together with kitchen string)

Sea salt and freshly ground black pepper to taste

For the lentil sauce:

½ pound smoky bacon

2 large onions, finely chopped

2 cups chicken stock, plus a few tablespoons for deglazing the pan

2 tablespoons best-quality Italian tomato paste

4 cups veal stock reduced to 2 cups (or use 2 cups frozen
   veal stock concentrate, thawed)

Sea salt, freshly ground black pepper, and freshly
   squeezed lemon juice to taste

1 bunch watercress for garnish

To cook the guinea hens:

1. Preheat the oven to 450 degrees.

2. Mix the butter and fat or oil together. Loosen the skin around the breast and thighs of the birds with your hands, being careful not to tear it. Force half the butter mixture under the skin and rub the rest all over the outside of the birds. Then season inside and out with salt and pepper. Place the hens, breast-side down, on a rack in a roasting pan.

3. Roast for 15 minutes in the oven. Turn the birds breast-side up, and lower the heat to 350 degrees. Pour the chicken stock into the roasting pan.

4. Cook until done, another 30 to 50 minutes, basting frequently. Cover the breast loosely in foil if it is browning too quickly.

5. The hens are done when juices are clear rather than pink when the point of a knife is inserted into the thigh.

6. Transfer the cooked birds to a cutting board and cover loosely with foil. Let them stand at least 10 minutes before serving. While the birds are resting, degrease the pan juices and deglaze the roasting pan with a few table-spoons of chicken stock and set aside.

To cook the lentils and lentil sauce:

1. While the hens are in the oven, cook the lentils. Place the lentils in a medium saucepan and add cold water to cover by 2 to 3 inches. Bring to a boil. Add the onion wedges, garlic, and bouquet garni. When the water comes back to a boil, reduce the heat to very low. Just before the lentils are done to al dente, add salt and pepper and finish the cooking, which will take approximately 20 minutes total (but check after 10 and 15 minutes just in case). Remove the onion, garlic, and bouquet garni. Drain and set aside.

2. While the hens and lentils are cooking, make the sauce for the lentils. Cut the bacon into half-inch squares. Place them in a medium sauté pan or skillet. When the bacon is just beginning to take on color, add the chopped onion. When the onion mixture is golden, deglaze with the chicken stock, then add the tomato paste and reduced veal stock. Simmer and continue to skim off the grease that comes to the surface. When most of the fat is removed, turn the heat to high and boil to reduce by two thirds, stirring occasionally. Adjust the seasonings, then add the reserved lentils. Reheat and adjust the seasonings once more.

To serve:

1. Cut each hen in half and arrange the halves on a warm platter. If using Rock Cornish hens, serve one bird per person, whole. Adjust the seasonings of the degreased pan juices—reheated if necessary—and stir half into the sauced lentils and pour the other half over the birds.
2. Reheat the lentils until very hot and spoon them onto the platter under or next to the birds. Garnish with watercress and serve right away while hot.

JANE GRIGSON'S

Pheasant

WITH APPLES, CREAM, AND CALVADOS

Jane Grigson (1928–1990)—on a par with Robert May, Eliza Acton, and Elizabeth David—was one of Britain's great culinary writers. Bemoaning the fact that "intelligent housewives" felt it their duty to be bored by cooking (and domesticity in general), Grigson was determined to teach the British to "enjoy food." Why eat canned or frozen food or worse when "anyone who likes to eat, can soon learn to cook well"? She wondered how we could "brutishly" reduce the "exquisite results" of centuries spent cultivating delicious varieties of wild fruit to mediocre "cans full of syrup and cardboard-wrapped blocks of ice." Grigson was an early advocate of seasonal cooking, slow food, and environmentally sound agriculture. As far back as 1970, in the introduction to *English Food* she wrote, "The encouragement of fine food is not greed or gourmandise; it can be seen as an aspect of the anti-pollution movement in that it indicates concern for the quality of environment."

Born Jane McIntyre in Gloucester in 1928, she attended Cambridge University before spending three months in Florence indulging her passions for poetry, music, and art, as well as for good food and wine, before returning to England to work in art galleries and then publishing. In 1953, as picture researcher for the encyclopedic *People, Places, Things and Ideas* to be published by

Thames & Hudson, she fell in love with the book's editor, poet and controversial critic Geoffrey Grigson. Twenty-three years younger than he, she became his third wife, and their remarkable partnership, mutual adoration, and grand passion lasted until Geoffrey's death in 1985.

It was not until the early 1960s, when Jane began summering in a cave cottage in Troo, France, with Geoffrey and their young daughter, Sophie, that her interest in food and cooking deepened. Grigson's first cookbook, *Charcuterie and French Pork Cookery*, was published in 1967 to rave reviews, and she went on to write six other cookbook classics. In addition, her popular food column for the magazine section of London's Sunday newspaper, *The Observer*, had a twenty-one-year run, from 1968 until her untimely death at age sixty-one. The happy and productive association with the paper led to some of her best books, including *Good Things, Food with the Famous*, and *The Observer Guide to British Cookery*. Her *Vegetable Book* and *Fruit Book* both won prestigious awards, and in 1977, she was voted Cookery Writer of the Year for *English Food*.

Grigson's wit and modesty and the generous nature of her personality were evident in her writing. The stylish prose was scholarly and authoritative, yet despite an intellectual, upper-crust tone, never intimidating nor patronizing. In an obituary for the *Independent,* Alan Davidson wrote: "Jane Grigson left to the English-speaking world a legacy of fine writing on food and cookery for which no exact parallel exists . . . She won to herself this wide audience because she was above all a friendly writer . . . the most companionable presence in the kitchen; often catching the imagination with a deftly chosen fragment of history or poetry, but never failing to explain the 'why' as well as the 'how' of cookery."

In her *Fruit Book*, Grigson proclaims *Faison à la Normande* (*à la Normande* usually signifying the inclusion of apples and cream) the best way to cook this flavorful bird, which tends to dry out even when you're careful. Placed in a covered casserole and surrounded by apples, onions, calvados, and cream, it cannot help but remain succulent and juicy—and taste marvelous. Ideally, make it in October when apples are at their peak; but it's great all through the cool months and is particularly festive around the holidays, pheasant offering an unconventionally welcome choice at Thanksgiving or Christmas. Serve with white rice or egg noodles; anything else detracts from the clean, simple flavors of the dish. A salad of mixed chicories and toasted walnuts is good either before or after the pheasant, and a slice of a dark chocolate or lemon tart provides an ultra-smooth finale. One capon or two 3-pound chickens can replace the pheasants with excellent results.

Serves 4 to 6, depending on the size of the birds

½ cup (1 stick) unsalted butter

2 large oven-ready pheasants, 2½ to 3 pounds each

¼ teaspoon dried thyme

Sea salt and freshly ground black pepper to taste

1 large Spanish onion (or 2 medium yellow onions), peeled and very thinly sliced

3 pounds good eating apples, peeled, cored, and cut into 10 wedges each

⅛ teaspoon ground cinnamon

1¼ cups crème fraîche or sour cream

5 tablespoons calvados or apple brandy (fresh apple cider or half cider and half poultry stock can be substituted for a different also delicious result)

4 tablespoons apple cider or extra apple brandy

Approximately 3 tablespoons finely minced fresh flat-leaf parsley or fresh chives for garnish

1. Preheat the oven to 350 degrees. Melt half the butter in a skillet large enough to comfortably hold both pheasants.

2. Brown the birds on all sides until nicely golden. Sprinkle with the thyme and season generously with salt and pepper.

3. Melt the remaining butter in another pan, add the onions and apples and sauté, stirring frequently, until the apples are golden. Sprinkle with the cinnamon and salt and pepper.

4. Spread one quarter of the onion-apple mixture over the bottom of a round or oval casserole just large enough to hold the pheasants. Lay the birds, breast-side down, on top of the apples. Pack the remaining apple-onion mixture down the sides.

5. Mix the crème fraîche with the calvados and cider and pour half of the mixture over the pheasants. Cover the casserole tightly with foil and then with a lid and place in the oven for 50 minutes. Turn the birds, breast-side up, replace the cover, and continue baking until very tender, about 20 minutes more.

6. When done, remove the casserole from the oven. Raise the oven temperature to 450 degrees. Pour 2 tablespoons of the remaining crème fraîche mixture over the pheasants and stir the rest into the apples. Taste and adjust the seasonings. Replace the cover and cook for 5 more minutes. Remove from the oven and let rest for 10 minutes. If necessary, the pheasant will stay hot up to 30 minutes at this point if kept covered in a turned-off oven with the door slightly ajar. Serve from the casserole or carve the birds and place on a platter with the saucy apples on top. Strew with parsley for a bit of color and serve, preferably with white or brown rice.

GOLD AND FIZDALE'S

Turkey Fillets

The world-famous musical duo of Gold and Fizdale—partners in life as well as work—performed as brilliantly behind typewriters and stoves as at the piano. Robert Fizdale and Arthur Gold met at Juilliard, and even before graduation had become a musical team. Focusing on contemporary music, they made their 1944 debut in New York with a program of John Cage. Although they played Mozart, Brahms, Mendelssohn, and Bartok to perfection, what they particularly enjoyed was persuading living composers—Francis Poulenc, Paul Bowles, Virgil Thomson, and Germaine Tailleferre as well as Cage—to write new works specifically for them. By the time they left the concert stage in 1982, virtuosos Gold and Fizdale were responsible for greatly extending the breadth and scope of the duo piano repertory.

The two men shared a passion for traveling, cooking, and writing as well as for music. In their homes in Manhattan and the Hamptons, they were known for their exceedingly gracious and generous lifestyle. Poets Marianne Moore and Elizabeth Bishop, choreographers George Balanchine and Jerome Robbins, and writers Louis Begley and Truman Capote were among the many intimates who delighted in their food and hospitality. One friend is quoted as saying, "With very little money, they showed the rich how to live." After Leonard Bernstein and his wife spent a weekend with them in Water Mill, the maestro wrote this sonnet, which says it all:

> Gastronomic Gurus, Grands Seigneurs,
> Old-fashioned enough to counteract
> La Nouvelle Cuisine, Les Nouvelles Moeurs;
> Dynamic Chefs, you are in fact
> A culinary wonder, perhaps the most
> Naturally joyous, deeply delighting
> Dear, considerate double-host
> For miles around. And while I'm writing,
> I might just add these qualities:
> Zest, wisdom, and utter ease.
> Dear duo, from Felicia and me,
> All thanks to you, most tenderly.
> Long life, good health, and all the rest,
> Ever, your grateful double-guest.

Even before retirement, Gold and Fizdale had begun a second career as writers. In addition to two definitive biographies—one on Misia Sert, the Parisian pianist, patron of the arts, and Diagelev intimate, and the other on Sarah Bernhardt—they penned a food column for *Vogue* for ten years and were contributing editors of *Architectural Digest*. In 1984, they wrote *The Gold and Fizdale Cookbook*, an award-winning work dedicated to George Balanchine "in whose kitchen we spent so many happy hours," a stylishly written compilation of over three hundred marvelous recipes gleaned from their extensive travels and many friends.

Over the years, I've made most of the book's recipes and recommend everything. Their substitution of turkey scallops for the hard-to-find and more expensive young milk-fed veal is surprising and an especially useful find. The authors describe "the Great Turkey Breakthrough," when they complimented the chef at a fancy Milanese restaurant on his exquisite veal and complained that there was nothing to compare in the United States. He leaned forward to make sure no one was within earshot and whispered, "Signori, I have a dark confession to make. I will tell you my secret. I make my veal out of turkey!"

Gold and Fizdale present excellent recipes for "veal" scaloppini, *tonnato,* and s*altimbocca alla romana*, all replacing veal with turkey breast. I have adapted the first two recipes here. The scaloppini is an Italian classic combining the mild (turkey or veal) with the salty (capers and anchovies), and can be thrown together last minute. The *tonnato* takes forethought, as the turkey must rest in its tuna bath for at least six hours before eating. However, it too is simple and the unusual sauce—a light tuna mayonnaise—is always a hit. An ideal warm-weather lunch—beachside or by the pool—*tonnato*, a visual ten when strewn with its garnish of fresh herbs, tomatoes, olives, and hard-boiled egg, makes an elegant first course in the evening or as a beautiful addition to a buffet.

You will save time and aggravation if you have the butcher pound the scaloppini for you. However, it is quite do-able at home. Put one turkey cutlet at a time between two pieces of waxed paper, and using a kitchen mallet or rolling pin, pound until evenly flat and very thin. Make sure that the meat is cold—right out of the refrigerator (ten minutes in the freezer is even better). Otherwise, it will turn into a mush when pounded and tear while being removed from the paper. Once pounded, keep the scaloppini refrigerated between sheets of waxed paper until ready to bread.

Turkey Scaloppini

Garnishing these scaloppini with "instant" tomato coulis—a sauce I learned from Puglia's Chef Leonardo at the Michelin one-starred Il Poeta Contadino in Alberobello, Italy—provides an extra hit of flavor and beautiful color. Leonardo uses the sauce to adorn individual artichoke flans, but when you see how easy and delicious it is, you'll find endless ways to use it.

Gold and Fizdale suggest serving buttery mashed potatoes with chopped chives and a squeeze of lemon juice stirred in alongside the scaloppini.

Serves 4 to 6

6 thin slices very cold fresh turkey breast, each weighing
    4 to 6 ounces each
2 eggs, lightly beaten
Approximately ¼ cup all-purpose flour
Approximately ¾ cup fine bread crumbs
1 teaspoon fine sea salt, or to taste
½ teaspoon freshly ground black pepper, or to taste
½ teaspoon paprika
6 tablespoons unsalted butter
3 tablespoons tasteless vegetable oil
½ lemon, plus 6 thinly sliced lemon rounds

6 rolled anchovies
1 tablespoon small capers, rinsed and well-drained
Tomato Coulis (optional, see recipe page 96)

1. Remove the skin, tendons, and fat from the turkey slices. Place each one between 2 pieces of waxed paper and use a rolling pin, heavy frying pan, or wooden mallet to pound as thin as possible. You can also have your butcher do this for you.
2. Put beaten eggs in a large shallow bowl or small baking dish. Combine flour, bread crumbs, salt, pepper, and paprika, and spread mixture on a large platter.
3. Heat 2 tablespoons of the butter and 1 tablespoon of the vegetable oil in a large heavy skillet until very hot.
4. While the butter and oil are heating, dip each fillet lightly in egg and then in the bread-crumb mixture. Place as many fillets in the pan as will fit without crowding, and sauté until golden on both sides and cooked through (1 to 2 minutes per side depending on their thickness). Add more butter and oil as needed and continue until all 6 fillets are cooked. As they are done, transfer the fillets to a warm serving platter. Squeeze the halved lemon over all. Center a lemon slice topped with a rolled anchovy on each fillet and sprinkle all of them with a few capers.

TOMATO COULIS

Makes approximately ⅔ cup

All ingredients should be at room temperature.
1 large very ripe tomato
⅓ cup olive oil
Sea salt and freshly ground black pepper to taste
Fresh basil and/or other fresh herbs of choice, capers,
   and/or garlic, to taste (optional)

1. Put everything in a blender. Purée well—for several minutes—until the sauce emulsifies, is completely smooth, and turns bright orange. It will have the consistency of mayonnaise. Adjust the seasoning.

Turkey Tonnato

Serve with a simple rice or pasta salad and/or toasted garlic bread, a green salad, and a chilled Italian white wine, preferably an Orvieto.

Serves 6

6 thin slices very cold fresh turkey breast, each weighing
   4 to 6 ounces
Sea salt and freshly ground black pepper to taste
6 tablespoons extra virgin olive oil
Tuna Sauce (recipe follows)

For the garnish:
2 tablespoons finely minced fresh flat-leaf parsley
4 scallions, cut into thin rounds
2 lemons, cut into thin rounds
4 ripe tomatoes, peeled and cut into thin wedges
2 hard-boiled eggs, peeled and quartered
Black Italian, Greek, or French olives

1. Remove any skin, tendons, and fat from the turkey slices. Place 1 slice between 2 pieces of waxed paper, and use a rolling pin, heavy frying pan, or kitchen mallet to pound it to approximately a ³⁄₁₆ inch thickness. Repeat with other slices. Or a butcher can pound them for you.

2. Season turkey fillets lightly with salt and pepper. Heat oil in a large skillet, and sauté fillets for 1 to 3 minutes per side, until tender. You will probably have to do this in batches. Do not let the turkey brown. Lay the fillets in one layer on a serving platter and cool completely.
3. When the turkey fillets have cooled, spread them with half the tuna sauce and then turn them over on the platter. Spread the rest of the sauce on the other side. Cover with plastic wrap, pressing it against the surface of the sauced turkey airtight to prevent the sauce from darkening. Refrigerate for at least 6 hours, preferably overnight, or for up to 48 hours.
4. Remove from the refrigerator 3 hours before serving. The turkey must be at room temperature to fully appreciate its special flavor. When ready to serve, sprinkle the parsley and scallions over all, and decorate the platter with lemons, tomatoes, egg slices, and olives.

TUNA SAUCE

All ingredients must be at room temperature.
1 large egg yolk
2 tablespoons freshly squeezed lemon juice
⅛ teaspoon cayenne pepper
¾ cup extra virgin olive oil
One 3-ounce can Italian tuna packed in olive oil
4 anchovy fillets, roughly chopped
¼ cup heavy cream
Approximately ¼ cup poultry or veal stock
2 tablespoons capers, rinsed and drained
Sea salt and freshly ground black pepper to taste

1. Combine the egg yolk, lemon juice, cayenne, olive oil, tuna, and anchovies in the container of a blender or food processor. Process to a smooth purée.
2. Transfer the mixture to a bowl, and slowly whisk in the heavy cream. The sauce will be quite thick. Thin it further with the stock, a bit at a time, until the sauce has the consistency of heavy cream. The sauce should not be so thick that it would coat the turkey fillets rather than penetrate them.
3. Stir in the capers, and add salt and pepper if desired. You may not need salt, as the anchovies and capers are quite salty.

Braised Rabbit

WITH PRUNES, FENNEL, AND ORANGE

"Multiplying like rabbits." Rabbits are everywhere—in the country, in the desert, in the woods, in the mountains, at the seaside. And in urban areas, rabbit can be found in abundance at the butcher. Why isn't there one in every pot in the United States as there still is in Italy, France, and Spain? Maybe our association with the Easter bunny is too strong. Or is it the rabbit-as-pet issue? Americans are not keen on eating anything four-footed and furry that even vaguely resembles man's best friend. I'm less sentimental and find rabbit delicious.

When I became an empty nester and could cook rabbit at home, the first dish I made was one I'd eaten several years earlier when visiting my friend Inigo de la Huerta on his parents' (the Duke and Duchess of Mandas's) *dehesa,* El Verdugal, in Spain's Extremadura. Once a lucrative farm property, the vast acreage was still dense with beautiful cork oaks and studded with sheep. Most interesting to me, however, were the *dehesa*'s black pigs. Fed on acorns, these special pigs, once killed and processed, emerged as Spain's *jamon ibérico,* arguably the most highly prized ham in the world. Once a year, the Duke gave each of the hundred or so workers on the farm a huge black pig for himself and his family. In the vast El Verdugal basement, the duke showed me hams from previous years—hanging from the ceiling as far as the eye could see—curing, and awaiting their moment of glory on the table. He explained that each June, the hams were taken to the country and hung for three months in the mountain air before returning in the fall, sun-tanned and rested, to their basement home. Thinly sliced and eaten like prosciutto, the Spanish ham also enriches soups and stews, such as this braised rabbit.

Despite El Verdugal's marvelous ham and other pork products, this hauntingly delicious Catalan-inspired rabbit and prune dish is what I remember best. Redolent of fennel, orange, garlic, and brandy, it is intensely flavorful and eminently satisfying.

After some trial and error, my own version of this dish now matches my memory of the original. As with all stews, it's tastier made a day or two in advance. Be sure to warn your guests to watch out for small bones. If you've never loved rabbit, there's a good chance this dish will convert you.

Serves 8 to 10

2 rabbits (2½ to 3 pounds each), each cut into 8 pieces
Sea salt and freshly ground pepper to taste

For the marinade:
1 bottle full-bodied dry red or white wine (preferably a
    Spanish Rioja)
2 large bulbs fresh fennel, trimmed and cut in quarters
    vertically
3 large carrots, peeled and cut into ½-inch rounds
3 large yellow onions, peeled and thickly sliced
6 cloves garlic, peeled and crushed
⅓ cup chopped fresh flat-leaf parsley
Several sprigs fresh thyme
2 bay leaves, crumbled
1 teaspoon whole black peppercorns, crushed
½ teaspoon dried rosemary, or 2 sprigs fresh rosemary
1 tablespoon whole fennel seeds
½ teaspoon ground cinnamon
⅛ teaspoon hot Spanish paprika, red pepper flakes, or a
    few drops of Tabasco sauce
20 pitted prunes
Approximately 6 tablespoons extra virgin olive oil
Approximately ⅔ cup all-purpose flour for dusting
½ cup brandy
3 cups chicken stock
½ pound cured ham—preferably Spanish Serrano or
    Ibérico, cut into ½-inch dice (Italian prosciutto is a
    good substitute)
2 tablespoons finely grated orange zest
Freshly squeezed lemon and/or orange juice to taste
¼ cup finely minced fresh fennel leaves, flat-leaf parsley,
    and/or chives for garnish
Toasted pine nuts or coarsely chopped toasted blanched
    almonds for garnish

1. To marinate the rabbit, rub the pieces with salt and pepper. Place the rabbit pieces, wine, fennel, carrots, onions, garlic, parsley, thyme, bay leaves, peppercorns, rosemary, fennel seeds, cinnamon, paprika, and pitted prunes in a large nonreactive bowl. Cover and refrigerate for 4 to 6 hours, turning the rabbit pieces occasionally.

2. Use tongs to remove the rabbit pieces and the prunes from the marinade. Reserve them in separate bowls.

3. Heat half the olive oil in a large casserole set over medium-high heat. While the oil is heating, dry rabbit pieces with paper towels and coat them with flour, being sure to shake off excess. When the oil is hot, in batches brown the floured rabbit pieces on all sides, being careful not to crowd. As each piece becomes golden brown, use tongs to transfer to a large bowl or platter.

4. Add the remaining oil, and when hot, add the reserved vegetables from the marinade. Cook, stirring often, for about 10 to 15 minutes, until lightly golden and somewhat soft. Add the brandy and boil for 1 minute, scraping up the flavorful bits stuck to the bottom of the pan.

5. Add the reserved marinade, chicken stock, and ham. Bring to a boil and simmer for 5 minutes, skimming fat, foam, and scum from the surface.

6. Add the rabbit pieces, cover the casserole, and simmer over low heat, skimming occasionally and turning the rabbit pieces, until the rabbit is tender, about 1 hour.

7. Use tongs or a slotted spoon to transfer the rabbit pieces to a bowl. Cover loosely with foil to keep warm. Add the orange zest to the pan liquid, and reduce by at least one third until somewhat thickened and sauce consistency. Season with salt, pepper, and lemon and/or orange juice. Return the rabbit to the pan, add the marinated prunes, and simmer for 5 to 10 minutes to heat through and blend the flavors.

8. Serve the rabbit from the casserole or transfer to a large heated platter. Strew the fresh herbs and toasted nuts over the top. Or plate and garnish each plate with the herbs and nuts.

9. Serve immediately with noodles or rice.

Note: The rabbit may be made through Step 7 up to 2 or 3 days ahead and stored, covered, in the refrigerator. It will improve with age. To serve, bring to room temperature, then place the covered casserole in a 300-degree oven for about 30 minutes, until piping hot. Adjust the seasoning again with salt, pepper, and orange and/or lemon juice.

BEEF, VEAL, LAMB, and PORK

Robert Carrier's Beef Wellington

Delmonico's Steak and Potatoes

Perino's Steak Diane

The Grand European's Beef Stroganoff

Luchow's Hash à la Lübeck with Anchovy-Caper Sauce

Napoleon Bonaparte's Veal Marengo

Jack Savenor's Leg of Lamb with Mustard and Ginger Coating

Julia Child's Navarin of Lamb

Craig Claiborne's Braised Lamb with Basil and Garlic Stuffing

Hafida's Lamb Tagine with Saffron, Dates, Olives, and Cilantro

The Russian Tea Room's Luli Kebabs

Charles Ranhofer's Crown Roast of Pork with Sausage Stuffing and Glazed Onions

Monsieur Dodin-Bouffant's Pot-au-feu

Apicius's Cassoulet

Beef Wellington

A "celebrity chef" long before the term was coined, Robert Carrier—with his spectacular food and natural flamboyance—convinced the British that enjoying a good meal was not a crime. Epitomizing fine dining in 1970s Britain, Carrier's restaurants, cookbooks, and television programs introduced truffles, brandy, and saffron to people still shaking off the memory of war rationing and canned fruit. As influential as Elizabeth David and Delia Smith, he is considered the link between them.

Carrier, an American, was born in 1923 into great wealth. Despite losing their money and their servants during the Depression, his parents kept their Tarrytown mansion, determined to maintain their grand lifestyle. His father, a property lawyer of Irish descent, and his gregarious and stylish mother, a German-American heiress, learned to prepare their own elaborate meals. Young Robert set the table and early on developed a passion for cooking and entertaining. Making do with less, he recognized the importance of expert showmanship, of being able to manipulate the appearance of things.

This interest in "show" drew him briefly to the Broadway stage, but he soon joined the army, ending up based in Paris with a fancy desk job. Having fallen in love with Europe, Carrier stayed on after the war and moved to London in 1953, cooking and entertaining nonstop. One night, a dinner guest, bowled over by an amazing meal, offered him a culinary editing job, which led to a weekly food column in the Sunday *Telegraph*. Before long, he'd established himself as the spokesperson for modern cookery, his voice launching a million dinner parties.

The public could not get enough of this charming and charismatic man who promised that anyone could learn to cook well. "There's nothing to it," he said. "It's really simple. People tend to flap about cooking, but there is no need to worry . . . anyone can do it." One thing led to another and before long this natural entrepreneur had his own television show, a successful PR company, and a weekly magazine in America.

Carrier's lunch and dinner parties felt like theater—well cast, flatteringly lit, and scripted with panache. "I entertain several nights a week," he said. "It's my life." But soon what Carrier really wanted was a restaurant. The pleasures previously experienced by his friends were shared with a wider clientele in 1959 when he opened Carrier's in Camden Passage, Islington, an area that had become a chic center of the London antiques trade. Small, relaxed, intimate, expensive, the eatery soon became the "in" meeting place for British and American celebrities alike.

The following year he opened a cook shop in Harrods, the first of a succession of Carrier shops in department stores in both Britain and America. Throughout the 1960s and '70s, he produced a stream of cookery books, all continuing to promote his idea that anyone could be an excellent cook. The most famous of these books was his 1963 *Great Dishes of the World,* a collection of recipes obtained on a tour of the world's best restaurants, eventually translated into fourteen languages and selling more than eleven million copies.

Always restless and wanting more, in 1971 Carrier jumped at the chance to buy Hintlesham Hall in Suffolk, to use as a country retreat. Initial plans to leisurely refurbish the dilapidated stately home quickly changed when he realized the decrepit edifice was about to collapse; he employed a crew of sixty to save the house on a shoestring. The conversion was sensational and a forerunner of many to come. Carrier opened Hintlesham as a hotel and restaurant the following year, offering luxurious dining that few could rival. Carrier's and Hintlesham Hall each were awarded two Michelin stars, and all was going swimmingly until he opened a cooking school at Hintlesham in the mid-1970s. This endeavor ended in financial disaster and forced him to close the entire Hintlesham operation at the end of 1982, just one year after opening his school. He sold the property the following year and bowed out of the restaurant in Camden Passage in 1984. After spending increasingly more time in his ornately restored mansion in Marrakesh as well as in France and in his native America, he died in 2006 at age eighty-two.

Fillet of Beef *en Chemise* ("in a nightshirt") was the idiosyncratic name Carrier gave to Beef Wellington, a descendent of the recipes for beef encased in decorative, flaky crusts so common in eighteenth- and nineteenth-century Britain. Named for Arthur Wellesley, First Duke of Wellington, the English soldier and statesman who defeated Napoleon at Waterloo, this *en croute* classic is an impressive presentation piece when brought to the table in all its golden glory. Fillet of beef, the ingredient being showcased, is slathered first with foie gras, and then with a mushroom duxelle before being wrapped in puff pastry. Ironically, the signature crust started out as a throwaway paste wrapped around the fillet to guarantee that it cooked without browning, in accordance with a short-lived fad for insipid meat.

Like *La Negresse sans Chemise,* his decadent chocolate truffle cake, Carrier's Beef en Chemise represented the unrestrained indulgence so typical of the famous chef. In the 1960s, Beef Wellington was the party dish of the decade on both sides of the Atlantic. A favorite of Richard Nixon, it was prepared by Julia Child in front of hundreds of thousands on television. Because the encased fillet was costly, dramatic, and relatively time-consuming to prepare, some believe that Beef Wellington's popularity had more to do with amateur cooks trying to outdo one another than with a real passion for the dish. Before long, all sorts of shortcut versions cropped up—I specifically remember one that substituted refrigerator crescent rolls for the puff pastry—and by the 1980s, Beef Wellington had lost its cachet. However, time has passed and Carrier's version is well worth reviving.

For a lighter and less expensive dish, foie gras can be replaced with sautéed chicken livers or ham, or left out completely, using layers of vegetables instead—caramelized onions, red bell peppers, fennel, or a combination of all three. Whichever version suits your fancy, each bite of the crisp and buttery pastry melds with the rare and tender beef and is as tasty served at room temperature on a summer picnic table as piping hot during the winter holidays.

Serves 6 to 8 generously

1 fillet of beef (approximately 2½ to 3 pounds)
2 tablespoons brandy, cognac, or Armagnac
6 tablespoons unsalted butter
2 tablespoons vegetable oil
Sea salt and freshly ground black pepper to taste
½ teaspoon dried thyme
4 cups finely minced white button mushrooms (porcinis, chanterelles, morels, or a mixture can be substituted)
1 large onion, peeled and finely chopped
¾ cup pâté de foie gras or ½ pound prosciutto or Serrano ham, very thinly sliced
1 cup diced fresh fennel bulb, sautéed with 2 tablespoons butter, salt, pepper, and a pinch of sugar for 20 to 30 minutes, until soft and beginning to caramelize (optional)
1 cup diced red bell pepper, sautéed with 1 tablespoon butter, salt, and pepper for 15 to 20 minutes, until beginning to caramelize (optional)
1 pound frozen puff pastry, thawed but still cool
1 egg yolk, lightly beaten with 1 tablespoon heavy cream

1. Trim the fillet of beef neatly, removing the ends, and brush it with the liquor. Let it stand for at least 30 minutes and up to 24 hours if refrigerated.

2. Melt 2 tablespoons of the butter with the vegetable oil in a skillet large enough to hold the meat over high heat. Season the meat with salt, pepper, and the dried thyme, and brown it well on all sides. Lower the heat if the oil is in danger of burning. When the meat is nicely browned all over, transfer it to a platter to cool. Once cooled, refrigerate it until cold, at least 2 hours and up to 24 hours. When cold, remove the butcher's string from the meat.

3. Melt the remaining 4 tablespoons butter in a medium skillet set over medium heat. Add the mushrooms and onions and sauté until the onions are soft and golden. Season with salt and pepper. Set aside.

4. Cut the foie gras into slices about ³⁄₁₆ inch thick. Use the slices to make a layer to cover the chilled meat, or wrap the chilled meat in prosciutto. Spread the mushroom and onion mixture over the foie gras or ham. If desired, make a layer of sautéed fennel and/or peppers on top of the mushrooms. Set the meat aside while you roll out the puff pastry.

5. Dust the cool pastry on both sides with flour, and place it between 2 large sheets of kitchen parchment paper to keep it from sticking to the rolling pin. Roll into a rectangle approximately 13 by 17 inches. If at this point the dough is too sticky to continue, place it in the freezer or refrigerator for a few minutes until it firms up. When it is no longer sticky, place the rolled dough on a parchment-covered baking sheet. Center the fillet on the rectangle of dough and wrap the dough up around the meat and pinch together the long seam running from end to end. Now fold the ends up over the meat and press down to seal, or if there is not enough dough for that, just pinch the ends together well. Turn the dough package over so the seam is underneath and use a knife to cut some small slits in the top side of the pastry to let the steam escape. The meat can sit in the refrigerator for several hours at this point.

6. When ready to bake, preheat the oven to 400 degrees. Using a pastry brush, paint the top of the dough with the egg-yolk mixture, and continue baking until the crust is golden brown and an instant-read thermometer inserted into the middle of the meat registers 122 degrees for rare, 130 degrees for medium rare. This will take anywhere from 30 to 60 minutes.

7. Remove the meat from the oven, let it rest for at least 10 minutes, then slice and serve. The meat can rest for up to 45 minutes and be served tepid or rest a little longer and be served at room temperature.

DELMONICO'S

Steak and Potatoes

In 1827, Delmonico's, the first freestanding dining establishment in America, opened its doors near Wall Street. One Delmonico's or another was considered the *sine qua non* of American restaurants until the doors finally closed in 1923, almost a century later. The saga began in 1824, when, after years spent sailing the triangle trade route between Cuba, New York, and the West Indies, Swiss schooner captain Giovanni Del-Monico relinquished his boat, turned landlubber, and opened a modest wine store on the Battery. In less than two years, a huge profit allowed him to close shop, take the money, run, and persuade his brother Pierre, a confectioner living in Berne, to partner with him in a European-style pastry shop and café at 23 William Street. The brothers anglicized their names, pooled their skills and resources, and set out to capture the just-emerging New York City luxury market.

Del-Monico and Brother, a unique spot to relax, snack, eat, and drink in a cozy, family-run atmosphere, represented a brand-new concept. It was just what the neighborhood needed. Emulating France, dishes were ordered off a "carte." Tablecloths, printed menus, individual tables, private dining rooms, a star chef, and a separate wine list were first experienced at Delmonico's, as was a long list of food firsts, including Delmonico Steak, Delmonico Potatoes, Eggs Benedict, Lobster Newburg, and, reputedly, the first ground beef patty ever served between slices of bread as a sandwich.

The establishment soon expanded into an adjacent room, and just three years after opening, took over the entire building. In 1831, nephew Lorenzo arrived from Switzerland to provide much-needed assistance, and in 1834, a 220-acre farm in Williamsburg was purchased to supply the restaurant with fresh meat, poultry, eggs, and vegetables. Never phased, when 23 William Street burned to the ground in the Great Fire of 1836, Peter and John imported three additional nephews and rebuilt—larger this time around—a few blocks away. The exorbitantly expensive construction at 2 South William Street vied with Paris's finest and was soon nicknamed "the Citadel" by its society clientele. Two stories of lavish "saloons" with inlaid floors, gilt walls, and imported damask draperies, as well as several private dining rooms and a kitchen one flight up stamped the Delmonico name indelibly on the map. China, glassware, and cutlery were the best available, and the basement wine cellar held 16,000 bottles of the most sought-after wines. For many, the greatest coup of all was the pair of marble columns excavated from Pompeii that flanked the entrance.

In 1842, John Delmonico died in a freak hunting accident. Business went on as usual, but now nephew Lorenzo (soon to be known as Lorenzo the Great) was titular head of all Delmonico enterprises. After another fire in 1845, he chose to go with the trend, moving to various venues up and across town. In 1861, he bought the Grinnell mansion on the corner of Fifth Avenue and Fourteenth Street; and after a year of the most outrageous renovations to date, Delmonico's once again reopened to an adoring public. This location bragged of both a restaurant and a café. Women were finally a regular part of the New York dining scene, and this new space was designed to accommodate them. It was here that Lorenzo hired the soon-to-be-legendary Charles Ranhofer.

As with many culinary histories, the story and nomenclature of Delmonico's Steak is confusing. We do know that Alessandro Filippini, hired by Delmonico's in 1849, and Charles Ranhofer, hired in 1862, served as *chefs de cuisine* of the restaurant empire until Ranhofer retired in 1896. Both men wrote epic cookbooks—*The Table* and *The International Cook Book* by Filippini and *The Epicurean* by Ranhofer—and each book contained virtually the same recipe for Delmonico Steak, a simply broiled boneless sirloin.

By 1868, the United States had recovered from the Civil War, the economy was booming, and there were four Delmonico restaurants in New York City. Word of these destination eateries spread. Based on unsurpassable quality and reputation, the word "Delmonico" was generalized and came to mean "the best of the best." Well into the twentieth century, people across America—even those who had never been to New York, let alone eaten at one of the restaurants—might name something "Delmonico" to mean "superlative." Butchers and chefs obliged their demanding patrons with the best they had on hand. Thus, the many different meanings of a "Delmonico steak."

Methods of cooking also differed, but here is the original recipe as set down by both Filippini and Ranhofer. The steak was served with a variety of sauces, though most commonly with sauce Bordelaise or maître d'hôtel butter. Whether you do or do not choose to sauce, Delmonico's Potatoes (see recipe page 109) alongside will give "meat and potatoes" an entirely new and utterly sublime twist. At the restaurants, each person was served an entire sirloin. In this age of daintier eating, a pound of meat per person may be more than you or your guests can handle. However, there is something to be said for Gilded Age generosity.

Delmonico's Steak

Serves 4 to 8

4 boneless top loin or strip steaks, 2 inches thick, weighing 1¼ pounds each (or substitute rib-eye or other highest-quality steak), at room temperature
Sea salt and coarsely ground black pepper to taste
4 tablespoons unsalted butter, melted
Sauce Bordelaise or Maître d'Hôtel Butter (recipes follow)

1. Preheat the broiler or grill.
2. Wipe the meat dry with paper towels. Season the meat with salt and pepper, then use a pastry brush to coat both sides with half the butter. Cook on each side for 4 minutes. Brush with the remaining butter and cook, turning frequently, on each side for 3 additional minutes, or to desired doneness, taking into consideration that the meat will cook a few degrees more while resting.
3. When done, let the meat rest for 5 minutes before slicing.
4. Serve sliced with or without Sauce Bordelaise or a generous pat of Maître d'Hôtel Butter.

Note: I suggest using an instant-read meat thermometer: 120 to 125 degrees for rare; 130 to 140 degrees for medium rare to medium. Well done is no way to eat a good steak.

SAUCE BORDELAISE

This rich and deeply flavorful old-fashioned sauce is delicious on any cut of steak, especially in colder weather.

For a richer Sauce Bordelaise, add a beef-marrow garnish. Soak 1 pound of beef marrow in ice water for 4 hours. Drain and cut the beef marrow into small dice. Place in a small saucepan with lightly salted cold water to cover, and bring to a boil over medium heat. As soon as a boil is reached, remove from the heat, wait 30 seconds, and then gently drain. Season with salt and pepper. Add to the sauce just before serving.

Another traditional option is to add ½ cup of good homemade tomato sauce with the stock.

Makes enough for 8 servings of Delmonico's Steak

1 cup minced shallots
16 whole white peppercorns (or half black, half white), crushed
2 cups good red Bordeaux wine
2½ cups homemade or best-quality store-bought veal or beef stock (demi-glace can be substituted; veal and beef stocks and veal demi-glace can be purchased frozen in some good supermarkets or ordered online)
3 sprigs fresh thyme, or ¼ teaspoon dried thyme
6 stems fresh flat-leaf parsley
1 bay leaf
1 clove garlic, peeled and thinly sliced
4 tablespoons cold unsalted butter, cut into ½-inch dice
Salt and freshly ground black pepper to taste

1. Put the shallots, crushed peppercorns, and wine in a medium saucepan set over high heat. Reduce by one third.
2. Add the veal stock, thyme, parsley, bay leaf, and garlic, and simmer gently for about 20 minutes, until the sauce coats the back of a spoon.
3. Strain into a clean saucepan, pressing down on the solids with a spoon to extract as much flavor as possible. Cool, then set aside or cover and refrigerate for up to 3 days.
4. Once the steaks are cooked, remove them from the pan, pour the sauce into the same pan, and deglaze over medium heat, scraping up all the coagulated juices.
5. Whisk in the cold butter, bit by bit, and season with salt and pepper. Just before serving, stir in any meat juices accumulated on the cutting board or platter and adjust the seasoning.

MAÎTRE D'HÔTEL BUTTER

Whether you choose to grill or broil, a pat of flavored butter placed on top of a hot steak greatly enhances it. Maître d'hôtel butter, with its clean, fresh taste, is the simplest of these condiments, containing nothing but butter, parsley, lemon juice, salt, and a pinch of cayenne.

In addition to transforming a piece of steak, chicken, or fish, flavored butters can enrich and add intensity to a soup, stew, or sauce and can perfect a baked potato or a medley of steamed vegetables. Additions to these butters are endless but include capers, anchovies, citrus zests, and virtually any fresh herb.

Makes approximately ¾ cup

½ cup chopped fresh flat-leaf parsley
10 tablespoons unsalted butter, softened
Freshly squeezed juice of ½ lemon
Pinch of cayenne pepper
Fine sea salt and freshly ground black pepper to taste

1. Use a food processor or a wooden spoon to blend the parsley with the butter. Add the lemon juice and season with the cayenne and salt and pepper. Using plastic wrap, roll the butter into one or two "sausages." Refrigerate for up to 3 days, or freeze—with aluminum foil wrapped around the plastic wrap—for up to 2 months.

Note: Adding half a crushed ice cube while processing helps the herbs stay green.

Delmonico's Potatoes

For over a hundred years and the world over, many versions of gratinéed potatoes have been called "Delmonico," the common denominators always being cream and some form of cheese. Luscious and rich—plentiful Gruyère and thick cream interspersed with tender layers of nutmeg-spiked potatoes—this recipe elevates the potato from lowly spud to something else entirely.

Charles Ranhofer is often credited for first serving the dish, but it was more likely a creation of Chef Alessandro Filippini, whose tenure in the Delmonico kitchen predated Ranhofer's by thirteen years. Filippini gave a recipe for these potatoes in his 1906 *The International Cook Book*, while Ranhofer's *The Epicurean,* published in 1894, does not mention them at all. Chef Filippini served them alongside Delmonico's Steak, and for decades, the combination was one of the most popular items on the menu.

For variety of taste, color, and texture, strew julienned carrots, celeriac, or fresh herbs; sautéed mushrooms, onions, or spinach; or smoky ham or crisp bacon among the layers of potatoes and cheese.

Serves 8

1¾ cups whole milk
2 cups heavy cream
4 cups well-washed and finely sliced leeks, white part only (or substitute chopped onions)
4 cloves garlic, peeled and put through a garlic press or very finely minced
¼ teaspoon freshly grated nutmeg
½ teaspoon dried thyme, or 2 teaspoons fresh thyme leaves, chopped
Sea salt and freshly ground white pepper to taste
10 tablespoons unsalted butter, at room temperature, in pieces
8 large Yukon gold potatoes, peeled and cut crosswise into ⅛-inch slices
½ cup freshly grated Parmigiano-Reggiano cheese mixed with ½ cup coarsely grated Gruyère cheese

1. Preheat the oven to 400 degrees.
2. In a large saucepan, combine the milk, cream, leeks, garlic, nutmeg, thyme, salt, and pepper over medium heat and bring to a simmer. Whisk in 7 tablespoons of the butter, a little at a time.
3. Remove the pan from the heat and keep warm (or you can rewarm when ready to use). This can be done up to 1 day ahead and covered and refrigerated once cooled.
4. Use the remaining 3 tablespoons of butter to grease an oval ceramic gratin dish approximately 18 inches long.
5. Use half the potatoes to cover the bottom of the buttered dish, slightly overlapping the slices. Season generously with salt and pepper.
6. Pour half the warm milk mixture over the potatoes and sprinkle with about three quarters of the cheese mixture.
7. Repeat with rest of the potatoes, milk mixture, and cheese.
8. Bake in the middle of the oven until the potatoes have absorbed the liquid and are deep gold and very tender when pierced with the point of a knife, about 1 hour or a bit more. Remove from the oven and let sit for at least 10 minutes before serving. The potatoes will stay hot for at least 25 minutes.

PERINO'S

Steak Diane

As a child, I looked forward to my grandmother coming to town. I would don an organdy party dress and patent-leather Mary Janes and go to lunch with her at Perino's, the genteel Wilshire Boulevard landmark and restaurant to the stars. Before Chasen's, before Romanoff's, before Scandia, and even before the Brown Derby, there was Perino's. As Cecilia Rasmussen wrote in the *Los Angeles Times*, "Only a dreamer would have opened a restaurant that charged $1.25 for a dinner at a time when Angelinos could eat a full and hearty meal for 5 or 10 cents." The dreamer was Alexander Perino, who borrowed $2,000 from a friend at the height of the Depression and opened the city's most expensive restaurant. Perino's soon became the benchmark for fine dining and remained an icon of culinary excellence for fifty years. Rasmussen goes on to write, "Perino referred to his establishment . . . as The Place, and for well-heeled Angelinos, it was. Some diners wore tuxedoes and carried engraved cigarette cases. Women made entrances wearing evening gowns, diamonds, and furs. Perino's drew diners with its Steak Diane, chicken quenelles, and pumpernickel cheese toast served by a waiter wearing white gloves."

Perino often told his favorite story about a customer tripping over a hat rack that fell onto another diner who then drew a gun. Perino knocked the weapon out of the man's hand and ordered a waiter to hide it. Later, when things had calmed down, Perino asked him where he'd put the gun. "In the soup," was the reply.

Looking back, I think Grandma was probably there to catch a glimpse of regulars Bette Davis, Frank Sinatra, Dean Martin, Elizabeth Taylor, and Cole Porter. I was too young to care about celebrities; the number one attraction for me was a multicolored spun sugar basket glistening like Murano glass and filled with Perino's special handmade chocolates. Attraction number two was the signature Steak Diane. Alexander Perino captivated me with the story of the dish's namesake, beautiful Diana, sister to Apollo and Roman goddess of the hunt. I loved the elegance of the steak pounded thin and flamed tableside just for me. High drama for a small child. But Steak Diane's main attraction was—and remains to this day—the classic combination of steak, butter, shallots, Worcestershire sauce, mustard, cognac, and fresh chives.

In the 1950s and '60s, Steak Diane was a signature dish of fine dining establishments coast to coast, part of a trend to flamboyantly prepare dishes tableside. There are many different versions of this steak, but almost all call for chafing dish theatrics that, surprisingly, are not merely for show. The heat of the burning alcohol caramelizes the sugars and melds the flavors of the components, thereby intensifying the taste of the finished sauce. I prefer the simple unadorned version. However, cream, veal stock, mushrooms, parsley, and/or thyme appear in some recipes and are worthy additions, so go ahead and experiment, with some or all of the listed optional ingredients.

It is generally accepted that Steak Diane sprang up in Manhattan in the early '50s—probably at either the Drake or the Sherry-Netherland Hotel or at the Colony Restaurant—and took the country by storm. This was a time of economic boom—Julia Child; the Kennedy White House; and Restaurant Associates' first "theme restaurant," Forum of the Twelve Caesars, with its pseudo-Roman menu, centurion helmets used as ice buckets, waiters scantily dressed in Roman-style jerkins, and flaming everything. French cooking and rich wine sauces—especially if on fire—were all the rage. These days it is rare to see Steak Diane on a menu, but try it at home—you don't have to flame it tableside—and you'll love it, as will your guests. And it's quick and easy to boot.

Game lovers, please note that a Steak Diane antecedent was Sauce Diane, which in the nineteenth century traditionally accompanied venison. The Steak Diane recipe works perfectly substituting venison noisettes for the beef fillet. And it is also good with chicken paillards.

Serves 4

Four 6-ounce filet mignon medallions, pounded between
    two pieces of waxed paper to a ½-inch thickness
Sea salt and freshly ground black pepper to taste
6 tablespoons unsalted butter
½ cup minced shallots
4 teaspoons minced garlic
2 cups very thinly sliced white mushroom caps
    (optional)
⅓ cup cognac or brandy
4 teaspoons Worcestershire sauce
4 teaspoons Dijon mustard
4 drops of Tabasco sauce or other hot red pepper sauce,
    or to taste
½ cup heavy cream (optional)
3 cups beef or veal stock, reduced to ½ cup (optional)
¼ cup finely minced fresh chives
2 tablespoons finely minced fresh flat-leaf parsley

1. Season the pounded meat on both sides with salt and pepper.
2. Place a skillet large enough to hold all the steaks in one layer without touching over medium-high heat. Add 2 tablespoons of the butter. When it has melted and the foam begins to subside, add the meat and cook for 2 minutes on each side, or until the meat is the desired doneness. Transfer the steaks to a plate and cover to keep warm.
3. Add the shallots and garlic to the skillet and cook, stirring, until the vegetables are soft and just beginning to color. Add the mushrooms, if using, and cook, stirring, until soft, about 5 minutes more. Remove from the heat.
4. Warm the brandy in a small pan. Add it to the sauce and ignite with a long kitchen match. Return the pan to the heat, and stir. When the flame has burned out, add the Worcestershire sauce, mustard, and Tabasco sauce.
5. At this point, either add the meat back to the pan and stir over medium-low heat just to warm through, or add the cream, mix thoroughly, and cook, stirring, for 1 minute. Add the veal stock and simmer for 1 minute. Return the meat and any accumulated juices to the pan and turn the meat to coat with the sauce.
6. Adjust the seasoning and serve with the sauce poured over and sprinkled with the fresh herbs.

THE GRAND EUROPEAN'S

Beef Stroganoff

Late one July afternoon when my two daughters were still young, we innocently boarded the Grand European at the Westbahnhof in Vienna, having no idea we were stepping into an expensive hoax. Having been assured by our travel agent that the unique and glamorous train voyage was well worth the money, we had prepaid in full. The trip turned out to be "more unique" than expected. For this maiden voyage, there were no other guests on the entire train. The thirteen additional passengers were either staff or members of one of several television crews given a free trip in exchange for publicity.

The Grand European was billed as an updated, more exclusive version of the Orient Express, traveling from Vienna to Prague and back with stops along the way. Seeing the refurbished navy blue cars—with their gleaming brass and elegant gold insignias—filled us with happy anticipation. Our mahogany-paneled cabins spoke of an era when railroad was king. Our car had been built in 1959 for the president of Hungary and used solely to transport heads of state. Richard Nixon had been an early passenger.

The train left the station on time, and the gorgeous countryside seen out the window took center stage. Unfortunately, outside soon merged with inside. No one had mentioned that "the most luxurious train in all of Europe" had no air-conditioning. As it was over ninety even in the late afternoon, we had no choice but to open the windows and leave them open. Covered in soot, we reached the Hungarian border around eight that first evening and were asked to disembark. Soon, a close cousin of the Little Engine That Could appeared and pulled our train a few feet and into Hungary. Starving and having been told that the food on the train would be excellent, we were more than ready to climb back on board and have dinner. No such luck. The train was pulled back and forth across the border for at least two hours while the television crews jostled for photo ops.

The 1927 dining car glowed seductively with soft, warm light emanating from the original wall sconces. Old-world elegance, however, was marred by noise from the tracks and dirt blowing in the still-open windows. And it did not help matters that the only thing on the menu was a piping hot beef stroganoff, something I had always associated with snow-on-the-ground weather. When I realized the dish included local girolles, the most sought-after member of the chanterelle family, I had several helpings—and not just because it was late and there had been no first course.

We were not thinking about the previous night's stroganoff until it appeared again—as the only option for lunch—the next day. That evening we had dinner in Budapest, but the following night, the stroganoff reappeared for our last meal on the train. When we returned to New York and were asked about the caviar, foie gras, and other elaborate food "as advertised," we spoke of more chanterelles than we could possibly eat, neglecting to mention there was nothing else.

I had no interest in eating anything resembling beef stroganoff for some time. However, on a dark, cold, and depressing January day a few years later, the thought of that delicious meal came back to me, and I felt the need to re-create the Grand European's one tour de force. I trotted off to the store, only to be informed that chanterelles were seasonal, and that winter was the wrong season. Patience was required, but when spring arrived, so did the mushrooms. The local farmers' market had plenty, and I used the sketchy notes dictated by the train's chef to create something truly delicious. Actually, try the stroganoff even if chanterelles are out of season or financially out of reach. Use whatever mushrooms are on hand. And if you can throw in a handful of rehydrated dried chanterelles, morels, or cèpes, so much the better.

There are as many recipes for beef stroganoff—small pieces of tender beef coated with a sour cream–based mushroom and onion sauce—as there are chefs to make it. The one unanimous inclusion is sour cream, as even the beef is questioned by the few who prefer their "stroganoff" mushrooms only. Those who include meat agree that the delicate beef must be cooked quickly, nicely browned on the outside, while remaining rare within. The original Russian garnish was straw potatoes (much like our French fries), but by the time the dish became popular in North America—post–World War II with the end of meat rationing—the more common accompaniment was buttered noodles.

Braised meats finished with sour cream were typical of Russian cuisine as far back as the Middle Ages and reflected the influence of nomadic people from the Steppes whose diet depended primarily on what their herds produced. *Larousse Gastronomique* states that this traditional Russian dish has been known in Europe since the seventeenth century, but that the "Stroganov" nomenclature was first seen in 1861 when a more refined recipe appeared in Elena Molokhovets's classic Russian cookbook, *A Gift to Young Housewives*.

There are three major theories about the naming of the dish, all three involving the Stroganovs, a family of peasants who by the fifteenth century had become wealthy merchants, financiers, and patrons of the arts. Continually striving for upward mobility, descendants helped Ivan the Terrible annex Western Siberia, lent huge sums of money to Peter the Great, and consequently became barons and counts.

Theory number one has Count Pavel Stroganov, a diplomat and 1890s St. Petersburg celeb, gourmet, and great friend of Alexander III, stationed in Siberia. His French cook, Charles Brière, discovered their beef was frozen solid and could be used only by cutting it into very thin strips. The second theory has Briére inventing the dish for a competition in St. Petersburg. Either of these theories sounds plausible until you realize that the recipe with the Stroganov name attached appeared in *A Gift to Young Housewives* several decades before Count Pavel came on the scene. Thus the third theory makes the most sense. Count Alexander Grigory Stroganov (1770–1857), previously known for Lucullan feasts—herring cheeks, salmon lips, poached bear paws, roast wildcat, cuckoo birds, and halibut livers being just a sampling of his exotic favorites—was old and had lost his teeth. He asked his chef to create something easy for him to chew. The chef reworked an earlier recipe by cutting the beef into small pieces and named it after his employer.

Serves 8

3 pounds filet mignon, cut into 1-inch chunks
Sea salt and freshly ground black pepper to taste
1 teaspoon sweet paprika
¼ cup brandy
6 tablespoons unsalted butter
1 large yellow onion, peeled and very thinly sliced
3 pounds chanterelles (other mushrooms may be substituted), wiped clean with a damp towel and halved (If using large mushrooms of another sort, slice them.)
½ cup rich beef or veal stock
⅓ cup heavy cream
⅓ cup sour cream
1 tablespoon Dijon mustard
2 tablespoons best-quality Italian tomato paste
¼ cup finely minced fresh dill
3 tablespoons finely chopped fresh flat-leaf parsley
Freshly squeezed lemon juice to taste

1. Heat a large, heavy skillet over high heat until very hot. Season the meat with salt, pepper, and paprika, and add it to the hot pan, a few pieces at a time. Don't crowd the pan. Sear the meat for 1 to 2 minutes per batch on each side, until quite brown. Then toss continually with a pancake turner until nicely browned but still quite rare, 3 to 5 minutes total per batch. As each batch is done, transfer it to a platter.

2. When all the steak has been seared, put it back in the hot pan. Warm the brandy in a small saucepan. Pour it over the meat and light with a long kitchen match. Flame while stirring and deglazing the pan. Place the contents of the pan in a colander set over a large bowl.

3. Wipe out the skillet and melt 4 tablespoons of the butter over medium heat. Add the sliced onion, season with salt and pepper, and sauté, stirring occasionally, until the onions have softened and turned light gold. Raise the heat to high and add the mushrooms. Sprinkle with salt and pepper and cook, stirring frequently, until the mushrooms are tender and quite brown, about 20 minutes.

4. Stir in the stock, heavy cream, sour cream, mustard, tomato paste, and reserved meat juices. Simmer for about 5 minutes, until the sauce thickens. Do not boil.

5. Return the meat to the skillet, and heat for 1 minute in the sauce. Do not overcook the meat. Stir in the dill and parsley, and season with salt, pepper, and lemon juice. Serve at once over buttered noodles or rice.

Hash à la Lübeck

WITH ANCHOVY-CAPER SAUCE

Luchow's, gone but not forgotten, remains the most famous of the many German eateries once dotting Manhattan. It was founded in 1882 when Guido August Luchow, a twenty-six-year-old German waiter, with financial help from piano magnate William Steinway, purchased the Union Square beer gardens of Luchow's employer, Baron von Mehlback. Steinway, who worked nearby, was the restaurant's guardian angel, appearing with his senior executives for the forty-five-cent lunch five days a week, often with visiting musicians in tow. At night, Steinway hosted exquisite fetes in the Hunt Room, which was decorated with mounted deer heads shot by Luchow himself, or in the Nibelungen Room with its lush wall murals peopled by heroic figures from Richard Wagner's Ring cycle. As years passed and Luchow's grew to eight times its original size, Steinways continued to patronize the restaurant, and it was not unusual to find several generations of the family dining there simultaneously. Luchow's survived two world wars and the Depression, remaining in operation for a full century, the only major New York City restaurant to outlast Prohibition.

With seven public dining rooms and two private ones upstairs, Luchow's sprawled a full block and was for many years New York City's largest restaurant. In the late 1800s, Union Square was a quiet, shady park, bordered on the west by fashionable Tiffany's, Macy's, and Brentano's, and on the south by the succession of German beer halls and Italian wine gardens that was Fourteenth Street. Luchow's itself faced a five-block stretch of Irving Place "where there were more luminaries of the theater, art, and literary worlds in residence than in any other neighborhood in the nation, perhaps in the world." With the Academy of Music and Steinway Hall nearby, and Tony Pastor's Theater around the corner, the area was the cultural center of Manhattan.

The ex-saloon was soon the favorite hangout of writers H. L. Mencken, O. Henry, Theodore Dreiser, and Thomas Wolfe, as well as musicians Arthur Rubinstein, Enrico Caruso, Richard Strauss, and Toscanini. Out-of-towners arrived in droves to ogle John Barrymore, Judy Garland, Lillian Russell, and other theater celebrities and to be part of "Sunday nights at Luchow's," which was for many years "the thing to do" in New York for both uptown café society and old-time

neighborhood residents who remembered the days of glory when Fourteenth Street happenings were the talk of the town.

A complete overhaul in 1914—handsome oak paneling, huge baroque mirrors, etched glass, skylights, and major collections of art and antique beer steins—made Luchow's a visual magnet, while good food and German *gemütlichkeit* (jolly conviviality) made it a second home to yet another generation of celebrities and colorful characters. Financier, gambler, and glutton Diamond Jim Brady—who hosted wild banquets where ladies of the chorus, engaged as dinner companions for the guests, often found five hundred dollars and pieces of diamond jewelry tucked under their napkins—was among them. And there was other wildness. On one occasion an aging lion, seduced by the restaurant's delicious aromas, escaped from his cage at the Herbert Museum next door. The fact that he was toothless and barely ambulatory did not prevent the diners from losing their *gemütlichkeit*. Everyone screamed, and those who could not flee leapt up onto the tables. The noisy crashing of glassware, china, and priceless knickknacks caused the poor animal, tail between his legs, to hotfoot it back to the museum without snagging a single sausage.

From the beginning, however, nothing contributed to Luchow's success as much as Luchow himself. This robust, good-natured, handle-bar-mustachioed man ate and drank with a zeal surpassing even his best customers. By evening's end, after downing wiener schnitzel and spaetzle for ten, and draining the dregs from his six-quart stein, August Luchow required four busboys to carry him to the quarters he shared with his sister above the restaurant. When Luchow died in 1923, this irrepressibly generous man was deeply mourned by friends, family, customers, and staff alike.

His heirs ran the restaurant until 1950, when it was purchased by Jan Mitchell, a well-to-do Swede who had dined there years before when a cadet in the Swedish navy. Mitchell had anticipated life as a country squire, but after a meal at Luchow's, turning on a dime, he decided to enter the restaurant business. He succeeded in purchasing the renowned eatery, but only after many years and only with a solemn promise to preserve its legendary traditions. Complying with a vengeance, Mitchell brought back the early menus, which people had enjoyed in the gaslight era, featuring wiener schnitzel, sauerbraten, dumplings, wild game, and German desserts. He thrilled many by reviving the pre-Prohibition weeklong galas with their German band music and special menus— the Venison, Goose, Bock Beer, May Wine, and Mid-Summer Forest Festivals—and reinstated the custom of installing a twenty-four-foot Christmas tree at the start of each holiday season. In 1952, he wrote *Luchow's German Cookbook*, a heartwarming and fascinating compendium of traditional recipes and restaurant lore. I've adapted the recipe for Hash à la Lübeck from this book.

By encasing rare beef, capers, and anchovies in a golden pastry crust, this recipe elevates "hash" to an elegant brunch, lunch, or supper entrée. And the tart, vinegary cucumbers perfectly complement the rich and hearty meat pie. Served with some gherkins alongside instead of the salad, the hash makes a great first course.

Serves 6

1 recipe The Brown Derby's Pastry for Covered Pies (see
    recipe on page 51), or 2 pounds frozen puff pastry,
    thawed
3 pounds cooked, very rare roast beef or steak, diced
    (approximately 6 cups)
5 tablespoons chopped capers
6 anchovy fillets, chopped
6 eggs, beaten (plus an additional egg if needed)
6 tablespoons fine bread crumbs
¾ teaspoon freshly ground black pepper, or to taste
¼ teaspoon freshly grated nutmeg
1½ teaspoons sea salt, or to taste
1 egg yolk whisked with 1 tablespoon heavy cream
    (optional)
Anchovy-Caper Sauce (recipe follows)
Cucumber Vinaigrette Salad (recipe follows)

1. Divide the dough into two parts, one about twice as big
as the other. Between large pieces of parchment, roll both
pieces of dough into rough circles approximately ³⁄₁₆ inch
thick. Make sure the larger circle is at least 16 inches
across and the smaller one at least 11 inches. Place the
smaller piece in the refrigerator to rest, and use the larger
piece to line a lightly greased 9-inch springform pan.
Refrigerate for at least 1 hour and up to 48 hours.
2. While the dough is resting, in a medium bowl, combine
roast beef, capers, anchovies, eggs, bread crumbs, pepper, nutmeg, and salt. If necessary, add another beaten
egg to achieve a smooth, slightly moist consistency. Pour
the mixture into the cold pastry-lined pan.
3. Preheat the oven to 350 degrees. Cover the top with
the rested smaller piece of pastry. Cut to size and crimp
the bottom and top pastries together to form a decorative
edge. Make some slits in the top to allow the steam to
escape. If you want a shiny crust, paint the top crust
with the egg yolk-cream mixture.
4. Bake in the oven for 45 minutes to 1 hour, until the
crust is deep gold. Let rest for 10 to 15 minutes, then
remove the sides of the springform pan and transfer the
pie to a large platter. Serve with Anchovy-Caper Sauce
and Cucumber Vinaigrette Salad.

ANCHOVY-CAPER SAUCE

Makes approximately 2½ cups

3 tablespoons unsalted butter
3 tablespoons all-purpose flour
½ teaspoon Worcestershire sauce
2 cups hot unsalted beef or veal stock
2 teaspoons chopped anchovies
1½ tablespoons chopped capers
1 tablespoon finely chopped fresh flat-leaf parsley
Sea salt and freshly ground black pepper to taste

1. Melt the butter in a medium saucepan set over
medium heat. Whisk in the flour and then the
Worcestershire sauce and cook, continuing to stir, for 2
minutes. Whisk in the hot stock and cook for a few minutes more, until thickened and smooth.
2. Stir in the anchovies and capers and simmer for 1 minute to allow the flavors to combine. Stir in the parsley and
season with salt and pepper. Serve hot.

CUCUMBER VINAIGRETTE SALAD

Serves 6

4 long, thin cucumbers, peeled and sliced paper-thin
1½ tablespoons salt
4½ tablespoons extra virgin olive oil
6 tablespoons white wine vinegar, or 3 tablespoons each of
    white wine vinegar and freshly squeezed lemon juice
¾ teaspoon freshly ground black pepper
1 tablespoon sugar
2 tablespoons minced fresh flat-leaf parsley, fresh dill, or
    fresh chives

1. Place the cucumbers in a nonreactive bowl and toss with
the salt. Set aside for at least 1 hour and up to 4 hours.
2. While the cucumbers are marinating, whisk together
the olive oil, vinegar, pepper, sugar, and parsley to make a
dressing.
3. Rinse and drain the cucumbers. Squeeze them dry in a
large kitchen towel, and mix them with the dressing.
Season with salt and pepper and marinate for 6 to 12
hours in the refrigerator before serving. The salad can be
eaten as soon as it is dressed but is better if you can wait.

Veal Marengo

Named after the Battle of Marengo—where Napoleon defeated the Austrian army near Turin on June 14, 1800—this veal dish includes the unlikely garnishes of crayfish and fried eggs. Seeing the narrow victory as a talisman, an indication of destiny, and a sign that the gods were on his side, the young Corsican saw the day as a triumph and named his favorite horse Marengo along with preparations of both chicken and veal.

Legend has it that in the confusion of fighting, supply wagons did not arrive, and Dunand, Napoleon's chef, found himself in a serious predicament. Because the general never ate on battle days, Dunand knew he would arrive exhausted and hungry at dinnertime. The chef is said to have scrounged up a chicken, some tomatoes, onions, garlic, eggs, and a few crayfish in a nearby village. With pearl onions and mushrooms already on hand, Chicken Marengo was born, with a veal variation to follow soon after.

The Marengo recipes, however, did not appear in contemporary accounts or cookbooks until twenty years later, and most likely, Dunand was not even in Bonaparte's employ until long past the events of June 14. It is telling that Louis Antoine Fauvelet de Bourrienne, Napoleon's private secretary, when writing in his memoirs about the evening of that spectacular day, said simply that, "Supper [was] sent from the Convent del Bosco."

Veal Marengo, nonetheless, is a French classic well worth revisiting. The crayfish or shrimp are easier to eat if shelled in the kitchen, but heads-on they are more decorative. Toasts and potatoes traditionally accompany this hearty dish, though rice or noodles work well also. Nothing green is necessary, but a mixed salad with a caper-anchovy vinaigrette or a simple sauté of green beans adds visual appeal to the plate as well as a pleasantly contrasting crunch.

Serves 6

3 pounds veal stew meat (breast, shoulder, short ribs, neck, shank, and/or round), cut into 2-inch pieces
9 tablespoons extra virgin olive oil
3 cloves garlic, peeled and sliced
1½ cups minced onions
1 teaspoon sea salt
½ teaspoon freshly ground black pepper
Dash of cayenne pepper
5 teaspoons all-purpose flour
2¼ cups dry white wine

1 pound fresh tomatoes, peeled, seeded, and chopped, or one 16-ounce can tomatoes (preferably San Marzano)
6 sprigs fresh flat-leaf parsley
1 bay leaf
½ teaspoon dried thyme, or several sprigs thyme
2 large sprigs fresh basil
1 strip of orange zest, approximately 3 inches long and ½ inch wide
½ pound button mushrooms or sliced larger mushrooms
1 cup pitted green olives

6 eggs

36 crayfish (18 small or medium shrimp can be substituted), cooked and (optionally) shelled

3 tablespoons chopped or julienned fresh basil

1. Preheat the oven to 350 degrees. Dry the veal on paper towels. Heat the oil until almost smoking in a large skillet set over high heat. Add the meat and brown on all sides, a few pieces at a time. As ready, transfer the browned pieces of veal to a 4- to 6-quart casserole. When all the meat has been browned, pour all but a tablespoon of oil out of the skillet and reduce the heat to medium. If the oil has burned, wash the skillet and start over with a fresh tablespoon of oil. Add the garlic and minced onions and sauté for 10 minutes, or until golden, stirring often.

2. While the onions and garlic are cooking, toss the meat in the casserole with the salt, pepper, cayenne, and flour. Then place the casserole over medium heat and continue to toss until the flour is lightly browned, about 3 to 4 minutes. Remove from the heat.

3. Add the wine to the skillet with the browned onions and garlic and boil for 1 minute, scraping up the coagulated juices from the bottom of the pan.

4. Pour the wine and vegetable mixture into the casserole along with the tomatoes, parsley, bay leaf, thyme, basil, and orange zest. Bring to a simmer over medium heat, stirring often to mix the liquid with the flour.

5. Cover the casserole, set in the lower third of the oven, and bake until the meat is almost tender when pierced with a fork, approximately 1½ hours. Add the mushrooms and the olives to the stew and stir down into the sauce. Put the casserole back in the oven for 25 to 45 minutes, until the meat is meltingly tender.

6. Pour the contents of the casserole into a large sieve set over a saucepan. Discard the orange zest, bay leaf, and herb sprigs. Place the saucepan over high heat and immediately remove any visible fat that rises to the top. If necessary, boil the sauce until it is slightly thickened and a rich red-brown. Correct the seasoning, and pour the sauce back into the casserole over the veal. The stew can be made in advance to this point. Cool, uncovered. Then degrease and refrigerate for up to 48 hours. To serve, bring to room temperature, and then simmer for 5 to 10 minutes to heat through. Then proceed with Step 7.

7. Fry the eggs in a little olive oil.

8. To serve, pour all the casserole contents into a large, hot serving dish and top with the shrimp and eggs. Strew with the chopped basil, and serve, piping hot, accompanied by rice, noodles, or mashed potatoes.

JACK SAVENOR'S

Leg of Lamb

WITH MUSTARD AND GINGER COATING

Living in Cambridge in the 1970s, I frequently ran into Julia Child at Savenor's Market. She was friendly and outgoing and we'd chat—she offering cooking tips in a motherly fashion, while I hung on every word, trying to figure out how many questions I could ask without seeming rude.

Jack Savenor owned a high-end grocery store on Kirkland Street. His parents had set up shop in 1939 with Rockefellers, Kennedys, and Schlesingers as regular customers. Savenor's prided itself on selling the finest quality meat and produce in the state. Julia and I and other die-hard carnivores bought whole steers and lambs that Jack would butcher before storing in individually labeled freezer compartments. Jack could always be found behind the counter fussing with his huge scale, its ten-pound meat hook sunk into a side of beef. In the late seventies, culinary Cambridge was rocked by scandal when it was discovered that Jack had been weighing the meat hook along with the meat. A small price to pay, as the beef was great and so was the lamb and so was Jack.

Julia, in reference to Jack—who became a celebrity in his own right after many guest appearances on her shows—was often quoted as saying, "Every woman should kiss her butcher." Jack took this literally and was always kissing Julia, which was fine as they were close friends. I, on the other hand, just out of college, found this dictum problematic. Though I could have gone elsewhere, I continued to wait in line for the delectable meat that was the Savenor trademark. Savenor's thrived, Jack survived the scandal, and there was no shortage of kissing.

This leg of lamb is juicy, succulent, deeply flavorful, and easy to prepare. Although I've adapted the recipe from *Mastering the Art of French Cooking*, I used to buy the meat from Jack and have always associated it with him. Emerging from the oven redolent of mustard, ginger, rosemary, and soy, and beautifully browned, this straightforward dish never fails to please and is one of those rare culinary finds where the divine result seems even more so due to the simplicity of the preparation. To intensify the flavor even further, slather the lamb with its coating a couple of days in advance. But even if you wait until right before roasting, the meat will be tender and flavorful. I serve it with sautéed green beans—which, in season, I mix with fresh shell beans; a pan-roast of potatoes; and broiled cherry tomatoes. Smashed potatoes with basil are another good accompaniment. Julia reminds us to "serve the lamb on hot plates as lamb fat congeals when cold."

Serves 6 to 8

½ cup Dijon mustard

2 tablespoons soy sauce

1 to 2 large cloves garlic, peeled and finely chopped or put through a garlic press

1 tablespoon dried rosemary leaves (dried thyme may be substituted)

¼ teaspoon powdered ginger

2 tablespoons extra virgin olive oil

One 6-pound, bone-in leg of lamb

1. Blend the mustard, soy sauce, garlic, rosemary, and ginger together in a small bowl.

2. Whisk in the oil by droplets to make a mayonnaise-like cream, or in a food processor, blend everything but the oil, adding it slowly through the feed tube while the motor is running.

3. Using a large pastry brush, paint the lamb with the mixture. The meat will pick up more flavors if coated in advance—several hours and up to 2 days, refrigerated until ready to use.

4. When ready to cook, bring the meat to room temperature and place it on a rack set in a roasting pan, and preheat the oven to 350 degrees.

5. Roast for approximately 1 hour for rare (125 degrees), 1¼ hours for medium rare (135 degrees), and 1½ hours for well done (150 degrees). Use a meat thermometer to check the temperature, and remember that the meat will continue to cook a bit as it rests, so take it out of the oven 2 or 3 degrees short of the temperatures given.

6. Cover the meat loosely with foil and let it rest for 20 to 30 minutes before carving.

Navarin of Lamb

In 1961, with the publication of *Mastering the Art of French Cooking,* Julia Child became a household name; and in 1963, WGBH in Boston launched *The French Chef,* Child's Peabody and Emmy award–winning television show. With her frank, no-nonsense manner, her down-to-earth charm, and her sometimes hilarious and always informative cooking demonstrations, Julia attracted huge audiences. Her thirty-minute cooking lessons could soon be seen on stations across America. Watching Child fumble and then correct her mistakes made viewers less fearful of disasters looming in their own kitchens. The producer, Ruth Lockwood, stated: "We wanted to let Julia be herself at any cost."

Julia's goofily comedic, larger-than-life on-screen persona captivated the country at a time when television was just becoming the great American pastime. Child was a cult figure coast to coast. Pied Piper–like, she led a generation of baby boomers and their parents to the stove and to the market. She did the nation an invaluable service—for a time almost single-handedly—in dramatically raising culinary standards and expectations across America.

In her memoir *The Tenth Muse,* Judith Jones, editor of *Mastering the Art of French Cooking,* states that the minute she received the manuscript and started turning its pages, she was "*bouleversée,* as the French say—knocked out." Child would not compromise the vision she had of her book; it had to work for Americans as lacking in knowledge as she had been when she first moved to France and learned to cook. The key to Child's success was her ability to teach foolproof culinary rules while simultaneously demystifying and adapting the French kitchen for Americans in a completely nonintimidating and nonpatronizing manner.

This delicious stew, technically a *navarin printanier* or spring *navarin,* is defined by *Larousse Gastronomique* as "a ragout of lamb or mutton with potatoes, and/or various other vegetables, particularly young spring vegetables." Legend has named it after the 1827 Battle of Navarino, when, during the Greek War of Independence, British, French, and Russian fleets destroyed those of the Turks and Egyptians. But as it existed long before the battle, the name probably comes from *navet,* the French word for turnip, originally a main ingredient in the dish. For some chefs, the term "navarin" means any type of ragout (fish, poultry, beef, or seafood) incorporating the requisite turnip or using it as a garnish.

Julia—differing from *Larousse*—suggests cutting the potatoes, carrots, and turnips into tidy, same-size ovals. As this is fairly taxing, I recommend using baby spring vegetables if available, or just cutting the peeled vegetables into uniformly-sized chunks. You can also drop the *printanier* concept and use shell beans or lentils instead. Or experiment with beef instead of lamb. All versions can be made up to three days ahead, refrigerated, and reheated for serving. Vegetables and starch are included in this one-dish meal, so all that's required is lots of hot French bread to mop up the sauce. An optional garnish of minced chives or chopped parsley strewn over the top is fresh and colorful.

Frequently butchers try to sell the leg or loin meat for lamb stew. You will pay more, and those cuts do not have the ideal proportion of fat and sinew recommended for slow braising. The result will still be good, but possibly a bit drier and less tender. Rather, try to find shoulder meat, or even better, as Julia suggests, a mixture of shoulder, breast, short ribs, and neck.

Much of the navarin's flavor originates in the initial browning of the meat pieces. Be sure to dry them with paper towels just before cooking, and heat the oil to almost smoking before adding a few pieces at a time. Crowding the pan causes the meat to steam and turn grayish, in direct opposition to the desired result. The amount of meat you cook per batch depends on the size of the pan—the bigger the pan, the quicker the process. The tablespoon of sugar tossed with the meat and caramelized just subsequent to browning adds depth of both flavor and color.

Serves 6

4 tablespoons tasteless vegetable oil, such as canola

3 pounds lamb stew meat, cut into 2-inch cubes (see recipe headnote: buy 4 pounds, as you end up with some short ribs, which have bones), excess fat and fell (the covering or filament) removed

1 tablespoon sugar

1 teaspoon sea salt

½ teaspoon freshly ground black pepper

3 tablespoons all-purpose flour

3 to 4 cups lamb or beef stock

2 cups canned tomatoes (preferably San Marzano)

3 cloves garlic, peeled and chopped

½ teaspoon dried thyme, or a few sprigs fresh thyme

1 bay leaf

½ pound French green beans (haricots verts), trimmed

18 small boiling potatoes, all approximately 2 inches long, peeled (If you cannot get potatoes the same size, buy bigger ones and cut them into same-size chunks after peeling.)

6 large carrots, peeled and cut into 1½-inch lengths

6 medium turnips, peeled and cut into thirds

One 10-ounce box frozen pearl onions, thawed

2 cups frozen green peas, thawed

Chopped fresh flat-leaf parsley or minced fresh chives for garnish

1. Preheat the oven to 450 degrees. Heat the oil in a large skillet over medium-high heat. Dry the meat well with paper towels and brown as much meat at a time as can fit in the pan while leaving at least an inch between pieces. Turn to brown all sides. As each piece becomes deep brown, use tongs to transfer it to a lidded casserole large enough to hold the meat and all the vegetables with some room to spare for liquids and stirring. Set the skillet aside to re-use in Step 4.

2. When all the lamb has been browned and transferred to the casserole, sprinkle with the sugar and toss over medium heat for 3 to 4 minutes, until the sugar has caramelized.

3. Add the salt and pepper and toss, then repeat with the flour. Place the uncovered casserole in the middle of the oven and bake for 5 minutes. Toss the meat and return to the oven for 4 more minutes. The flour should be evenly browned and the meat coated with a light crust. Remove the casserole from the oven and reduce the temperature to 350 degrees.

4. Pour the fat out of the skillet used in Step 1. Pour 2 cups of the stock into the skillet and bring to a boil over high heat, scraping up the coagulated sauté juices (if these juices have burned, then eliminate this deglazing step). Pour the liquid from the skillet into the casserole. Stir to mix everything together and bring to a simmer. After a minute or two, add the tomatoes, garlic, thyme, and bay leaf. Simmer for 2 minutes. The meat should be almost covered by stock. If it isn't, add more stock.

5. Cover the casserole and place it in the lower third of the 350-degree oven. Regulate the heat so the casserole simmers slowly and regularly for 1 hour.

6. While the stew is cooking, bring a saucepan of salted water to a boil, add the green beans, and boil rapidly

until al dente, about 5 minutes. Drain in a colander and run cold water over the beans to stop the cooking.

7. After an hour's cooking, pour the contents of the casserole into a large sieve set over a bowl. Rinse out the casserole, discarding any loose bones. Return the contents of the sieve to the casserole.

8. Skim as much fat as possible off the top of the sauce in the bowl, correct the seasoning, and pour the sauce back into the casserole.

9. Add the potatoes, carrots, and turnips. Press the vegetables into the casserole around the pieces of lamb and baste with sauce. Bring to a simmer on top of the stove, cover, and return to the oven. After 30 minutes, add the thawed onions and put the casserole back in the oven.

10. Cook for another 30 minutes, or until the vegetables are tender when pierced with a fork and the meat is also very tender but not yet falling apart. Remove from the oven. Tilt the casserole and spoon off as much fat as possible.

11. To serve, bring the stew to a simmer on top of the stove. Gently stir the peas and green beans into the bubbling stew. Cover the casserole and simmer for about 5 minutes, until the green beans and peas are hot and cooked through.

12. Serve the navarin from the casserole or arrange it on a very hot platter. Garnish with freshly minced herbs.

Note: This dish may be prepared through Step 10 up to 2 days in advance. Cool, uncovered, and then refrigerate, covered. Refrigerate the peas and green beans separately.

CRAIG CLAIBORNE'S

Braised Lamb

WITH BASIL AND GARLIC STUFFING

Although Craig Claiborne (1920–2000)—legendary *New York Times* food editor, author of the famous *New York Times Cookbook* series, and serious bon vivant—was for most of his adult life a fixture of the New York–East Hampton social scene and an inveterate globe-trotter, he always kept a culinary foot solidly rooted in the Deep South of his birth. When he was quite young, his father's financial reversals led the family to settle in Indianola on the Mississippi Delta, where his mother opened a boardinghouse to help make ends meet. Claiborne, a timid and awkward child, found hanging out in the kitchen, surrounded by the all-embracing black staff, the perfect antidote to the brutal teasing of his peers, the smothering love of his overprotective mother, and the abuse of his father. Like so many other great American cooks—James Beard, Edna Lewis, Gene Hovis, and James Villas, and even the Duchess of Windsor—it was in his childhood kitchen that Claiborne began a lifelong involvement with the process of cooking. This passion eventually expressed itself in restaurant criticism, food writing and editing, and an endless search for unfamiliar—often exotic—recipes to re-jigger and make palatable, accessible, and pleasing to an American public reared on meat and potatoes.

In 1942, just out of journalism school, Claiborne joined the navy, and after the war worked—briefly and somewhat unhappily—in public relations. In 1949, he moved to France, where the epiphany of French food changed his life. In the navy once again for the Korean conflict, Claiborne had a good deal of time to contemplate his future. As the two things he cared most about were words and food, he decided to try his hand at culinary writing. When the war ended, he used his G.I. Bill scholarship to attend the prestigious École Hôtelière in Lausanne.

Returning to New York from Switzerland, he was hired as a receptionist by *Gourmet* and soon promoted to editor. Claiborne worked his way up the food-publishing ladder, and in 1957, landed the plum job of food editor for the *New York Times*, where he remained in one capacity or another for twenty-nine years. The first man in America to oversee the food page of a major newspaper—previously a woman's domain—Claiborne was responsible for numerous innovations, the most important of which was the now famous four-star rating system, imitated by publications worldwide and used by the *Times* to this day. Drawing on his culinary expertise and international experience, Claiborne redirected the paper's food pages away from general entertaining columns for the upscale homemaker toward a broader social and cultural agenda.

Claiborne authored or edited more than twenty cookbooks, often with his professional partner, *New York Times* chef Pierre Franey; and his *New York Times Cookbook*, published in 1961, sold more than a million copies. His cookbooks, columns, and reviews introduced a generation to a variety of ethnic cuisines at a time when the average American had never heard of guacamole, quiche Lorraine, or even a baguette. Claiborne demystified unfamiliar foods, making them look easy and fun to make. In addition to his cookbooks, Claiborne wrote *A Feast Made for Laughter*, an autobiography in which he discusses good times and successes as well as the conflicts arising from his homosexuality.

In 1975, a wining bid on a television fundraiser led to Claiborne's most notorious culinary adventure. News of the $4,000 thirty-one course Parisian meal attracted criticism while boosting his panache quotient at the same time. This exuberant eating came to an end when his doctor put him on a diet. Readers followed his progress like a soap opera, and the ensuing book *Craig Claiborne's Gourmet Diet* introduced the concepts of low-sodium and low-fat cooking.

Craig Claiborne's recipe for Braised Lamb with Basil and Garlic Stuffing was the one recipe given in his *New York Times* obituary. Lamb was Claiborne's favorite meat, French his favorite cuisine, and a slow braise his favorite cooking method. Despite very few ingredients and almost no active preparation time, this flavorful lamb—redolent of basil, garlic, and bacon—is one of the all-time great recipes for the cooler months. It is even better made a day or two ahead and reheated in the oven when ready to serve. Rice, noodles, or roast potatoes are good accompaniments, as are potatoes, mashed alone or with turnips, celery root, broccoli, or zucchini.

Serves 12 to 16

½ pound bacon or salt pork
12 cloves garlic, peeled and finely minced
½ cup fresh flat-leaf parsley leaves, plus more if desired
1 cup fresh basil leaves, plus more if desired
One 7- to 8-pound leg of lamb, boned, giving about
    6 pounds of meat
Sea salt and freshly ground black pepper to taste
Reserved bones from the lamb, cut by the butcher into
    pieces approximately 2 inches long
¼ cup extra virgin olive oil
2 cups coarsely chopped onion
1 cup coarsely chopped carrot
1½ cups dry white wine
4 cups chopped, peeled tomatoes, best-quality fresh, or
    canned San Marzano

1. Combine the bacon, garlic, parsley, and basil in a food processor or blender. Blend the ingredients to a fine purée.

2. Sprinkle the lamb inside and out with salt and pepper. Spread the bacon-herb mixture on one side of the lamb and roll it up. If some of the stuffing oozes out, don't worry. Use kitchen string to tie up the lamb, tucking in torn pieces of lamb as necessary. Skewers can also help hold the meat together. Rub the lamb with any excess bacon-herb mixture.

3. Put the olive oil in a heavy casserole just large enough to hold the lamb and bones snugly. Heat the oil to almost smoking over high heat. Place the lamb in the hot oil and arrange the bones around it. Brown the lamb and bones on all sides. Then sprinkle the chopped onion and carrot over the bones and toss with the bones and oil. Cover and cook for 5 minutes. Toss the vegetables again and cook for 5 minutes more.

4. Carefully pour off and discard all the fat that has accumulated. Add the wine and tomatoes and season with salt and pepper. Cover and bring to a boil. Cook over medium-low heat, at a brisk simmer, for 2 to 2¼ hours, until the lamb is meltingly tender when pierced with a knife or fork.

5. Remove the lamb and discard the bones. Set the lamb on a cutting board to rest, covered loosely with foil to keep warm. Bring the sauce to a boil, skimming the surface as necessary to remove as much fat as possible. Cook the sauce down until it is sauce consistency. Adjust the seasonings. Slice the meat, and spoon a little of the sauce over each serving. Sprinkle with extra chopped parsley and/or basil if desired.

Note: The lamb is even more delicious made a day or two ahead. Refrigerate, then bring to room temperature before reheating the meat and the sauce, covered in the original casserole, in a 350-degree oven for 30 to 40 minutes, until piping hot.

Lamb Tagine

WITH SAFFRON, DATES, OLIVES, AND CILANTRO

My friend Gordon Watson—a London-based art and antiques dealer and an expert on every-thing visual—used to have a house in Ireland, not far from Waterford. When I visited, we beach-picnicked on huge local crabs that we cracked on the rocks, slathered in homemade mayon-naise, and ate with chunks of Irish brown bread. I was sad when Gordon sold that house, but he soon bought again—this time in Tangiers—a roomy, European-style abode with an overgrown Arab gar-den, a short walk up a steep hill from the medina.

I don't see him much these days and have not been to Tangiers in several years. I miss the house with its own *hammam*; Gordon's eccentric mélange of European, Asian, old Roman, and North African collectibles; the terraces from which you see and smell the Mediterranean; and the restored gardens filled with citrus, bougainvillea, pomegranate, jasmine, and hundreds of flickery, fairy-tale candles to mark the paths at night. What I do still have, from those days in Tangiers is the best recipe ever for lamb tangine, given to me long ago by Gordon's cook Hafida.

A smiling kitchen presence always ready with a cup of mint tea, Hafida is magic behind the stove. Her version of lamb tagine, the traditional North African stew, is the most flavorful I've eaten. Incorporating dates, olives, saffron, and preserved lemons, as well as the meat itself, the dish is an entire *souk* on a plate. Serve it like Hafida does, preceded by a salad of red onion, avocado, orange, and cilantro. Like all stews, this one is even better made one or two days ahead of time and reheated for serving.

The recipe that follows is adapted for the American kitchen and makes use of a casserole, assuming you do not have a tagine. For enhanced flavor, the meat is browned before cooking. Traditionally, this is not the case, so you can eliminate the browning if you wish.

Moroccans would start this meal with a selection of hot and cold mezze, or small plates. I suggest serving two or three of Hafida's favorites from the selection below as a first course, and then leaving the platters on the table throughout the meal as refreshing accompaniments to the rich tagine. But these little salads are not necessary, as the complex flavors of the lamb, dates, olives, saffron, and cilantro really require nothing alongside other than couscous or rice pilaf.

Mezze choices include: a relish of chopped fresh lemon, onion, and flat-leaf parsley with or without tomatoes; fresh orange segments combined with chopped onions and fresh mint; roasted eggplant mashed with garlic, olive oil, and pre-served lemon; grated carrots dressed with olive oil and lemon; mixed bell peppers, roasted, diced, and combined with Spanish onions, tomatoes, garlic, and olive oil; and flat-leaf parsley leaves tossed with thinly sliced red onions, capers, and mint.

Serves 6 to 7

For the spice mixture:
5 cloves garlic, peeled and minced
2 tablespoons extra virgin olive oil
2 tablespoons ground cumin
1 tablespoon ground ginger
1½ teaspoons sea salt
2 teaspoons ground turmeric
2 teaspoons sweet paprika
1 teaspoon ground cinnamon
1 teaspoon freshly ground black pepper

For the lamb:
3 pounds lamb shoulder, cut into 3- to 4-inch cubes
2 tablespoons extra virgin olive oil
2 large Spanish onions, peeled and thinly sliced
¼ teaspoon sugar
2 cups homemade beef stock plus ½ cup water, or
  2½ cups best-quality store-bought beef stock
½ teaspoon crumbled saffron threads
20 Moroccan, Greek, kalamata, or other pitted imported
  black olives, cut in half vertically if large (You can use
  pit-in olives, but then be sure to warn your guests.
  I like the Greek ones with chile flakes or Sicilian
  spiced olives.)
2 preserved lemons, cut into small dice
One 15- to 16-ounce can chickpeas, rinsed and drained
  (optional)
12 to 16 cups cooked rice or couscous as an
  accompaniment
1 bunch fresh cilantro, coarsely chopped, plus ¼ cup
  for garnish
¼ cup chopped pitted dates
¼ cup chopped roasted almonds to sprinkle
  over the top

1. Combine all the spice mixture ingredients in a bowl large enough to comfortably hold the lamb.

2. Add the lamb pieces and toss to coat well.

3. Heat the olive oil in a large casserole. Brown the meat in batches so as not to crowd them, placing the pieces back in the bowl as browned.

4. Add the sliced onions and sugar to the pan, adding a little more oil, if necessary, and cook, stirring frequently, for 10 minutes. Add the meat back to the pan and continue to cook and stir until the onions turn light gold, approximately 5 more minutes.

5. Add the stock (and water if using) and saffron. Bring to a boil, then immediately reduce the heat to a simmer. Cover and simmer for 1 hour.

6. After an hour, remove from the heat and skim off the fat that has risen to the surface. Add the olives and preserved lemons. Cover and simmer for 30 minutes more or cook, uncovered, if the sauce seems too thin. Skim off the fat again. The meat should be very tender and almost falling apart. If it is not, replace the cover and simmer until it is. Add the chickpeas, if using, and cook for another few minutes, until they are heated through. At this point, you can let the tagine cool, uncovered, and then cover and refrigerate for up to 3 days. When ready to serve, remove any fat that has congealed on the surface, bring to room temperature, leave uncovered, and reheat on the top of the stove over medium-low heat, stirring often. Continue with Step 7. As with soups, stews and tagines develop flavor and are therefore better when made at least a day ahead.

7. When the meat is very tender, serve in bowls over couscous or rice and sprinkle with the cilantro, chopped dates, and almonds. Alternatively, the condiments can be passed or they can be stirred into the finished tagine right before serving.

THE RUSSIAN TEA ROOM'S

Luli Kebabs

Madonna worked in the cloakroom until she was fired for inappropriate dress; Leonard Bernstein wrote the initial bars of "Fancy Free" sitting at his favorite table; Elizabeth Taylor Burton chose the restaurant to debut her thirty-three-carat Krupp diamond, a fortieth birthday gift from Sir Richard. In its heyday, New York City's Russian Tea Room—which the *New York Times* called a "preserve of infused vodka, glinting caviar and buttery blini"—served almost six thousand liters of the Russian liquor and more than a ton and a half of those special little eggs each year, not to mention 15,867 pounds of sour cream and eight thousand pounds of beets. Known worldwide for its opulence, the restaurant's impressive clientele mix included kings and presidents; writers and critics; theater, music, and dance luminaries; and the international political elite. Regulars such as Marilyn Monroe, Woody Allen, Rudolph Nureyev, George Balanchine, William Faulkner, Henry Kissinger, Helen Gurley Brown, Barbara Walters, Michael Douglas, and hundreds of other big-name celebrities chose this "light-filled palace" for power meals, tête-à-tête trysts, and movie locations.

The Russian Tea Room, however, began humbly. In 1927, in the midst of Prohibition and the same year that Babe Ruth hit sixty home runs, Viennese choreographer Albertina Rasch opened a chocolate and tea shop at 150 West Fifty-seventh Street. She planned to cater to former dancers of the Imperial Russian Ballet who, having fled the Bolsheviks, were arriving in New York City in droves. It was thrilling to find a spot with a *samovar* where they could gather, drink tea spiked with cherry preserves, and share stories of home. By 1929 "the Russian tea room" had moved across the street and set up shop in an Italianate brownstone next door to Carnegie Hall, where it remained—despite an invitation in the late 1950s to join the New York Philharmonic in its move to Lincoln Center—until it closed.

Alexander Maeef, a Siberian émigré, came on board in 1930 and ruled the roost. He initially shared the space with a hosiery shop, but when Prohibition ended, he turned an unused horse stable next door into a series of exotic eating venues. To provide his czarist émigrés with an over-the-top home away from home, Maeef imported the finest caviars, vodkas, and teas for them, while creating a red, green, and gold decor to simulate Russian Christmas all-year-round.

In the mid-1940s, Sidney Kaye, a high-school chemistry teacher, put together a group of investors to purchase the Tea Room; but by 1955, Kaye was running the legendary showbiz hangout on his own and did so until his premature death in 1967. The restaurant then prospered for almost thirty years managed by Kaye's widow, Faith Stewart-Gordon, until 1996 when she sold to Warner LeRoy. But the Tea Room could not survive his death in early 2001, followed a few months later by 9/11; and in 2002, the restaurant folded. Eventually, it reopened under new management, but—to quote Judy Collins in her 2002 *New York Times* op-ed piece—"[The Russian Tea Room] is no longer the ante-room to all the glamour and gifts, sizzle and pulse, art, intelligence and determination of this great city."

As a child, Joel Kaye, Sidney Kaye's son, aspired to join him in the family business. He spent summers working in the office, the cloakroom, and behind the cashier's desk at the restaurant, as well as trotting off daily to the green grocer, butcher, and fishmonger. He grew to understand restaurant operations inside and out, spending two years at Cornell's School of Hotel Management, only to realize that despite loving food, cooking, and especially eating, he had no interest in taking over the Tea Room.

Nonetheless, Joel well remembers his youthful summers spent there. A macaroon, mocha buttercream, and chocolate concoction called a *lodichka* was his favorite menu item back then. A close second, however, and usually his choice for a main course, was Luli Kebabs. Even now, he makes these ground lamb patties at home—bathed in Mushroom Sauce, and sometimes with Georgian Sour Plum Sauce in addition. Joel completes the plate with a pilaf, incorporating dried cherries, walnuts, and parsley. Alternatively, serve the kebabs, like Joel's father did at the restaurant, accompanied by plain rice, sautéed red and green peppers, and a flavorful eggplant and tomato salad. Be sure to have a dish of hot mustard on the table for those who prefer to spice things up.

To provide extra flavor, I add fresh parsley, mint, and garlic to my ground lamb mix. For casual events, the kebabs are delicious sandwiched inside hot pita bread with bowls of tomatoes; sliced red onions; a garlicky mix of yogurt, chopped cucumbers, and dill; shredded lettuce; and extra fresh herbs offered alongside.

Serves 6

3 tablespoons unsalted butter
2 large onions, peeled and minced
3 cloves garlic, peeled and finely minced
3 pounds ground leg of lamb (the butcher can grind it
  for you)
2 teaspoons fine sea salt
¾ teaspoon freshly ground black pepper
2 teaspoons ground coriander
2 teaspoons ground cumin
3 eggs, lightly beaten
½ cup chopped fresh mint, flat-leaf parsley, and cilantro,
  or a mixture of the three (optional)

1. Heat the butter in a large saucepan over medium heat. Add the onions and garlic and cook until softened, approximately 3 to 5 minutes.
2. Remove from the heat and cool. Add the meat, salt, pepper, spices, eggs, and fresh herbs, if using. Knead together with your hands thoroughly. The ingredients must be very well incorporated. Refrigerate for at least 1 hour and up to 12 hours.

3. Use a ½-cup measure to divide the mixture into 12 equal portions. Shape each portion into an oval approximately 3 by 5 inches.
4. Broil or grill the patties, turning frequently, until cooked through. This should take 10 to 15 minutes. Joel Kaye likes to cut the kebabs in half horizontally at this point and cook them another minute or two until the edges are just beginning to crisp.
5. Serve on a bed of hot rice or pilaf, accompanied by sautéed peppers, an eggplant and tomato salad, a red onion salad, and a sauce (options follow).

Note: A mushroom or brown sauce traditionally accompanied The Russian Tea Room's Luli Kebabs, but a sour plum sauce (*tkemali*) and/or Greek yogurt mixed with garlic, onion, fresh herbs, and diced cucumber is also delicious. Toasted pita is a nice addition, and don't forget hot mustard (recipes follow).

MUSHROOM SAUCE

Makes approximately 2 cups

1 ounce dried mushrooms (chanterelles, porcinis, morels,
    or a mixture), rinsed and then soaked in 1½ cups
    warm water for at least 1 hour
2 medium yellow onions, peeled and chopped
2 cloves garlic, peeled and chopped
5 tablespoons unsalted butter
2 tablespoons all-purpose flour
2 cups good chicken or veal stock
Sea salt and freshly ground black pepper
Lemon juice to taste
3 tablespoons chopped fresh flat-leaf parsley or chives
    (optional)

1. Strain the mushrooms over a bowl. Reserve the soaking liquid and finely chop the mushrooms.
2. In a large skillet or sauté pan over medium heat, cook
the onions and garlic in 4 tablespoons of the butter until
very soft and beginning to color. Sprinkle with the flour,
and continue to cook, stirring, for 2 minutes. Add the
stock and then the soaking liquid, being careful not to add
any dirt that may remain in the bottom of the bowl. Bring
to a boil, then turn down the heat and simmer, stirring
occasionally, while preparing the mushrooms.
3. In small skillet, melt the remaining 1 tablespoon butter
and cook the chopped mushrooms, stirring frequently,
until soft and cooked through, about 10 minutes. Add
them to the onion mixture and continue to cook until a
light gravy consistency is reached. Season with salt, pepper, and lemon juice.
4. Off the heat, add the fresh herbs and serve hot.

THE RUSSIAN TEA ROOM'S HOT MUSTARD

¼ cup dry mustard
1 tablespoon brown sugar
2 teaspoons white or cider vinegar
2 teaspoons hot water
1 teaspoon dark sesame oil

Combine all the ingredients thoroughly. Let rest at least 1
hour and chill before using. The mustard will keep in the
refrigerator for months, so if you like it, make extra.

GEORGIAN SOUR PLUM SAUCE

Georgian Sour Plum Sauce, or *tkemali*, is named after
the regional plums from which it is traditionally made
and has always been a staple of the local kitchens, used
ubiquitously, a bit like ketchup in America. Joel Kaye likes
the condiment with Chicken Kiev, and the Russian Tea
Room served it with grilled meat and fish as well as with
kebabs. The Tea Room made it from dried prunes, though
most other sources suggest that unripe red plums plus
lemon juice best captures the flavor of the *tkemali*. The
rhubarb-like color of the finished product is divine. Traditionally, the cooked plums are put through a food mill
before continuing with the recipe, but I prefer the texture
and the appearance of this chunkier sauce. The plum sauce
will keep for several weeks in the refrigerator and freezes
well if you want to stock up for winter.

Makes approximately 3 cups

1½ pounds unripe red plums, pitted and cut into
    ¼-inch dice
3 tablespoons freshly squeezed lemon juice, or to taste
1½ teaspoons ground coriander
¼ teaspoon ground fennel
¼ teaspoon fenugreek or dry mustard
Large pinch of cayenne pepper
4 cloves garlic, put through a garlic press
Sea salt and freshly ground black pepper to taste
¾ cup chopped fresh cilantro

1. Put the plums in a large nonreactive saucepan with
2 tablespoons of water and 1 tablespoon of the lemon
juice. Bring to a boil, then reduce the heat, cover, and
simmer until the plums are soft, 10 to 15 minutes.
2. Add the spices, garlic, salt and pepper, and the remaining 2 tablespoons of the lemon juice. Bring to a boil, then
reduce the heat and simmer for 5 minutes. Add the cilantro and simmer for 3 minutes more, still covered. Remove
from the heat and season with more lemon juice, salt,
and pepper.
3. Cool the sauce, then cover and refrigerate. Wait at least
6 hours before serving.

Crown Roast of Pork

WITH SAUSAGE STUFFING AND GLAZED ONIONS

When Charles Ranhofer joined Delmonico's in 1862, the restaurant reached its apogee of success and fame. Ranhofer invented or reworked numerous dishes, developing an elaborate seven-page "carte," written in both French and English. Steak Delmonico, Delmonico Potatoes, Lobster Newburg, Baked Alaska, Eggs Benedict, and Chicken à la King remain synonymous with both Ranhofer and Delmonico's to this day. In addition, Ranhofer piqued his customers' curiousity as well as their palates by introducing the first avocados, or "alligator pears," in the United States; two versions of bird's-nest soup; and a "soya sauce" that would be accepted even now, almost 150 years later, as an up-to-the-minute component of a fusion feast.

Dishes were named after prominent people—especially those who dined at Delmonico's—as well as after friends and current events. There were "Sarah potatoes" for Sarah Bernhardt; Peach pudding "à la Cleveland," honoring the president; and in 1871, Grand Duke Alexis of Russia was presented with Lobster Duke Alexis. Ranhofer also gave recipes regional American names such as Striped Bass à la Manhattan and Philadelphia Style Clams.

This third-generation chef was born in 1836 in St. Denis, France. At twelve, he began culinary education in Paris and at sixteen took his first job working as *chef de cuisine* for an Alsatian prince. Barely twenty, he cooked for the Russian Consul in New York before taking jobs in Washington, D.C., and New Orleans.

In 1860, after four years in the United States, Ranhofer returned to Paris to orchestrate grand balls at the court of Napoleon III. Back in New York a year later, his tenure as Master Chef at the brand new hot spot Maison Dorée lasted just a year before Lorenzo Delmonico stole him away from his Union Square neighbor. With only one short interruption, Ranhofer ruled the Delmonico's kitchens for thirty-four years. The saying in New York was that Charles Ranhofer was the city's first chef, and there was no second.

Ranhofer favored an abundance of game—all species of duck, geese, pheasant, and smaller birds such as thrush and woodcock—that exemplified the Gilded Age. In addition, there were hare and rabbit and, of course, chicken, fish, and every imaginable kind of shellfish, with an emphasis—

again era-appropriate—on oysters and lobster. Sauces too found center stage. There were bécha-mels and other flour-thickened sauces à l'Escoffier, as well as lighter, more modern sauces based on "essences"—chicken, duck, fish, game, mushroom, and truffle.

Some things, however, were not state of the art. Many dishes were convoluted—reminiscent of the European palace cooking whence Ranhofer emerged—food that no one would think of mak-ing or eating today. One out of hundreds of examples is *Volière Galatine of Pheasants à la Casimir Perier*, which sets two feathered pheasants—wired together into some sort of "natural appear-ance"—on top of socles made of "tin covered with noodle paste" after cooking them with truffles, game glaze, foie gras, forcemeats, livers, white game breasts, and pistachios.

In his biography of Ranhofer, Lately Thomas described his subject as "one who moved among the great chefs of France as peer and equal." Ranhofer, certainly the greatest cook America ever knew and probably one of the most important chefs of all time, was informed by the past. However, in looking steadily toward the future, he changed what Americans ate and the way they ate it forever after.

Lavish enough for the most elegant dinner party and the perfect alternative to Christmas goose, recipe number 1,798 in Ranhofer's *The Epicurean* is Rack of Pork Crown-shaped with Small Onions (*Carré de Porc en Couronne aux Petits Oignons*). I've adapted this ring of succulent pork chops, with its flavorful "farce" and garnish of glazed baby onions, a banquet favorite at Delmonico's from early on. The rich sausage stuffing is traditional and extends the number of people the roast will serve. I prefer cooking the stuffing separately and filling the roast with it once they are both cooked. Both the pork and the stuffing cook more rapidly and evenly this way. Alternatively, the cooked roast can be filled with herbed mashed potatoes or a mushroom risotto; or a bit lighter, fill the cooked crown with mixed baby vegetables, sautéed or creamed spinach, sautéed red cabbage, or buttered green peas. Or just toss the recipe's glazed baby onions with fresh herbs and use that combination to fill as well as garnish the roast. Have your butcher trim the two racks and tie them into a crown.

Serves 12 to 16, depending on the rest of the menu

1 large onion, peeled and quartered

6 cloves garlic, peeled

4 sprigs fresh thyme

1 sprig fresh marjoram (optional)

2 carrots, peeled and sliced

2 ribs celery, thinly sliced

½ cup sliced fresh fennel fronds

2 bay leaves

1 crown roast of pork, 20 ribs weighing approximately 10 pounds, ribs frenched by your butcher

Sausage Stuffing (recipe follows), at room temperature

Approximately ¼ cup extra virgin olive oil mixed with 2 cloves of garlic put through a press

Sea salt and freshly ground black pepper to taste

2 teaspoons dried thyme

½ teaspoon sugar

1 teaspoon red wine or sherry vinegar

¾ cup dry white wine

1 cup chicken or pork stock, plus extra if needed

¼ cup freshly squeezed orange juice

Pinch of cayenne pepper or several drops Tabasco sauce

1 tablespoon finely minced fresh flat-leaf parsley

Glazed Onions (recipe follows)

1. Preheat the oven to 450 degrees. Strew the onion, gar-lic, thyme, marjoram, carrot, celery, fennel, and 1 of the bay leaves on the bottom of a large roasting pan. Place a rack on top of the vegetables and the pork roast above.

2. Fill the roast loosely with stuffing. Do not pack down. If there is extra stuffing, cook covered in a separate casserole.

3. Paint the roast, stuffing, and vegetables with garlic oil and season all with salt, pepper, and dried thyme.

4. Cover the bare ends of the rib bones with small pieces of aluminum foil to prevent burning, and roast in the middle of the oven for 20 minutes.

5. Lower the oven temperature to 350 degrees, and pour 1 cup of water into the bottom of the pan. Roast for 1½ to 2 hours more, or until an instant-read thermometer reads 140 degrees when stuck into the thickest part of the meat. This may take less time if cooking all the stuffing separately. If the stuffing gets too brown and dry before the meat has finished cooking, moisten with a bit of stock, paint with more garlic oil, and cover loosely with foil.

6. When the roast is done, transfer it to a platter or cutting board and cover loosely with foil to keep warm. The roast must rest at least 15 minutes before cutting.

7. While the meat is resting, remove any visible fat from the drippings. Place the pan on the stove over medium heat. Add the sugar, vinegar, and wine, and bring to a boil while deglazing the pan. After 2 or 3 minutes, add the stock, orange juice, and cayenne or Tabasco sauce. Simmer, stirring frequently and mashing the vegetables into the sauce, for approximately 5 to 10 minutes, until a sauce consistency is reached. If the sauce is not thick enough, you can mash a tablespoon or two of stuffing into it at this point. Strain the sauce through a coarse sieve into a sauceboat, add the parsley, and adjust the seasoning.

8. Present the roast at the table. Carve into chops and serve with the stuffing, sauce, and glazed onions.

SAUSAGE STUFFING

8 cups whole wheat, multigrain, or white bread cubes (or a
    mixture), dried on a cookie sheet in a 325-degree oven
6 tablespoons unsalted butter
3 medium onions, peeled and chopped
4 ribs celery, finely sliced crosswise
1 large bulb fresh fennel, chopped (include some of the
    fronds if possible)

3 cloves garlic, peeled and thinly sliced
1 tablespoon whole fennel seeds, toasted
2 teaspoons dried thyme
3 tablespoons minced fresh flat-leaf parsley
1 tablespoon minced fresh marjoram
1 pound ground pork, crumbled
Approximately 1½ to 2½ cups chicken or pork stock
1 cup raisins
Sea salt and freshly ground black pepper to taste
2 eggs, lightly beaten

1. Place the dried bread cubes in a large bowl. Set aside.

2. Melt the butter in a large skillet set over medium-high heat. Add the onions, celery, fennel, garlic, fennel seeds, thyme, and half the parsley and marjoram. Cook, stirring frequently, for 15 to 20 minutes, until the vegetables are just beginning to color.

3. Add the ground pork and cook, stirring frequently, until cooked through, about 10 more minutes. Stir in ½ cup stock.

4. Scrape the mixture into the bowl of bread cubes. Add the reserved parsley and marjoram, and the raisins. Toss to combine. Add enough of the remaining broth to make a moist, but not at all wet, stuffing. Season with salt and pepper. If not using right away, cool and then cover and refrigerate. Bring to room temperature. Stir in the beaten eggs before cooking.

GLAZED ONIONS

3 tablespoons unsalted butter
Two 1-pound bags frozen pearl onions, thawed
1 cup chicken or pork stock
Sea salt and freshly ground black pepper to taste
1 tablespoon finely minced fresh flat-leaf parsley

1. While the roast is cooking, make the glazed onions. In a large skillet over medium heat, melt the butter. Add the thawed onions and sauté until lightly golden, about 10 minutes.

2. Add the stock and boil to reduce until the onions are just glazed. Season with salt and pepper and set aside. When ready to serve, reheat over medium-high heat and toss with the parsley.

MONSIEUR DODIN-BOUFFANT'S

Pot-au-feu

In Marcel Rouff's classic French novel *The Passionate Epicure*—dedicated to and based loosely on the life of Jean-Anthelme Brillat-Savarin (1755–1826), author of *The Psychology of Taste*—we are introduced to confirmed bachelor Monsieur Dodin-Bouffant, a retired magistrate now devoting himself solely to the high arts of romantic love and French cuisine. Renowned as France's most celebrated gastronome, "the Napoleon of gourmets, the Beethoven of cooking" represents "the apotheosis of French grand cuisine." In her January 23, 2003, *New Yorker* article reviewing the *Modern Library Food*'s new edition, Francine du Plessix Gray calls Dodin-Bouffant "the Robespierre of the dinner table," citing his exacting gustatory judgments that have disqualified hundreds of prominent men from supping at his house for sins as minor as "having unrestrainedly praised the badly buttered toast under a partridge of the wrong age."

Marcel Rouff (1877–1936), novelist, poet, critic, and historian, was a founding member of the Academie des Gastronomes and a longtime friend of Curnonsky, "le Prince des Gastronomes." Together they wrote the masterwork *La France Gastronomique,* a near-perfect examination of French cookery. *The Passionate Epicure* takes itself seriously and at the same time indulges in parody at the expense of Rouff's compatriots as represented by Dodin, a man constantly making a case for cooking being on par with the major arts and comparing himself as a gourmet to Claude Lorraine as a painter and Berlioz as a musician. He gives himself credit for "culinary inventions of courage and brilliance" such as "daring to wed fish and fowl . . . and enhance the aroma of a capon, copiously marinated, by a stuffing in which the dominant notes were the flavours of shrimp and turbot."

The novel opens with Dodin grieving the death of Eugenie Chatagne, his cook and "devoted collaborator" of many years. After months of punishingly bad food at the local café and disappointing interviews to fill the vacant position in the kitchen, Adèle Pidou appeared on his doorstep. Her short, stocky body and her "fat thighs, overfull bodice and somewhat faded hair" did not force him to stuff his hands in his pockets as was often the case "to save them from the wanderings of tempta-

140

tion." But Adèle could cook and almost immediately became "the mistress of the house [and] . . . the handmaiden of his brain." From then on, Dodin lived in an "uninterrupted dream of veal birds and scented stuffings, unbelievable legs of mutton . . . jugged goose livers, stewed cockscombs . . . savory sausages of suckling pig trotters in milk . . . patties of perch, baby-quail tarts . . . larks au gratin, moulds of pheasant . . . jellied boar [and] . . . snipe à la poulette."

News of Adèle's culinary prowess spread. Thus, when "the heir to the throne of Eurasia" was taking the waters nearby, he invited Dodin to dinner with the hope of a return invitation. The much-anticipated repast disappointed Dodin, for whom it represented quantity rather than quality. With more than fifty overly complicated dishes, their flavors drowned in elaborate sauces and thirty wines, Dodin viewed the dinner as highly imperfect and totally lacking in harmony, "abundant, thickset, rich, but without light, without brilliance . . . Custom, but no rules. A parade, but no organization. What mistakes in the succession of flavours and textures!"

Dodin invited the Prince and his entourage back, and in an attempt to teach the ostentatious foreigner a lesson, served a mere four courses, the centerpiece of which was pot-au-feu, a dish epitomizing the spirit and frugality of the French bourgeoisie. When Dodin read out the menu, the Prince was outraged, insulted, and incredulous, as "this meager programme would hardly have provided the first course of his ordinary meals." However, he soon learned that Adèle's version of the national dish was like no other:

"The beef itself . . . was carved into slices of a flesh so fine that its mouth-melting texture could actually be seen. The aroma it gave forth was not only that of beef-juice smoking like incense, but the energetic smell of tarragon with which it was impregnated and the few, very few, cubes of transparent, immaculate bacon in the larding. The rather thick slices . . . rested languidly upon a pillow made of a wide slice of sausage, coarsely chopped, in which the finest veal escorted pork, chopped herbs, thyme, chervil . . . this delicate triumph of pork-butchery . . . was itself supported by ample cuts from the breast and wing fillets of farm chickens, boiled in their own juice with a shin of veal, rubbed with mint and wild thyme. And, to prop up this triple and magnificent accumulation . . . was the stout, robust support of a generous layer of fresh goose-liver simply cooked in Chambertin."

The Prince was duly impressed and humbled. In leaving, he addressed his host saying, "From no one but you . . . could I have accepted the lesson I have just been taught. Comfort my somewhat bruised vanity by giving me a single formula your genius alone has discovered." With a deep bow, Dodin responded that great cookery "is a choice work which demands great love . . ." An unfortunate outcome of this transcendent meal was the Prince's campaign to woo Adèle away from Dodin-Bouffant who won out in the end, but only by understanding that to retain Adèle he had to marry her.

Although pot-au-feu, the national dish of France, has been called "the foundation of empires," it is essentially just a boiled beef and vegetable "knife-and-fork soup." The dish has ancient origins and innumerable variations (*petite marmite, poule au pot, bollito misto*, among others). With Dodin-Bouffant, it reached unimaginable heights of taste and complexity. As Rouff did not grace us with Adèle's exact recipe—and opinion differs whether to start cooking the meat in boiling water to seal in flavor or in cold water brought slowly to a simmer, resulting in intensely flavored broth but less tasty meats—I suggest a compromise: Place the meat in cold broth brought quickly to a boil and then immediately turned down to a simmer. Broth rather than water gives the soup a jumpstart on intensity; and by bringing it to a boil rapidly, the meats retain their flavor.

Whether you decide on a simpler preparation or attempt to emulate Dodin-Bouffant and go whole hog, pot-au-feu is a meal in itself. The flavorful broth or bouillion is served as a first course, often dotted with croutons and sprinkled with Gruyère. The main dish, or *bouilli*—a platter of boiled meats and mixed vegetables, often but not always including boiled potatoes and cooked cabbage—follows, with gherkins and a variety of mustards and sauces served alongside. Possibly gilding the lily, some people include slices of poached marrowbone accompanied by toasts upon which to spread the marrow and fleur de sel to sprinkle over. Although not traditional, I strew a handful of fresh chervil, parsley, or chives over the arranged platter. As well as a bright taste, the fresh herbs impart a lively visual counterpoint to the long-cooked vegetables and succulent meats.

Dodin-Bouffant wowed his dinner guests right off by floating artichoke hearts atop the broth "like treasure islands . . . laden with a butter fried-stuffing in which carps' roes and mushrooms were mashed up together with cream." And under the surface were "small rissoles of shrimp-tails laced in melted cheese." Those marvels are probably best left to the fictional Adèle, but you might want to try—like Monsieur Dodin-Bouffant and especially around the holidays—poaching a whole foie gras in Chambertin, and then slicing and adding it to the platter. However, neither "floating islands" of goodies nor expensive goose liver is necessary. Even the most basic pot-au-feu represents elegant but deeply satisfying comfort food. On a cold winter day, you may for a moment imagine yourself in Paris sitting in a cozy Belle Epoque bistro partaking of the country's "national dish."

Pot-au-feu is tastier when made a day or two ahead. Cook the recipe through Step 6 and cool. Dampen the cooled meats and vegetables with a few ladlefuls of broth and then refrigerate solids and broth separately. After several hours, skim the fat from the broth, and taste it for intensity. If it is not highly flavorful, boil to reduce until it is. Adjust the seasonings. If desired, you can chop and brown a large onion and add it to the broth for color and flavor before rewarming.

The following recipe easily serves sixteen. For eight people and/or for ease of preparation, you can eliminate the pork, chicken, and sausage. Another option is to omit the pork and chicken but retain the sausage (which adds significant flavor), putting it in the pot only for the last half hour of cooking. Don't forget to tie pieces of kitchen string around the chicken and around each package of meat to facilitate removal from the pot when testing for doneness.

Serves 16 to 20

1 veal knuckle bone (optional but suggested, as it adds
    flavor and body)
2 pounds beef or veal bones (optional but suggested, for
    flavor and body)
8 chicken livers, plus 1 to 2 pounds (optional) necks,
    gizzards, poultry scraps, and/or carcasses
1 large marrowbone (optional but suggested)
4 pounds boned beef—a combination of at least two
    of the following: brisket, shoulder, chuck, and top rib,
    all excess fat removed (All pieces of meat should be
    tied up in string by the butcher so that they do not
    fall apart during cooking.)

2 pounds shin of beef, both meat and bone (all excess
    fat removed and tied with string as instructed for
    boned beef)
One 4-pound piece of pork either butt, picnic, rolled
    shoulder, or fresh ham
One 4-pound stewing hen (If unavailable, use a roasting
    chicken, but only cook for 1 hour.)

Soup vegetables:
3 medium yellow onions, peeled and each one stuck with
    1 whole clove
3 carrots, peeled

3 ribs celery

2 parsnips, peeled

2 whole leeks, washed

1 head garlic, unpeeled and cut in half crosswise

1 bouquet garni (8 sprigs fresh flat-leaf parsley, a bay
leaf, a few sprigs fresh thyme, and 8 black peppercorns wrapped in cheesecloth)

One 2-pound piece of mild, lightly smoked country or
Polish sausage

Enough room-temperature beef or chicken stock (or a
mixture of beef and chicken stock) to cover the meat
by 6 inches, approximately 12 cups (If this is not
enough, use cool water to make up the difference.)

2 teaspoons kosher salt or sea salt (more may be needed
later)

Garnish vegetables:

5 very large carrots, peeled and cut into quarters
lengthwise

5 large leeks, carefully washed and trimmed

3 medium turnips, peeled, trimmed, and cut into 4
wedges each

3 large parsnips, peeled, trimmed, and cut into quarters
lengthwise

1 small bunch fresh chervil, tied up in cheesecloth
(optional)

1 large Spanish or yellow onion, peeled, chopped, and
sautéed in butter or olive oil to a deep brown

1 small white cabbage, trimmed, cut into wedges, and
steamed or boiled until tender

10 medium boiled peeled potatoes, halved after cooking,
or 1 to 2 pounds noodles, cooked according to package directions and dressed with butter, sea salt, and
freshly ground black pepper to taste

Salsa Verde or Fresh Herb Mayonnaise (recipes follow) to
serve alongside

A variety of mustards (including Dijon, whole-grain, and/
or English)

Whipped heavy cream or crème fraîche mixed with grated
fresh or bottled horseradish to taste

Crème fraîche mixed with a mustard of your choice to
taste (I like Dijon and/or Zatarain's whole grain.)

1. Place the bones in the bottom of a stockpot or Dutch oven large enough to comfortably hold all the ingredients. Place the chicken livers on top of the bones along with any other poultry giblets, scraps, or carcasses you may be using. Tie a long piece of kitchen string securely around each piece of beef and pork, and also around the hen, and then add each one to the pot on top of the bones, leaving the strings hanging over the side of the pot so the meat can easily be removed to test doneness. Be sure the strings are short enough not to catch fire. Add the stock—and water if necessary—to cover by 6 inches.

2. Bring to a simmer over medium-high heat. When the water comes to a boil, turn down to a simmer and add the salt. A thick gray scum will slowly accumulate on the surface.

3. When the scum is thick and compact, remove it with a slotted spoon. Be sure to also remove any scum stuck to the sides of the pot. Add ½ cup of cold water to stop the simmering. The water will then come back to a simmer and scum foam will rise to the top. Skim it off and repeat this process for about 15 minutes, until all that remains is a bit of white froth. Add the soup vegetables, bouquet garni, and sausage, and continue simmering for 30 min-utes. Transfer the sausage to a bowl large enough to hold all the soup solids—meats and vegetables—later on. At this point, check the chicken also and assess whether it's done or how much longer it needs to cook. When done, transfer it to the bowl with the sausage. Cook the other meats 2 hours more.

4. While the meats are cooking, tie the garnish vegetables in one or more cheesecloth "packages." This will make it easier to get them in and out of the pot.

5. After the meat and bones have cooked for 2½ hours total, check on the doneness of each one. Remove any that are done to the bowl and continue simmering the others until all the meats are meltingly tender. This could take another hour or so (depending upon the size and cut of each piece of meat). Transfer each piece of meat—as it is ready—into the bowl with the sausage and chicken, and moisten with several ladlefuls of cooking liquid.

6. At this time, add the garnish vegetable "packages" and chervil (if using) to cook with the remaining meat or with just the bones if all the meat has been transferred to the bowl. The vegetables will take about 20 minutes to cook. When done, transfer the packages to a platter to cool. When the rest of the meat is done, transfer it to the bowl.

7. Discard the large bones and any other small bones that may have come loose during cooking. Strain the cooking liquid, discarding the bouquet garni, soup vegetables, and any other solids in the strainer. Reserve the broth. When cool, cover and refrigerate for several hours and then degrease. It is best—though not necessary—if you can wait 24 to 48 hours before continuing with the recipe.

8. To continue, simmer the broth with the sautéed onion for 5 to 10 minutes, until reduced and intensely flavorful. Adjust the seasonings and reheat the meat, chicken, sausage, garnish vegetables, cabbage, and potatoes in the reduced broth.

9. Remove the strings and cheesecloth and discard. Carve the chicken and slice the various meats and place them in the middle of a large, hot serving platter. Surround the meats with the garnish vegetables, grouped by color, and heap the cabbage at one side of the dish.

10. Serve the potatoes or noodles separately. I like to add a dusting of chopped fresh parsley, chervil, or chives over the top for taste but mostly for color. Pass the sauces of your choice separately. It is also a good idea to pass a bowl or pitcher of the broth to moisten and flavor the meat, vegetables, and potatoes.

SALSA VERDE

Makes approximately 2 cups

1 bunch each (leaves only) fresh flat-leaf parsley, fresh
    tarragon, fresh basil, and fresh chives
2 to 3 cloves garlic, peeled
3 shallots, peeled
½ cup extra virgin olive oil
Sea salt and freshly ground black pepper to taste
Freshly squeezed lemon juice to taste

1. Put the herbs in a food processor along with the garlic, shallots, and 2 tablespoons of the oil.
2. Blend to combine. Add the rest of the oil, and purée until quite smooth. Season with salt, pepper, and lemon juice.

Note: This sauce is best if made at least an hour before using.

FRESH HERB MAYONNAISE

Follow the instructions for the Garlic Mayonnaise (recipe on page 43), but use only ½ clove of garlic and add 1 cup of chopped fresh herbs of your choice. I particularly like a mixture of tarragon, shallots, basil, and a little parsley.

APICIUS'S

Cassoulet

Much is known but much is also unknown about Marcus Gavius Apicius, first-century Pompeian merchant and bon vivant. According to Athenaeus, Apicius " . . . spent myriads of drachmas on his belly." His extravagant banquets at the court of Tiberius were the source of much imperial gossip. The name Apicius, however, is most famously associated with *De Re Coquinaria* (*On the Subject of Cooking*), the first cookbook in the Western world.

Some historians believe Apicius wrote the ten-chapter tome himself, while others credit an antique compiler, drawing on a number of sources in addition to the writings of Apicius. Whatever its origins, the book is a fascinating document and a window into the culinary life of imperial Rome at the time of Tiberius. It shows antique Roman cookery to be quite sophisticated and most likely the foundation for classic French as well as Italian cuisine. Rouxs were used to thicken sauces; meat was stewed in wine; and truffles were coveted even two thousand years ago—evidently more plentiful back then, one recipe serving them whole in a sauce of wine, black pepper, and honey. Ingredients today resemble those of Apicius—lamb, beef, chicken, veal, fish and shellfish of all types, olive oil, milk, wheat flour, wine, many fruits, vinegar, honey, eggs, garlic, onions, leeks, dill, mint, pine nuts, lard, and a large array of exotic spices. And many recipes using these components are identical to those we make now: pancakes; savory soufflés; various chicken, veal, lamb, and beef dishes; boiled eggs dressed with a honey vinaigrette and pine nuts; and an ancient approximation of a hamburger—bun and all! The book also provides the names and concepts for both paella and cassoulet.

Apicius had a penchant for exotica. Therefore, many of his favorite foods are no longer in vogue. His addiction to flamingo tongues was well known, as was his love of boiled ostrich, *talons de chameaux* (which I can only translate as camels' heels), and foie gras of pig. He force-fed swine with figs and honeyed wine so they might die in ecstasy, their livers *ficcatum*, literally "figged"— the derivative of *fegato,* meaning liver in modern-day Italian.

Apicius spared no effort seeking out the finest food and drink. Bryan Miller of the *New York*

146

Times called him "a gastronomic Diogenes, wandering throughout the empire in search of satisfaction." Once, hearing that Libyan crayfish were far superior to those in his native land, he set sail immediately. His reputation preceded him, and after a lengthy and arduous voyage, the ship was met by fishermen carrying baskets of their best crayfish. Realizing the shellfish was no better than what he ate at home, and wasting no time, our gourmande told the captain to turn the ship around and head back to Rome without even setting foot on shore.

According to Seneca, Apicius poisoned his own wine when he realized that his assets were no longer ample enough to continue dining in his usual manner. He died young, but two thousand years later, his name lives on in association with arguably the most famous cookbook of all time.

Cassoulet—winter food for hungry guests—is a traditional specialty of southern France, where it's baked and served in an earthenware *cassole*. Richly sauced white beans slow-cooked with pork skin and a variety of succulent meats—typically goose, duck, pork, pork sausages, mutton, and/or partridge—is the perfect finale to a day on the slopes or a tramp through snowy woods. Only a green salad and crusty bread are called for, though fruit and a plate of good cheeses follow the cassoulet nicely, as does a tarte Tatin or something chocolaty.

Theories explaining the origins of the dish are numerous. The most fun—though not necessarily the most accurate—credits Apicius. In *De Re Coquinaria*, he makes his *Conchicula* by putting dried peas or beans, sausages, pork meatballs, and a shoulder of pork in an earthenware baking dish along with pepper, oregano, dill, onion, cilantro, wine, *liquamen* (a Roman fish sauce), and olive oil, and then simmering the entirety very slowly until done.

Years ago, I combined and reworked a number of my favorite cassoulet recipes with great success. I have re-created the result—possibly the best cassoulet I have ever tasted—many times since. Though time-consuming, it's an efficient and relatively inexpensive way to feed a large gathering (and 95 percent of the work can be done days in advance) and well worth the effort.

Serves 12 generously

1½ pounds boneless pork shoulder

2 pounds fresh pig's feet, quartered, or fresh ham hocks, or some of both

1 pound fresh pork skin with ¼-inch layer of hard fat attached

Sea salt and freshly ground pepper to taste

2 pounds dried white beans, preferably great Northern

A few sprigs fresh thyme

½ pound pancetta or lean salt pork

About 13 tablespoons fat from confit of duck or goose

4 cups diced onions

5 large carrots, peeled and sliced thinly crosswise

4 ribs celery, thinly sliced crosswise

1 whole head of garlic, unpeeled and halved crosswise

6 ounces cured or baked ham, in one piece

2 cups canned tomatoes, preferably San Marzano

About 3 quarts unsalted chicken, pork, or duck stock

Bouquet garni containing 8 sprigs of fresh flat-leaf parsley, 4 sprigs fresh thyme, and 1 bay leaf, all tied together

Finely grated zest of 1 orange

1 tablespoon whole black peppercorns

1 onion, peeled and stuck with 1 clove

1 pound fresh garlic-flavored pork sausage, such as cotechino

6 leg portions (thigh plus drumstick) confit of duck or goose

2 teaspoons chopped fresh garlic

¼ cup chopped fresh flat-leaf parsley

2 teaspoons chopped fresh thyme

½ cup fresh bread crumbs

1. Day One: Season pork shoulder, pig's feet or ham hocks, and pork skin with salt and pepper. Place in earthenware, enamel, or glass dish, cover, refrigerate overnight.

2. Day Two: Rinse the beans in cool water. Soak them with thyme sprigs in cool water to cover by at least 3 inches for 1½ hours.

3. Meanwhile, cut the pork shoulder into 1½-inch cubes. Set aside. Simmer the pork skin in water to cover until supple, about 30 minutes. Drain. Roll up like a rug and tie with kitchen string in several places. Blanch the pancetta or salt pork in simmering water for 3 minutes.

4. In a 5-quart flameproof casserole, heat 5 tablespoons of the confit fat, and brown the cubed pork shoulder. Add the onions, carrots, and celery and sauté over medium heat, stirring, until the vegetables are soft and the onions are golden, 15 to 20 minutes. Add the pig's feet or ham hocks and the blanched and drained pancetta or salt pork. Raise the heat and allow the meats to brown a little around the edges, turning the pieces occasionally. Add the whole garlic, the ham, and the tomatoes. Cook, stirring, for 1 minute. Add the stock and bring to a boil. Reduce the heat, add the bouquet garni, orange zest, peppercorns, and clove-studded onion, and simmer, covered, for 1 hour.

5. Drain and rinse the soaked beans and put in a 5-quart saucepan. Cover the beans with lukewarm water and slowly bring to a boil over medium heat. Reduce the heat to low and simmer for 10 minutes. Drain immediately and add to the simmering ragoût in the casserole.

6. Separately cook the sausage in simmering water for 30 minutes. Add to the ragoût, along with 1 cup of the sausage-cooking liquid and cook for 30 minutes more. (The total cooking time up to this point is about 2 hours.) Remove from the heat and cool. Remove and reserve as much of the fat that has risen to the top as possible.

7. Discard the clove-studded onion, bouquet garni, the fatty part of the salt pork, and all the bones. Separate the rinds, meats, and beans. Remove and discard the gristle and fatty parts from the meats. Strain the cooking liquid. Refrigerate the liquid, rinds, meats, and beans separately.

8. Day Three: Remove the liquid, meats, rinds, and beans from the refrigerator. Remove any remaining fat that has congealed on the top of the liquid. Place the cooking liquid, pig's feet, ham hocks, pork skin, and assorted rinds in a saucepan and simmer for 1 hour, or until fork-tender. Strain, reserving liquid and solids separately. Measure the liquid and add enough water to make 9 cups. Cool, then skim away all fat. Scrape away and discard all fat from assorted rinds. Chop all the rinds, skins, and meat solids into approximately ½-inch pieces. Set aside.

9. Prick the pork sausage and brown in 1 teaspoon of confit fat in a nonstick skillet. Pour off the fat and discard. Cut the sausage into bite-size pieces. In a large bowl, combine the sausage with the other meats. Generously season with salt and pepper. Refrigerate the mixed meats unless proceeding with the recipe.

10. Add 2 tablespoons of confit fat to same skillet used to brown sausage and heat until very hot. Brown skin side of the duck or goose confit until very crisp. Remove from pan, pat with a paper towel to remove excess fat, and cut thigh from the drumstick. You will now have 12 pieces of duck or goose. Season with pepper and cover with a damp cloth and then plastic wrap and set aside. Refrigerate if not continuing that day.

11. Later on Day Three or Day Four: Assemble the cassoulet: Spread pork rind squares all over bottom of a 7-quart wide, ovenproof enamel, earthenware, or ceramic serving dish. Cover with a layer of beans, then a layer of assorted meats (but not duck or goose confit). Combine garlic, parsley, thyme, and 1 teaspoon of pepper, and spread half over the beans. Repeat with rest of meats, then remaining herb mixture, and end with the remaining beans. Reheat cooking liquid, and pour enough over the top to cover beans. Be sure there is at least an inch of "growing space" between beans and rim of the dish. Reserve remaining liquid to baste cassoulet as it cooks. The dish can be prepared up to 24 hours ahead to this point. Leave in a cool place, or if more than a few hours, cover and refrigerate.

12. About 4 hours before serving, preheat oven to 450 degrees. Sprinkle half the bread crumbs over the beans and dot them with 2 tablespoons of fat from the confit. Set the dish in the oven and bake until a golden skin forms on top of the beans and the mixture is very hot and bubbly, approximately 30 to 40 minutes.

13. Reduce the heat to 300 degrees, and gently stir in the skin that has formed and baste the beans with a few spoonfuls of the cooking liquid. Continue to bake until another skin forms—about 30 or 40 minutes more. Repeat the process two or three more times. Continue to baste frequently to keep the beans from drying out. If you run out of cooking liquid, use more stock or water if necessary. You do not want the finished product to be dry—moist is important for a good result.

14. After the cassoulet has cooked for about 2 hours, break up the skin and press the pieces of duck or goose confit into the top layer of beans. The duck confit should remain just even with the beans' surface—indicating individual servings of confit. Sprinkle the beans and duck with the remaining bread crumbs and dot over about 3 tablespoons of the confit fat. Bake until a well-browned glaze forms on the top and the cassoulet is bubbling hot, about 20 minutes. Serve directly from the dish.

OMELETTES, MAIN COURSE SALADS, PASTA, and POLENTA

Auguste Escoffier's Old-fashioned Omelettes

Richard Olney's Warm Seafood Salad with Saffron and Curry

Wallis Simpson's Prince of Wales Salad

The Brown Derby's Cobb Salad

Robinson Family and Camille Glenn's Mixed Bean Salad with Ham and Smoky Bacon

Restaurant Dodin-Bouffant's Lamb Salad with Flageolets and Two Purées

Teresa Buongiorno's Favas and Chicory with Peppers and Sweet Onion Salad

Pellegrino Artusi's Spinach and Polenta Pasticcio

Pellegrino Artusi's Mushroom and Veal Pasticcio

Craig Claiborne's Chicken Tetrazzini

Bomba La Habana with Chicken and Potatoes

Old-fashioned Omelettes

Culinary magician and legendary restaurateur Auguste Escoffier (1846-1935) did more for the world of gastronomy than invent *Pêche Melba* and *Poires Belle Hélène*. He was the first great chef to work in restaurants rather than private homes. During his collaboration with César Ritz—in fine hotel dining rooms including both the Paris and London Ritz—he shepherded the professional kitchen out of the Middle Ages and into the twentieth century. He divided his kitchens into five interdependent geographical "stations" called *parties*. Second in command after Chef Escoffier was the *saucier*, responsible for saucing food prepared by the four other *parties*. Likewise, the *patissier* provided pastry for everyone, while the *garde-manger* assembled cold dishes and supervised supplies for the entire kitchen. Hot food came from the *entremetier* and *rotissier*. Gone was the inefficiency and duplication of non-communicating independent units. In addition, this gentle and compassionate man forbade the general brutality that had ruled kitchens for centuries, insisting that a calm workplace produced optimum results.

No less important were Escoffier's menu innovations. Ever since medieval times, grand meals had been served *à la française*; many courses—sometimes a hundred or more, both sweet and savory—were put on the table at once. The priority was an impression of great luxury rather than a harmonious combination of dishes; individual guests tasted only what happened to be within easy reach. In contrast to service *à la française*, Escoffier anticipated service *à la russe*, with the same dishes served to everyone, one after another in courses.

This Russian export was not new. Discovered by Carême a hundred years earlier, it was neither elegant nor grand enough for the times. Gradually, however, service *à la russe* did catch on, and by the time Escoffier wrote his *Livre des menus* in 1912, the number of dishes per menu had been drastically reduced. In addition, he stated that menus should allow flexibility and be appropriate for the occasion, the guests, the season, and the dining time available. Another huge first was

Escoffier's *à la carte* menu, soon to be introduced in America at Delmonico's.

Escoffier continued where Carême left off, lightening sauces and simplifying the food as well as the menu. With his admonition *"faites simple,"* Escoffier substituted a sprinkling of parsley and a few vegetables for the inedible garnishes of the previous century. He abolished the elaborate pedestals and architectural *pièces montées* of his predecessors, repeating Mallarmé's statement that "Food should look like food," not like Greek temples or jewelry or "specimens of taxidermy." Escoffier's philosophy of pared-down refinement has informed the cuisine of all who followed. Anne Willan, in *Great Cooks and Their Recipes*, states that after five hundred years, it was because of Escoffier that "quantity at last surrendered to quality, and gluttony to gourmandise."

The great chef's longstanding legacy is the groundbreaking 1903 *Le Guide Culinaire*, on a par with his brilliance in the kitchen. Five thousand recipes, written primarily for chefs of large restaurants, the *Guide* outlined his innovative ideas and principles, as new at the time as Carême in his day or nouvelle cuisine in the 1960s.

Thirty-one years later, in 1934—to please an ever-changing audience, now including a greater percentage of home cooks—Escoffier published the more manageable and compact *Ma Cuisine,* containing just half as many recipes as the *Guide.* Escoffier loved omelettes, which he described as "a special type of scrambled egg enclosed in a coating or envelope of coagulated egg and nothing else." I've chosen four that are no longer commonly prepared. The choice was difficult, as *Ma Cuisine* has twenty-eight omelette preparations and *La Guide Culinaire* a whopping fifty-seven—from the simple to the outrageous. All four are delicious and easy to make if you follow Escoffier's simple suggestions.

With omelettes, even more than with most things in life, practice makes perfect. But if you are careful not to burn your creation, it is virtually impossible to fail even the first time out. Once you get the technique down, experiment. Seasoned cooked vegetables make good fillings alone or in combination—tomatoes, onions, garlic, zucchini, asparagus, artichoke, endive, potatoes . . . the list is endless. Or try vegetables in combination with cheese and/or ham, bacon, fish, shellfish, game, and poultry. Eggs provide a blank but delicious slate.

A successful omelette depends on the fat in the pan being hot enough to set the exterior without being so hot that it toughens before the interior has cooked. Cooking lasts only two or three minutes, so be sure to have all your ingredients in place before beginning. When making more than one omelette, beat all the eggs together and then use a ½-cup measure to portion out each omelette. Serve as ready. Or if you work fast, you can keep the finished omelettes warm in a 200-degree oven. Paint with melted butter and serve.

In Escoffier's words: *"The preparation of an omelette:* Heat the butter in an omelette pan until it just begins to turn brown, this will not only give an excellent flavour to the omelette, but will also provide the required amount of heat necessary to ensure the correct setting of the eggs. Pour in the eggs, which have been well beaten until the yellow, and whites are thoroughly blended and seasoned, shake the pan and stir briskly with a fork at the same time so as to ensure even cooking. If the omelette is to be stuffed inside with a garnish this should be placed in the centre at this time and the omelette should be quickly folded, rolled into shape and turned over on to a suitable dish, then finished according to the requirements of its recipe. When the omelette is on the dish it is good practice to draw a piece of butter over it in order to make its surface glossy."

Omelette à la ménagère

Despite it being one of his most basic omelettes, containing nothing but large pasta and eggs, Escoffier claims the *Omelette à la ménagère* (Housewife's Omelette) as his favorite. The toasted, slightly chewy pasta combines with the creamy eggs to produce a divine and unexpected texture. Once you've tried it, like me, you may find the combination addictive.

Serves 1

3 eggs, at room temperature
Large pinch of sea salt
Large pinch of freshly ground black pepper
2 to 3 tablespoons unsalted butter
1 cup cooked (al dente) penne or other fairly large pasta
½ tablespoon cold butter to glaze the surface after
    cooking (optional)

1. Whisk the eggs with the salt and pepper until they are completely homogenous but not frothy.
2. Melt the butter in a heavy 9- or 10-inch omelette pan or heavy nonstick skillet set over medium-high heat. Add the cooked pasta and cook, tossing frequently, until pale gold, 3 to 4 minutes. Add the beaten eggs and cook, shaking the pan occasionally until just set, 1 to 2 minutes.
3. Slide the omelette out onto a plate and then invert back into the pan to brown the underside. This should just take about 30 seconds. Be careful not to overcook.
4. Slide the omelette onto a hot serving plate, and serve flat, cut into halves or wedges. Do not fold over. If desired, rub the top with a bit of the butter to provide a shine.

Sorrel Omelette

In spring when sorrel is abundant and at its best, treat yourself to Escoffier's Sorrel Omelette (*Omelette à l'oseille*). Sorrel is often served in combination with goose, duck, cream, sweetbreads, and fatty fish such as salmon, mackerel, and shad, as its acidity nicely balances rich foods. For the same reason, sorrel is perfect with eggs.

Serves 1

3 eggs, at room temperature
Large pinch of sea salt
Large pinch of freshly ground black pepper
2 tablespoons unsalted butter
3 to 4 tablespoons finely shredded sorrel, sautéed in
    butter until very tender
½ tablespoon cold butter to glaze the surface after
    cooking (optional)
1 teaspoon chopped fresh chervil (You can substitute
    ½ teaspoon chopped fresh tarragon or 1 teaspoon
    chopped fresh basil, or omit.)

1. Whisk the eggs with the salt and pepper until they are completely homogenous but not frothy.
2. Melt the butter in a heavy 9- or 10-inch omelette pan or heavy nonstick skillet set over medium-high heat.
3. When the butter begins to brown, add the beaten eggs. Grasp the handle of the pan and shake eggs back and forth while using a fork to stir eggs with your other hand. Hold bottom of the fork tines parallel to bottom of the pan and mix without letting the fork touch the bottom of the pan. Within about 30 seconds, curds will form and set firmly on the bottom (that is why you don't let the fork touch the bottom). Stop stirring and use the back of the fork to spread the eggs into an even circle, filling the pan.
4. With the surface still moist, add the sautéed sorrel in a stripe down the middle of the eggs.
5. Roll the omelette by tilting the pan away from you at a 45-degree angle and use the fork to coax the top third of the omelette away from the handle and down over itself to just cover the filling.
6. Have a warm plate ready, and slant the pan to at least 90 degrees. Make a second fold by sliding the omelette out

of the pan and letting it fall seam-side down onto the plate. If desired, rub the top with a bit of butter to provide a shine and garnish with chervil.

Omelette Lorraine

Chock-full of bacon and Gruyère cheese, accented with chopped chives, and enriched with a spoonful of cream, the old-fashioned Omelette Lorraine is hard to resist. The flavor combination is reminiscent of the quiche of the same name, but due to its concentrated flavor, even tastier. It is perfect for Sunday brunch.

Serves 1

3 eggs, at room temperature
2 ounces lean bacon, cooked and crumbled (Canadian bacon or flavorful ham cut into a tiny dice may be substituted.)
2 ounces Gruyère cheese, coarsely grated
1 teaspoon finely minced fresh chives
2 tablespoons heavy cream
Large pinch of sea salt
Large pinch of freshly ground black pepper
2 tablespoons unsalted butter
½ tablespoon cold butter to glaze the surface after cooking (optional)

1. Whisk the eggs with the bacon, cheese, chives, cream, salt, and pepper until they are completely homogenous but not frothy.
2. Melt the butter in a heavy 9- or 10-inch omelette pan or heavy nonstick skillet set over medium-high heat. When the butter begins to brown, add the beaten eggs.
3. As the omelette cooks, use a fork or a metal spatula to lift the edges of the omelette and tilt the skillet to allow the uncooked egg to run to the bottom. When all is an even consistency, place the stuffing in the middle and fold the omelette in half. Slide onto a warm plate and serve immediately. If desired, rub the top with a bit of the butter to provide a shine.

Chicken Liver Omelette

When you crave complex flavor but have no time for complex preparations, make this hearty omelette that can be thrown together in ten or fifteen minutes. If you have ten minutes more, consider adding a sauté of mushrooms and onions to the mix.

Serves 1

3 tablespoons unsalted butter
3 chicken livers, diced
2 teaspoons minced fresh flat-leaf parsley
Sea salt and freshly ground black pepper to taste
2 tablespoons veal demi-glace (heavily reduced veal stock), which can be purchased frozen
1 teaspoon dry white wine (optional)
3 eggs, at room temperature
½ tablespoon cold butter to glaze the surface after cooking (optional)

1. In a small skillet set over medium-high heat, melt 1 tablespoon of the butter. When the foam begins to subside, add the chicken livers, parsley, salt, and pepper. Cook for a minute, then add the demi-glace, and the wine, if using. Cook another minute or two, until very little liquid remains. Take the pan off the heat and set aside.
2. Whisk the eggs with salt and pepper until they are completely homogenous but not frothy.
3. Melt the remaining 2 tablespoons butter in a heavy 9- or 10-inch omelette pan or heavy nonstick skillet set over medium-high heat. When the butter begins to brown, add the beaten eggs.
4. As the omelette cooks, use a fork or a metal spatula to lift the edges of the omelette and tilt the skillet to allow the uncooked egg to run to the bottom. When all is an even consistency, place the cooked chicken livers in the middle and fold the omelette in half. Slide onto a warm plate and serve immediately. If desired, rub the top with a bit of the butter to provide a shine.

RICHARD OLNEY'S

Warm Seafood Salad

WITH SAFFRON AND CURRY

Having discovered Richard Olney's recipe for a warm seafood salad years ago in his cookbook *Ten Vineyard Lunches,* I've been making and gently tweaking it ever since. I replaced the original snow peas and mushrooms with julienned carrots and have added curry powder, shrimp, and extra aromatics. For a heartier salad, two cups of cubed cooked potatoes can be included in the final reheating. The dish lends itself to experimentation; substitute monkfish for the scallops, cockles for the mussels, or use the basic recipe plus the fish and clams. Or try clams, mussels, or shrimp alone. If just shrimp are used, replace the mussel cooking liquid with two cups of shrimp, shellfish, or fish stock.

When served as a summer lunch main course, no starter is required. Just pass hot baguettes and some good butter. Like Olney, who did not favor overly sweet desserts, finish the meal with a platter of French cheeses and a basket of stone fruit—plums, white peaches, apricots, and cherries. The salad makes an ideal first course at dinner whatever the season. And Olney suggests serving it with a Condrieu.

Serves 6 to 8

4 pounds fresh mussels
4 large carrots, peeled
1 large onion, peeled and minced
⅓ cup chopped shallots
1 clove garlic, peeled and minced
Several sprigs fresh thyme, or ½ teaspoon dried thyme
1 bay leaf
½ cup chopped fresh flat-leaf parsley
1 cup dry white wine
⅛ teaspoon saffron threads, crushed between your fingers
⅛ teaspoon curry powder
1 pound small shrimp, peeled and deveined
1 pound sea scallops, halved crosswise and rinsed
    in cool water
1 pound fresh squid, cleaned and bodies cut into
    ¼-inch rings
1 cup heavy cream
Sea salt and freshly ground white or black pepper to taste
Freshly squeezed juice of ½ lemon, or to taste
2 bunches frisée, shredded, or a mixture of shredded
    frisée and decorative salad leaves such as red leaf let-
    tuce, mâche, and arugula (approximately 8 cups total)
½ cup snipped chives or fresh fennel leaves—a mixture is
    even better

1. Discard any mussels with broken shells. Rinse them and soak them in icy, heavily salted water for about 45 minutes. Debeard the mussels just before cooking. Farm-raised mussels need no soaking or debearding, just a quick rinse in cool water.

2. Meanwhile, using the grater attachment of a food processor, a multi-hole citrus zester, or a sharp knife, cut the carrots into fine strips (julienne) and set aside.

3. In a large pot or saucepan, gently toss the mussels with the onion, shallots, garlic, thyme, bay leaf, parsley, and white wine. Set over high heat and cover the pot. Shake the pot frequently, and when most of the mussels are open—this just takes a few minutes—remove from the heat. Using a slotted spoon, transfer the opened mussels to a bowl, cover the pot again, and put back on the heat until the rest of the mussels have opened.

4. Transfer all the mussels and their cooking liquid to a large colander set over a large bowl. Rinse out the pan. When cool enough to handle, shell the mussels and place them in a medium bowl. Discard the shells. Spoon over a few tablespoons of the cooking liquid to keep them moist. Cover the bowl with a damp paper towel and set aside.

5. Strain the remaining cooking liquid through a fine sieve into the rinsed saucepan. Add the saffron and curry powder,

bring to a boil, and simmer for 1 minute. Add the shrimp, and as soon as they turn red, add the scallops and then the squid. Simmer until done—this should take about 3 minutes. Don't overcook. Using a slotted spoon, transfer the seafood to the bowl with the mussels.

6. Over medium-high heat, reduce the cooking liquid by half and add the cream. Continue to reduce, stirring occasionally, until the sauce is the thickness of heavy cream.

Season with salt, if needed, pepper, and lemon juice.

7. Divide three quarters of the salad greens among 6 to 8 individual soup plates. Add the remaining greens, carrots, seafood, and any accumulated juices to the sauce in the pan, stirring gently over very low heat for 1 minute. Do not let the sauce boil. Ladle the seafood with its sauce over the greens and top each portion with a sprinkling of chives or fennel.

WALLIS SIMPSON'S

Prince of Wales Salad

A sardine-lover's dream come true, this unusual salad is appreciated by my cooking students as fully as it was by the Parisian *haute monde* who ate it at the Windsor's table in the 1940s and '50s. Lemon, fennel, capers, anchovies, and sardines conjure up the Ligurian coast, while chervil and grated egg provide a soupçon of French refinement that reminds us of the original hostess. In smaller portions, this lunch main course is an ideal starter for dinner.

Serves 6

For the dressing:
5 tablespoons freshly squeezed lemon juice
1 tablespoon white wine vinegar
2 to 4 anchovy fillets, mashed
Finely grated zest of 1 lemon
Sea salt and freshly ground black pepper to taste
Pinch of cayenne pepper
2 teaspoons Dijon mustard
2 large cloves garlic, peeled and minced
2 shallots, peeled and thinly sliced
6 tablespoons extra virgin olive oil

For the salad:
12 ounces oil-packed sardines, oil wiped off, bones removed (or buy boneless), and broken or cut into bite-size pieces
1 head romaine lettuce, trimmed, outer leaves removed, and sliced very thinly crosswise before washing and spinning dry
2 large Belgian endive, sliced crosswise into 1-inch pieces
3 large bunches watercress, trimmed
1 small bunch chervil, chopped (optional)

½ cup capers
4 hard-boiled eggs, coarsely grated
4 ribs celery, sliced crosswise very thinly
1 bulb fresh fennel, trimmed, quartered vertically, and sliced crosswise paper-thin
Thin lemon slices for garnish
Fresh nasturtiums (if available) for garnish

1. Whisk together all the dressing ingredients except the oil. Wait at least 15 minutes for the salt to dissolve. Whisk in the olive oil and adjust the seasonings.

2. Place the salad ingredients in a large bowl and toss together with enough dressing to moisten and flavor. Adjust the seasoning. Garnish with lemon slices and nasturtiums. Serve right away.

Note: If you want a heartier salad, add sliced boiled potatoes and/or bite-size pieces of cooked swordfish, halibut, shelled shrimp, or cod marinated ahead of time in a bit of the dressing, if possible.

Cobb Salad

A tempting mix of chopped greens, chicken, hard-boiled egg, avocado, bacon, tomato, and Roquefort cheese, Cobb Salad—invented by and named after Bob Cobb, an owner of the Brown Derby—was the restaurant's most famous recipe. Legend has a hungry Cobb raiding the refrigerator one night, chopping up some leftovers and tossing them together with the Derby's famous French dressing. Hollywood friends in the dining room that evening—including Jack Warner and Sid Grauman—were intrigued with Bob's dinner. They loved the salad and requested it on their next visit; soon Cobb Salad was a menu fixture, one of the most sought-after salads since the discovery of lettuce.

My grandfather lived just a block from Hollywood and Vine. Growing up, I spent many Saturday afternoons lunching with him at the local Brown Derby. When I didn't order Shrimp Louie, chicken croquettes, or baked ham (the Saturday special), I ordered Bob Cobb's perfect salad. The delicate balances are just right—crunchy and soft, salty and mild, moist and dry. There was such demand for the French dressing that the restaurant bottled and sold it for home use. A real classic, and—along with Caesar, chef's, and Niçoise—one of the most famous salads of all time.

Serves 8

1 head iceberg lettuce

1 bunch watercress

1 head frisée

1 head romaine lettuce

2 pints cherry tomatoes, quartered vertically

2 whole chicken breasts (4 half breasts), poached or
    roasted, skinned, and cut into ½-inch dice

12 strips best-quality smoky bacon, cooked until crisp,
    blotted on paper towels, and crumbled

6 hard-boiled eggs, chopped

1 cup Roquefort or other crumbly blue cheese cut into
    small dice or coarsely grated

2 Haas avocados, cut into ½-inch dice (at the last minute
    so they don't discolor)

¼ cup finely minced chives

Approximately 1 cup of The Brown Derby's Old-fashioned
    French Dressing (recipe follows)

Sea salt and freshly ground black pepper to taste

1. Julienne or finely chop the iceberg lettuce, watercress, frisée, and romaine, and place in a large salad bowl.
2. Arrange the tomatoes, chicken, bacon, eggs, cheese, and avocados in 1 or 2 mounds, each attractively spaced, on top of the greens.
3. Sprinkle the chives over all.

4. When ready to eat, present the salad at the table, and toss with enough dressing to moisten and flavor. Season with salt and pepper if needed.

THE BROWN DERBY'S OLD-FASHIONED FRENCH DRESSING

Makes approximately 2 cups

½ cup red wine vinegar

¼ teaspoon sugar

Freshly squeezed juice of ½ lemon

1½ teaspoons sea salt

½ teaspoon freshly ground black pepper

1 teaspoon Worcestershire sauce

½ teaspoon English or Dijon mustard

1 small clove garlic, peeled and finely minced

1⅓ cups French (or other light) extra virgin olive oil

1. Shake all of the ingredients except the oil together in a large jar.
2. Add the oil and shake again. Set aside for at least an hour before using to allow the flavors to marry. Extra dressing can be stored in the refrigerator for at least 2 weeks.

Mixed Bean Salad

WITH HAM AND SMOKY BACON

The auspicious Kentucky pairing of Camille Glenn and her recipes with the Robinson family and their meat began in the early 1990s when Glenn—longtime food columnist for the *Louisville Courier-Journal,* cookbook author, and Louisville's preeminent caterer and cooking teacher—set out to find the best meat in town. Some of the city's most respected cooks were consulted, and all fingers pointed to Bert Robinson, a purveyor of high-end meats to award-winning restaurants and renowned chefs. First commerce and then friendship sprang up between Robinson and Glenn, who turned one hundred in October 2009. Glenn was soon using nothing but Robinson meat for her famous dinner parties; and the Robinsons, realizing early on that Glenn's recipes were the best in the South, have always consulted her or her cookbooks when preparing food for friends and for family gatherings. Like Glenn, I find Robinson meat unbeatable and use it for my own entertaining and classes whenever I can. And like the Robinsons, I've gleaned wonderful recipes from Camille's books. Well-worn copies of both *The Heritage of Southern Cooking* and *Camille Glenn's Old-fashioned Christmas* have prime spots by my stove.

Both Glenn and Robinson were raised in small Kentucky towns by food-oriented parents; and over the years, both have acquired a deep knowledge of things culinary and a serious respect for taking no shortcuts. Camille's family owned a small hotel in Dawson Springs, where as a young girl "intensely interested in food and its preparation," she hung out in the kitchen until old enough to study at Paris's Cordon Bleu. The Robinsons operated a grocery business in the farming community of Owensboro, and Bert too learned firsthand that good business depended on providing the highest-quality products to his customers at affordable prices.

This recipe for a ham, bacon, and mixed bean salad is the offspring of a long culinary friendship. My friend Ben Robinson, who now runs Robinson's Prime Reserve, got it from his father, who got it from Camille Glenn years ago when she came by to pick up a meat order. Bert asked if she had any ideas for using up abundant leftovers of Mamaw Robinson's ham. (Ben's grandmother's "secret" ham was coated in a bread crumb, brown sugar, and red wine paste before baking.) Glenn suggested adding chunks of the ham to her own warm bean and bacon salad. The Robinsons did so, taking a few more liberties along the way. The result—a harmonious combination of beans, herbs, walnuts, and smoky meats—is now a family favorite Ben makes for Sunday lunch during Robinson family-reunion weekends. He passes baskets of milk biscuits and crocks of honey-butter, and for heartier appetites, places the biscuits—toasted and buttered—on top of the salad, with a final garnish of hot poached eggs. To emulate the Robinsons, begin the meal with Kentucky Burgoo, a local specialty—mixed meats and poultry and up to ten kinds of vegetables in a rich broth. Dessert is always pie—pecan, Key lime, or Derby.

Serves 6

½ pound sliced lean smoky bacon

½ pound braised or baked ham, cut into ½-inch dice (cooked chicken, duck, or roast pork may be substituted)

1 small clove garlic, peeled and finely minced

2 cups fresh lima beans, or frozen lima beans, thawed, and/or 1½ pounds waxy potatoes such as Yukon gold or red bliss, boiled, peeled, and cut into ¼-inch slices

1¼ pounds green string beans, trimmed

1¼ pounds yellow wax beans (if unavailable, double the amount of green string beans), trimmed

8 scallions, cut into very thin rounds

¼ cup chopped fresh flat-leaf parsley

¼ cup minced fresh tarragon

¼ cup snipped fresh chives

½ cup Kentucky black walnuts (or substitute regular walnuts), broken into pieces and toasted

¼ cup sherry vinegar or cider vinegar

2 teaspoons Dijon mustard

1 tablespoon walnut oil (optional)

Up to ½ cup extra virgin olive oil

Sea salt and freshly ground black pepper to taste

1. Put the bacon in a skillet and fry until golden brown but not overly crisp. Remove the bacon, reserving the fat, and chop coarsely. Mix the chopped bacon with the ham and garlic. Set aside.

2. If using fresh lima beans, cook in boiling salted water until tender, 15 to 20 minutes. Drain well and transfer to a large salad bowl.

3. Meanwhile, drop the green string and yellow wax beans into a large pot of boiling salted water and cook until tender but still crisp, about 5 minutes. After 3 minutes, add the thawed lima beans, if using. Drain immediately. Dry the beans with kitchen towels and transfer to the large salad bowl with the fresh lima beans.

4. Add the bacon mixture to the warm beans followed by the scallions, parsley, tarragon, chives, walnuts, and potatoes, if using.

5. In a small bowl, combine the warm bacon fat (reheat if necessary), vinegar, mustard, walnut oil, if using, and enough olive oil to make ¾ cup vinaigrette. Mix thoroughly and season with salt and pepper.

6. Pour the dressing over the salad, toss, and adjust the seasoning. Serve while still warm.

Lamb Salad

WITH FLAGEOLETS AND TWO PURÉES

Boned and stuffed saddle of lamb for two—the stuffing and garnishes changing weekly—was a dinner menu constant at Dodin-Bouffant. In order to create a hollow for the stuffing, chef Bob Pritsker meticulously removed the fillets from each side of the loin, and employees begged him to include them in the staff meal. But the restaurant's "waste not, want not" mantra was strong—even in the glory days of New York circa 1978—and the Pritskers created their signature "Salade d'Agneau" around these morsels. As lamb fillets are hard to find, I suggest substituting two loin chops per person or a total of two pounds butterflied leg of lamb for the eight servings in this recipe.

Insatiable critic Gael Greene was an avid fan. Reviewing Dodin-Bouffant in *New York* magazine, she wrote, "By far their most stunning invention is lamb salad, rose pink and tender. Slices of the saddle are served still warm on green tongues of arugula in a subtle vinaigrette. With it comes a tiny hill of flageolets, purée of celery root, and something sharp and strange . . . purée of radish. And the scattered seeds that crack on your tooth are black mustard. In the writing, this may sound like a three-ring circus; in the mouth, it is dazzling and it works."

Serves 8

For the flageolets:
⅓ cup plus 2 tablespoons extra virgin olive oil
5 cloves garlic, peeled and minced
2½ cups dried flageolets, rinsed, picked over, soaked overnight in cold water, and drained
5 to 6 cups chicken stock
¼ cup snipped chives
Sea salt and freshly ground white or black pepper to taste

1. Place a large sauté pan over low heat, add ⅓ cup of the olive oil, and sauté the garlic without allowing it to color, until soft, about 5 minutes.

2. Add the flageolets and stir over medium heat for a minute or two. Add chicken stock to cover by about an inch, and bring to a simmer. Cover and cook at a bare simmer for 30 minutes. Remove the lid and continue cooking for another 30 minutes, or until the flageolets are done, adding more chicken stock if necessary. The flageolets should be tender but not soft.

3. Drain excess liquid. Dress with the chives, the remaining 2 tablespoons olive oil, and salt and pepper. Set aside.

For the radish purée:

6 tablespoons minced shallots

9 tablespoons unsalted butter

36 brightly colored radishes, trimmed and cut into
thin slices

3 tablespoons freshly squeezed lemon juice

3 to 4 tablespoons heavy cream

Sea salt and freshly ground white pepper to taste

1. In a large skillet set over medium heat, sauté the shallots in the butter until they are wilted.

2. Add the radish slices and lemon juice and continue cooking until the color of the radish skin has "bled" and the radishes are soft. This will take approximately 15 minutes.

3. Boil off any excess liquid and purée in a food processor, while gradually adding the heavy cream through the feed tube. Season with salt and pepper. Keep warm or reheat in a microwave when needed.

For the celery root purée:

2 pounds celery root, peeled, trimmed, and cut into
1-inch dice (approximately 4½ cups)

5 tablespoons unsalted butter

¾ cup heavy cream

Sea salt and freshly ground white pepper to taste

1. Blanch the celery root in boiling salted water until just tender, about 5 minutes. Drain.

2. Pass the blanched celery root through the fine screen of a food mill or purée in a food processor.

3. Dry the resulting purée in a saucepan by stirring over low heat until all excess liquid evaporates.

4. Stir in the butter and heavy cream and season with salt and pepper. Keep warm or reheat in a microwave when needed.

For the lamb:

5 lamb fillets, 2 pounds boned and buttterflied leg of
lamb, or 16 1½-inch-thick lamb loin chops

Sea salt and freshly ground black pepper to taste

2 tablespoons unsalted butter

1. Preheat the oven to 525 degrees. Pat dry whichever cut of lamb you are using and season with salt and pepper.

2. In a heavy skillet, heat the butter over high heat. Add the lamb and brown on all sides. If using the fillet, turn after 2½ minutes and cook for another 2 minutes for medium rare. If using the loin chops or butterflied leg, cook for 3½ minutes on each side for medium rare, possibly a bit longer for the leg.

3. Let rest while assembling the garnishes. As ready, transfer the lamb to a sheet pan and place the sheet in the oven.

For the greens:

16 cups arugula or mâche

½ cup walnut oil

2 tablespoons balsamic vinegar

Sea salt and freshly ground black pepper to taste

8 teaspoons black mustard seeds

Assembling the salad:

1. Just before serving, toss the salad greens with the walnut oil, vinegar, and salt and pepper.

2. Put a portion of the dressed greens in the center of each of 8 dinner plates and attractively arrange servings of each vegetable around the greens.

3. Slice the lamb fillets or leg and divide the slices among the 8 plates, laying the slices on top of the greens. Alternatively, place 2 whole chops, overlapping, on each portion of greens. Sprinkle each plate with 1 teaspoon black mustard seeds.

TERESA BUONGIORNO'S

Favas and Chicory

WITH PEPPERS AND SWEET ONION SALAD

Akin to spinning straw into gold, the Pugliese for centuries have turned basic, inexpensive ingredients into flavorful, marvelous meals. Perhaps a good lesson for our times. On my recent trip to southernmost Italy, I was taught a number of regional specialties by Teresa Buongiorno, chef of the Michelin-starred restaurant Osteria Già Sotto l'Arco, which she owns with her husband in the small town of Carovigno near the port of Brindisi.

Because their menus were dictated by poverty in times past, Pugliese farmers ate poultry or meat only once a week—Sunday at midday, and even then, primarily lamb, chicken, rabbit, and pork. Cows were needed for dairy products, and along with horses, were only eaten when old and useless for all else. The rest of the week this hearty vegetarian meal was the norm with *Fave e Cicorie* as its centerpiece. Now, however, because the region has the largest olive oil output in Italy and a burgeoning economy, this classic repast is no longer a daily mainstay.

In the past the fava bean purée was prepared in a terra-cotta container called a *pignata* and cooked directly on hot coals inside the fireplace, but a modern-day stovetop works just fine. Local supermarkets do not contain a plethora of wild chicory, but a sauté of bitter greens is a good substitute. Traditional side dishes include a platter of cut raw vegetables—fennel, cucumber, radish, carrot, and celery; a red onion salad; and a pan-fry of green peppers and cherry tomatoes—all in tasty and visually vibrant contrast to the mild, creamy favas and the soft, garlicky greens. With its varied components, this unusual and flavorful meal should appeal to even the most devoted carnivore. Like the Pugliese, be sure to set baskets of bread and dishes of almonds, olives, and olive oil on the table beforehand. And, best of all, *Fave e Cicorie* serves a crowd easily and, epitomizing *cucina povera*, costs next to nothing to prepare.

For the fava beans:
½ pound potatoes, peeled and cubed
1 pound dried skinless fava beans (may be packaged as
    split fava beans), soaked overnight in cool water to
    cover by 2 inches
½ teaspoon sea salt, plus more to taste
½ cup extra virgin olive oil
Freshly ground black pepper to taste

1. Place the cubed potatoes in the bottom of a large
saucepan. Drain the fava beans and put them on top of
the potatoes. Add enough water to cover the beans.
2. Place the pot over medium-high heat and bring to a
boil. Skim off all the foam that rises to the top, add ½
teaspoon salt, then partially cover the pan. Turn the heat
down to a high simmer and cook, stirring occasionally, for
about 1 hour, until the beans have dissolved into the
water, melded with the potatoes, and have reached the
consistency of a purée. Add boiling water if needed during
cooking to prevent scorching.
3. Stir in the olive oil and pepper. If you prefer a smoother
purée, beat in the oil with a handheld mixer, but don't
overmix or the potatoes may become gluey. Keep warm
while preparing the accompanying dishes.

For the Sweet Onion Salad:
4 large red onions, peeled, sliced paper-thin, and broken
    into rings
½ teaspoon sea salt, plus more to taste
1 tablespoon red wine vinegar
½ cup olive oil
Freshly ground black pepper to taste

1. Toss the onions with salt. Let stand at least 15 minutes, stirring occasionally, to wilt the onions.
2. Add the vinegar and toss. Then add the oil and season
with salt and pepper. If possible, make the salad at least
30 minutes before serving, stirring frequently while
waiting.

For the bitter greens:
2 pounds wild chicory, kale, dandelion greens, or
    broccoli rabe
½ cup extra virgin olive oil
Sea salt and freshly ground black pepper to taste

1. While the beans cook, rinse the greens in cool water,
then place the very wet leaves in a large saucepan over
high heat and cook them, stirring frequently, adding a
little more water if necessary to prevent scorching.
2. When the leaves are very tender, transfer them to a
colander and drain. Squeeze out the excess water, put the
greens back in the pan, and toss with ½ cup olive.
Season with salt and pepper. Keep warm while preparing
the other dishes.

For the peppers:
8 green Italian frying peppers (cubanelles or other
    mild green peppers), seeded, deveined, cut into
    ½-inch strips
3 tablespoons extra virgin olive oil
2 cups cherry tomatoes, cut in half
Sea salt and freshly ground black pepper to taste

1. Heat the peppers in a large skillet with the oil, tossing
frequently. After about 10 minutes, when they are tender,
add the cherry tomatoes.
2. Cook for 1 to 2 minutes, until the tomatoes are heated
through. Season with salt and pepper and transfer the
vegetables to a warm serving bowl.

To serve:
3 tablespoons coarse white bread crumbs fried in a little
    olive oil or butter (optional)

Place the purée on a warm platter with the sautéed
greens on top or alongside. If desired, sprinkle with the
fried bread crumbs for additional flavor and crunch.

Spinach and Polenta Pasticcio

Polenta, an inexpensive and amazingly versatile comfort food made from ground corn, can be grilled, fried, sautéed, baked, or just eaten in its natural porridgey state. Polenta imparts the taste of corn while simultaneously absorbing the flavors of the food with which it is served. Both Venice and Lombardy claim its invention, but no one knows for sure. It is certain, however, that maize arrived from the New World in the early sixteenth century, flourished on the Po River plain, and became the foundation of the northern Italian diet from the 1700s on. Southerners so identified the grain with the north that they disparagingly called the northerners *mangiapolenta*, or "polenta eaters." Only post–World War II affluence banished polenta as the region's dietary mainstay. Nonetheless, the historical importance of this corn product has not been forgotten. On the Friday before Lent, in Ponti in Italy's Piedmont region, townspeople still honor polenta, celebrating the feast of Polentone, when an enormous dish of *pasticcio di polenta*, layered with mushrooms and weighing more than a thousand pounds, is prepared and given to the poor.

Like Ponti's poor, I love casseroles where layers of polenta function much like the noodles in lasagna. Fillings can be as adventurous as your imagination allows. This version—spinach, with the addition of ricotta, spices, pine nuts, and raisins, perfectly paired with mild polenta in taste, texture, and color—is addictive. However, sautéed cabbage; a ragù of tomatoes, lentils, or dried beans; mushrooms sautéed with lots of onions and garlic; or something as straightforward as plain tomato sauce also make delicious vegetarian fillings. Meat eaters too can have a field day incorporating ragùs of beef, duck, pork, or chicken. Whatever the filling, typical proportions are three thin sheets of polenta club-sandwiching two layers of filling. Parmesan is sprinkled over all, and the dish is baked until piping hot and golden.

A small portion of pasticcio or even the spinach alone works well as a side dish to accompany roasted or grilled fish, meat, or poultry. The pasticcio is also excellent as a first course.

Serves 7 to 8

2 quarts liquid (water, vegetable stock, chicken stock, or a mixture)
2 tablespoons olive oil
Tabasco sauce to taste
2 teaspoons sea salt
Freshly ground black pepper to taste

One 1-pound bag or box unseasoned instant polenta
¼ cup heavy cream
Sautéed Spinach with Ricotta and Currants (recipe follows)
1¾ cups freshly grated Parmigiano-Reggiano cheese
1 tablespoon unsalted butter, cut into tiny pieces

To make the polenta:

1. Place the 2 quarts liquid, olive oil, Tabasco sauce, salt, and pepper in a large saucepan. Bring to a boil, lower the heat, and simmer for 2 minutes.

2. Off the heat, whisk in the polenta, a little at a time, to avoid lumps.

3. Return the pan to the heat, and simmer, stirring, for 6 minutes. If the polenta gets too thick, add more liquid.

4. Stir in the cream and simmer 1 more minute. Turn off the heat and adjust the seasonings. The polenta probably will need more salt. Let the polenta rest for 1 to 2 minutes before dividing it between two greased loaf pans. Once cool, refrigerate if not using right away.

Note: Make polenta at least 4 hours ahead to give it time to cool completely before slicing. It can be made up to 3 days ahead, cooled, covered, and refrigerated before using.

To assemble and bake the dish:

1. Use olive oil to generously grease the bottom and sides of a shallow baking dish or lasagna pan approximately 12 by 12 inches, 10 by 15 inches, or 8 by 16 inches (more or less 150 square inches).

2. Unmold the cooled polenta and cut into ¼-inch-thick slices. Cover the bottom of the greased baking dish with one layer of polenta slices. This may take some cutting and piecing, which is fine, but be sure to cover the entire surface.

3. Evenly spread half the Sautéed Spinach with Ricotta and Currants over the polenta, then sprinkle with ½ cup of the grated cheese.

4. Repeat with another layer of polenta, the rest of the spinach, and another 1 cup of cheese. Top with a third layer of polenta. Sprinkle with the remaining cheese and dot with the butter pieces. Cover with foil. Either bake right away or refrigerate for up to 24 hours. If refrigerated, bring near room temperature before baking.

5. Preheat the oven to 350 degrees. Bake, covered, for 1 hour, or until heated through and sizzling around the edges. Uncover, raise the heat to 450 degrees, and bake for another 10 minutes, or until the cheese on top is melted and beginning to color. Let sit for 10 minutes before slicing. Cut into portions and serve immediately on warm plates.

Note: There may be a few slices of polenta left over. Topped with butter and Parmesan and then broiled or toasted, they make a great snack or cocktail tidbit.

SAUTÉED SPINACH WITH RICOTTA AND CURRANTS

3 pounds fresh spinach, trimmed
5 tablespoons extra virgin olive oil
⅛ teaspoon red pepper flakes
3 medium onions, peeled and thinly sliced
4 large cloves garlic, peeled and minced
¼ teaspoon ground cinnamon
Scant ¼ teaspoon freshly grated nutmeg
½ cup pine nuts, toasted
5 tablespoons currants
1½ cups very fresh ricotta
½ cup freshly grated Parmigiano-Reggiano cheese
Sea salt and freshly ground black pepper to taste

1. Rinse spinach several times in cold water. When completely clean, place the dripping wet spinach in a large skillet or sauteuse. Cover and cook over medium heat for 3 to 5 minutes, until leaves are wilted but still bright green. Immediately turn the spinach into a large bowl of ice water to stop the cooking. Drain in a colander, squeeze out all the extra moisture, and chop coarsely.

2. Place the same skillet back over medium heat and add the olive oil and red pepper flakes. Add the onion and sauté, stirring frequently, for 10 minutes, or until golden brown.

3. Stir in the garlic and cook another 2 minutes. Add the spinach, cinnamon, nutmeg, pine nuts, and currants. Stir while sautéing for 2 to 4 minutes, until aromatic and very hot. Add the ricotta and cook for a minute or so, until heated through. Turn off the heat and toss in the grated cheese. Season with salt and pepper.

Note: The spinach can be made up to 24 hours in advance, cooled, covered, and refrigerated before using.

PELLEGRINO ARTUSI'S

Mushroom and Veal Pasticcio

Brilliant and eccentric Pellegrino Artusi was born in 1820 in a small town near Forli in the Emilia-Romagna. Thanks to his father's success as a textile merchant and drugstore owner, this only son among seven sisters grew up in comfort. As a young man working in the family business, he traveled all over Italy. At this time he developed a serious interest in food and collected much of the gastronomic lore he was later to incorporate into his magnum opus. A brutal assault on the town of Forli by a notorious Robin Hood–like brigand known as the Ferryman (an attack that left his sister Gertrude insane for the rest of her life) precipitated the family's move to Florence in 1851.

Artusi was perfectly suited to the larger world of the Tuscan capital. In just thirteen years he made enough money as an investment banker to retire and dedicate himself to intellectual pursuits. Settling into a permanent bachelorhood characterized by "a modest hedonism, an elegant wardrobe, and a real passion for food," and encouraged by friends, Artusi began compiling his collected recipes and accompanying food history. His wit, charm, and friendship combined with free professional service opened many useful doors.

Along with his housekeeper Francesco and his cook Marietta, Artusi developed and perfected the recipes in his small kitchen. As Artusi himself was "the tastemaker"—never touching a pot, pan, or kitchen utensil—all culinary tasks fell upon his two *semper fidelis*; Francesco is quoted as complaining, ". . . our master drives us crazy with his continuous experiments." These crazy-making kitchen adventures, however, led to the writing and publication of the best-selling Italian cookbook of all time, Artusi's masterpiece, *La Scienza in cucina e l'arte di mangier bene* (*Science in the Kitchen and the Art of Eating Well*).

Garibaldi was often quoted as saying, "It will be spaghetti, I swear to you, that unifies Italy." Only twenty years after Garibaldi's unification of the country, Artusi followed suit by uniting

"Italian" dishes from all parts of the emerging nation under one cover. In his long and scholarly introduction to the book, Luigi Ballerini explains that after centuries of domination by various foreign powers and the series of military campaigns and annexations that made up the Risorgimento, the people of the recently unified state shared very little, not even a common language. "From this perspective, the reclaiming of recipes, and the gastronomic ingenuity to which they bear witness, had to be motivated, at least in part, by the desire to see the newly established nation 'off to a good start.'" At the time of publication, in direct juxtaposition to contemporary cookbooks, which were written in French solely for professionals and focusing primarily on French cuisine, *La Scienza* provided recipes written in Italian for an audience of upper-middle-class Italian home cooks. An optimistic message from the author's preface states: "You need not have been born with a pan on your head to become a good [cook]. Passion, care, and precision of method will certainly suffice; then, of course, you must choose the finest ingredients . . . for these will make you shine."

In 1891, when Artusi, age seventy-one, completed his seven-hundred-page tome, he was laughed out of every publishing house he entered and in the end was driven to self-publish. He was shocked when his cautious first printing of only one thousand copies quickly sold out. There were numerous editions, and at his death in 1911, more than 200,000 copies had been sold, and they've been selling ever since. For well over one hundred years, the book has remained popular worldwide, and in Italy, *Artusi*, as it is lovingly nicknamed, is revered. Treated as an heirloom—virtually no home is without one—copies are passed down from one generation to the next.

Although *Artusi* contains 790 excellent recipes, the book promotes good taste at least as much as good cooking. The headers are filled with historical, sociological, and cultural information—sometimes wry, sometimes arbitrary, sometimes digressive, but always fascinating. Ballerini states, "Whatever else they may be, his pages read like a humorous collection of practical, naïve, and sometimes blasphemous, remarks . . . a meticulous compilation of culinary rules, means, and advice, tickled and bedazzled by a panoply of anecdotes and commentaries . . . [forming] a decidedly irresistible cocktail." Ballerini also credits Artusi with taking the first major step toward the evolution of the cookbook as a literary genre. Pellegrino opens a recipe for *spaghetti alla rustica* with a long ramble about the pluses and minuses of garlic—interesting but in no way useful when it comes to getting the spaghetti on the table. The same situation occurs in the header for Frog Soup: "Before describing the frog soup to you, I wish to say a few things about this amphibian of the batrachian order . . . the metamorphosis it undergoes is truly worthy of note. In the first part of its existence the frog can be seen darting around in the water like a fish, all head and tail . . ."

Truly exhaustive and at times a bit exhausting, even without recipes, there would be something for everyone in this cornerstone of modern Italian cookery.

In Italian, the word *pasticcio* means pastiche, jumble, hodge-podge, mess, or muddle, in addition to being a pie or casserole. In his recipe for *Pasticcio di Maccheroni*, Artusi indulges in a bit of wordplay when he suggests modifying the recipe "as you please because a pasticcio comes out well no matter how it is prepared." I have "modified" his recipe and chosen to omit the sweetbreads, cock's combs, testicles, and unlaid eggs.

In *La Scienza,* Artusi presents various pasticcio fillings, including meat, game, seafood, hare, liver, and artichoke. My favorite is this simplified version of a macaroni and meat pie popular on the tables of Ferrara's nobility beginning in the early 1700s. This flavorful mélange of pasta, celery root, tomato sauce, and a chunky meat and mushroom ragù all enclosed in a slightly sweet and lemon-perfumed crust harkens back to the Emilia-Romagna of long ago; and the pie's more elaborate cousin is still traditionally served at regional weddings to mark Fat Tuesday and on the last Sunday of Carnival before Lent.

Though a somewhat time-consuming recipe, all of its individual components can be prepared up to three days in advance and refrigerated until needed. In addition, well wrapped, the pastry, tomato sauce, and ragù can be made up to three months ahead and frozen. The dish becomes vegetarian and much simpler if you omit the ragù.

Serves 6

1½ recipes pastry for covered pies (see recipe for The Brown Derby's Seafood Pot Pie on page 51), with the addition of 1 tablespoon sugar and the grated zest of 1 lemon

1½ pounds peeled celery root, potatoes, or a mixture, cut into large chunks of approximately the same size

2 tablespoons unsalted butter or olive oil

Several tablespoons of milk, as needed

Salt and freshly ground black pepper

1 recipe Meat and Mushroom Ragù (recipe follows)

1 pound ziti or penne, cooked al dente, refreshed under cool water, and drained

Quick Tomato Sauce (recipe follows)

3 tablespoons freshly grated Parmigiano-Reggiano cheese, plus more for passing

1. Roll the dough into a very large circle, at least 17 inches. Carefully fit it into a greased 9-inch springform pan. If the dough is too soft to handle, refrigerate it until it hardens up a bit. If the dough breaks as you are working with it, just patch it back together. Let the formed dough rest in the refrigerator for at least 1 hour (longer is better) and up to 2 days. When ready to bake, preheat the oven to 400 degrees. Cover with aluminum foil, shiny-side down, weighed down with pie weights or dried beans. Bake for 20 minutes in the lower third of the oven, and then remove the weights and foil. Prick the pie crust all over with a fork, and continue to bake until the crust is deep gold, about 10 minutes more. Remove from the oven and cool or proceed with the recipe immediately while the shell is still hot.

2. While the crust is cooking, place the celery root and/or potatoes in a large saucepan of salted water. Bring to a boil, then reduce the heat and simmer until the vegetables are very tender when pierced with a fork. Drain them well and then mash them with the butter or olive oil. You should have a thick but not gloppy purée. If too thick, add milk, a tablespoon at a time, until the desired consistency is reached. Season with salt and pepper.

3. Spread a thin layer of the purée over the baked crust—either still hot or cooled. Cover with all the Meat and Mushroom Ragù, then use the remaining purée to make a final layer. The cooled dish can be refrigerated at this point for up to 24 hours. Bring to room temperature before proceeding.

4. To continue, preheat the oven to 350 degrees. Stick the ziti or penne into the purée so they stand straight up. Crowd them as much as possible so that they do not fall over and push them down into the purée, keeping the top as level as possible.

5. Pour two thirds of the Tomato Sauce evenly over the noodles, filling the pasta holes as much as possible. Sprinkle with half the cheese and bake until piping hot, 20 to 30 minutes if the ingredients were warm or hot to begin with, 40 to 60 minutes if made ahead and being reheated. Sprinkle with the rest of the cheese and serve, passing more Parmesan and the rest of the tomato sauce on the side.

MEAT AND MUSHROOM RAGÙ

Makes approximately 8 cups

2 ounces dried porcini mushrooms
1½ cups hot water
5 tablespoons unsalted butter
1 large onion, peeled and minced
2 ribs celery, minced
1 large carrot, peeled and minced
4 ounces prosciutto di Parma or boiled ham, or a mixture, minced
1 pound veal loin, cut into large chunks and coarsely ground in a food processor
½ pound lean ground beef
6 tablespoons dry Marsala
⅔ cup dry white wine
1½ cups strained porcini mushroom soaking liquid reserved from cooking the mushrooms
2 tablespoons best-quality Italian tomato paste
1⅓ cups strong chicken stock, preferably homemade

1. Rinse the dried porcinis well in cool water to remove any sand, then place them in a small bowl and cover with the hot water. Soak at least 30 minutes, or until softened. Use your hands to lift the mushrooms out of the bowl, squeezing out as much water as possible. Reserve the mushroom soaking liquid.

2. Coarsely chop the mushrooms and set aside. They can be refrigerated at this point for up to 3 days.

3. Heat the butter in a heavy 12-inch skillet over medium-high heat. Add the minced vegetables and chopped ham. Sauté, stirring frequently, until onion begins to color, about 5 minutes. Add the ground veal and beef.

4. Turn the heat up to high, breaking up chunks of ground meat and stirring to encourage even browning. A brown glaze should develop on the bottom of the pan. Take care not to burn it, as the glaze contributes important flavor to the sauce. The browning takes about 10 minutes.

5. When the meat is deeply browned, add the Marsala, reduce the heat to medium, and simmer until all the liquid has evaporated. Add the white wine and cook it off as you scrape up the brown glaze. This should take about 10 minutes.

6. Add the mushrooms, their liquid, and the tomato paste and continue to cook, stirring often, until there is no liquid left in the skillet.

7. Transfer the ragù to a large saucepan and stir in the stock. Bring to a boil over high heat, then adjust the heat so the ragù is just simmering. Cover and cook until it resembles a thick soup, 30 to 40 minutes. Remove from the heat and cool. At this point the ragù can be refrigerated for up to 3 days or frozen for up to 3 months.

QUICK TOMATO SAUCE

Makes 5 to 6 cups

1 large onion, peeled and chopped
3 tablespoons olive oil
4 cloves garlic, peeled and chopped
Two 28-ounce cans chopped or diced tomatoes (preferably San Marzano)
1 teaspoon sea salt, or to taste
Large pinch of sugar
Balsamic vinegar to taste
Freshly ground black pepper to taste

1. In a large saucepan, sauté the onion in the olive oil over medium heat for 5 minutes. Add the garlic and continue to sauté until the onion is golden.

2. Add the remaining ingredients and bring to a boil over high heat. Boil, stirring frequently, for 15 minutes. Remove from the heat and puree with a handheld blender or cool to lukewarm and purée in a blender or food processor. The sauce should not be too thick. If it is, thin with water, one tablespoon at a time.

Chicken Tetrazzini

The only thing we know with certainty about Chicken Tetrazzini is that it was named for the opera star Luisa Tetrazzini, brilliant coloratura soprano, who was born in Florence, Italy, in 1871, and began singing as soon as she could walk. After performing in the Italian provinces, Russia, Spain, and South America, this Florentine Nightingale made her United States debut in San Francisco in 1905. She was a huge success locally but did not become an international superstar until she performed in London's Covent Garden in 1907. The following year she debuted in New York and overnight was the talk of the town, commanding the highest fees and selling to standing room only.

Although some authorities believe Chicken Tetrazzini originated in the kitchens of Manhattan's Knickerbocker Hotel, and a few credit Escoffier, most agree with James Beard, who believed the dish was created for Luisa by Chef Ernest Arbogast at San Francisco's Palace Hotel where Tetrazzini was a long-time resident.

Less lucky in love than in her career, the last of her three husbands dissipated the fortune she had amassed, and her final years were marred by poverty and ill health. Her mantra at this time, repeated on numerous occasions was, "I am old, I am fat, but I am still Tetrazzini." By the time she died in Milan in 1940, she was penniless, her funeral by necessity paid for by the state.

There are many versions of this layered American casserole, the constants being pasta—usually spaghetti—mushrooms, butter, cream, Parmesan sauce, and chicken or turkey—though the poultry is sometimes replaced by tuna or another fish. Common additions are wine or sherry, stock vegetables, and toasted almonds sprinkled over the top. In the seventies I made Tetrazzini frequently—especially post-theater—as only tossing a salad and reheating the casserole were required. I usually took Vincent Price's suggestion and substituted sautéed chicken livers for the poached chicken or even used both, which I still recommend. Price gilded the lily and topped the dish with hollandaise sauce before the final gratinée. It was delicious, but in these leaner times, I prefer Claiborne's version, a bit lighter though still rich enough, moist, and delicious—which replaces the hollandaise with a light béchamel perfumed with Parmesan and sherry. The recipe scales up perfectly to feed a crowd.

Serves 6 to 8

Homemade or best-quality chicken stock to cover, approximately 5 to 7 cups

2 teaspoons sea salt (omit if your stock is salted)

1 large onion, peeled and cut into large chunks studded with 2 cloves

2 ribs celery, chopped

A few sprigs fresh flat-leaf parsley

3 cloves garlic, peeled and crushed

½ bay leaf

2 large carrots, peeled and cut into chunks

2 pounds boneless, skinless chicken breasts

7 tablespoons poultry fat or butter, plus 2 teaspoons to grease the casserole

2 cloves garlic, peeled and sliced

1 yellow onion, peeled and chopped

1½ pounds mushrooms, trimmed and sliced

Sea salt and freshly ground black pepper to taste

¼ cup all-purpose flour

8 ounces spaghetti

1 egg yolk, lightly beaten

2 tablespoons sherry, or to taste

Tabasco sauce to taste

1⅓ cups grated Parmigiano-Reggiano cheese

1 to 2 tablespoons cold unsalted butter, cut into small pieces

1. Place the chicken stock, salt, if using, onion, celery, parsley, garlic, bay leaf, and carrot in a medium-large saucepan or casserole and bring to a boil. Add the chicken breasts. If the stock does not cover them, add more until it does. Bring back to a boil, then turn the heat down so the liquid barely simmers. Partially cover and cook until done. After 10 minutes, cut into one of the breasts. It should be just barely pink in the center, slightly underdone, as it will continue to cook as it cools and when reheated later. However, if it is too underdone, cook a bit more and check again. For tender, juicy chicken, do not overcook. When ready, remove the chicken from the broth. Continue to simmer the broth, partially covered, for another 30 minutes.

2. While the broth is simmering, in a large skillet set over high heat, melt 3 tablespoons of the fat and add the sliced garlic and chopped onion. Cook until soft. Add the sliced mushrooms and salt and pepper. Stir and cook until they release their juices and then the juices evaporate, approximately 15 minutes. The mushrooms should be nicely browned. Set aside.

3. Cut the cooled chicken into large chunks. Reserve.

4. Once the stock has simmered for 30 minutes, strain it into a small saucepan. You should have 2¼ cups. Reduce or add water if you have too much or too little stock. Bring it to a boil in preparation for Step 5.

5. In a medium saucepan, melt 4 tablespoons of the fat. Add the flour and stir with a wire whisk until blended. Cook over medium heat, stirring, for 2 minutes. Add the boiling stock and whisk vigorously to avoid lumps. Continue to cook, whisking constantly until the sauce is smooth and thick. Set aside.

6. Cook the spaghetti according to package directions, drain, cool, and set aside.

7. Whisk 2 tablespoons of the simmering sauce into the beaten egg yolk and then stir the mixture back into the remaining sauce along with the sherry, chicken pieces, and mushrooms.

8. Simmer until the chicken and mushrooms are heated through, 3 to 4 minutes. Do not boil. Add Tabasco sauce, salt, and pepper. Do not underseason—this dish tastes best with plenty of salt and pepper.

9. Butter a 3- to 4-quart casserole and preheat the broiler. Evenly spread one third of the chicken mixture in the bottom of the casserole, then one third of the spaghetti on top, and sprinkle with 3 tablespoons grated Parmesan. Repeat twice more so you have 3 layers of the chicken mixture and 3 layers of the spaghetti, finishing with a spaghetti layer. Sprinkle with the remaining Parmigiano, and dot with butter.

10. Brown quickly in the broiler and serve right away.

Note: The dish can be made up to 24 hours ahead, cooled, covered, and refrigerated. To proceed, bring to room temperature. Bake, covered, in a 350-degree oven for approximately 30 minutes, until piping hot. Then proceed with Step 10, browning the casserole quickly under a hot broiler.

Bomba La Habana

WITH CHICKEN AND POTATOES

For millions of transplanted Cubans, many memories of their homeland revolve around food: the *lechón*, or roast pig, that is synonymous with Christmas Eve family dinners; the black beans served at nearly every meal; and everyone's favorite, *arroz con pollo*. Like Proust's fabled madeleine, a flaky guava pastry can instantly send the Cuban emigré back in time or ignite nostalgia for family and a lost way of life—comfort food not necessarily in its heartiness but in its ability to soothe the soul.

In old Cuba, children's birthday celebrations, christening parties, and even weddings traditionally featured a standard lunch menu. Tables on shaded terraces were spread with crisply starched and ironed white linen and then laid with plates of savory ham croquettes, pork and cornmeal tamales, sandwiches of deviled ham spread between triangles of fluffy crustless white bread, pâté-like *carne fria*, and this delicious chicken dish inspired by the mayonnaise and olive oil–sauced potato salads of Spain, the island's culinary antecedent. Even today, such fare is typical at daytime family celebrations for Cubans the world over.

My friend Raul Barreneche's Cuban-born mother, Chuchi, ate this chicken and potato combination as a young girl in 1940s Havana. Decades later, she made it for her own children's birthdays in suburban Philadelphia, and now—via Raul—has passed the recipe on to me. The original source was Nitza Villapol, who was Cuba's Betty Crocker, Julia Child, and Martha Stewart rolled into one, a household name with a popular cooking show on Cuban television in the 1950s. The program, called *Cocina al Minuto* (*Quick Cooking*), was based on Villapol's seminal cookbook of the same name. Like *The Joy of Cooking* in America, the book became a culinary bible for a generation of Cuban homemakers, codifying not only the definitive recipes of classic Cuban cookery like plantain soup, *papas rellenos*, and *ropa vieja*, but also international favorites of the era. Among the book's eight hundred recipes are Villapol's versions of osso buco, strawberry shortcake, chop suey, and Trader Vic's pork chops. In the early days of exile, such a large number of Cubans—including Chuchi—left the island with Villapol's book in hand that, especially in Miami, Nitza's version of anything was—and still is—considered the ultimate, the *sine qua non* of that particular dish.

Chuchi left Cuba in 1960, planning to return in a few months. Life and politics intervened, however, and she's never been back. Now at forty, Raul consults Villapol's recipes whenever he wants to rekindle a taste of his—and his mother's—childhood.

Despite the preponderance of cubed, boiled potatoes in this dish, Cubans refer to it as chicken salad. Americans might consider it potato salad with diced chicken; but in either case, it is comforting no matter where you were born. The parsley and chives are my additions, and I've changed Chuchi's proportions a bit. The salad is forgiving. Play with it and see what you prefer. Serve it simply mounded over lettuce on a platter or go all-out Cuban. Chuchi iced her molded salad with mayonnaise before decorating it with hard-boiled egg slices, canned asparagus, pimentos, sliced black and green olives, and canned green peas. I use fresh asparagus and fresh or frozen peas. Quite a spectacle, and with or without decor, the salad is a winner.

Serves 8

1 pound boiling potatoes, such as Yukon gold or red bliss

2½ pounds boneless chicken pieces, roasted or poached, skin removed and cut into ½-inch dice

3 hard-boiled eggs, peeled and diced

1 cup very thinly sliced celery

½ cup minced green or black olives, or a combination

1 cup frozen green peas, cooked according to package directions (be careful not to overcook)

2 crisp red apples, cut into ¼-inch dice

⅓ cup chopped fresh flat-leaf parsley

⅓ cup chopped fresh chives or scallions

2 to 3 cups best-quality mayonnaise, preferably home-made (see recipe on page 43; omit the garlic), or to taste

Sea salt and freshly ground black pepper to taste

Optional garnishes:

Lettuce (shredded iceberg would be era-appropriate)

2 to 3 cups mayonnaise for icing

Jarred red peppers, roasted red peppers, or pimentos

Pimento-stuffed green olives, cut into thin rounds

Pitted black olives, cut into thin rounds

Cooked green peas

Cooked green asparagus

2 to 4 hard-boiled eggs, sliced

Extra virgin olive oil for drizzling (optional)

1. Place the potatoes in a medium saucepan with generously salted cool water to cover. Add a heaping tablespoon of salt and bring to a boil. Lower the heat and simmer until just tender when pierced with a fork. Don't overcook, or the potatoes will not hold their shape when mixed into the salad. Drain, and when cool enough to handle, peel and cut into ½-inch dice. Cool completely before combining with the other ingredients.

2. In a large bowl, use a rubber spatula to gently fold the cooled potatoes together with all of the other salad ingredients except the mayonnaise, salt, and pepper. Add enough mayonnaise to flavor and bind the ingredients but not so much that the salad is gloppy. Adjust the seasoning.

3. Place whole lettuce leaves or shredded lettuce on a large round platter. Form the salad into a dome and use a metal spatula to spread the remaining mayonnaise over the salad to completely cover it, like icing a cake.

4. Garnish decoratively with the pimento strips, olive rounds, green peas, cooked asparagus, and egg slices. Drizzle olive oil over the top if desired.

Acknowledgments

There are many to thank. First off, it was a privilege to have worked with Eric Boman a second time. Without Eric's layout and brilliant photography, this book would have been different and certainly inferior. I am also grateful for his spot-on perfectionism, help beyond the call of duty, and close friendship.

Next I would like to acknowledge my editor and now-friend Sandy Gilbert. Her intelligence, tireless perseverance, close and thoughtful attention to detail, and sense of humor kept chaos at bay and me on track. Thank you to Charles Miers for enthusiastically agreeing to publish yet another book of mine. Lisa Queen, as always, has been an agent par excellence. I deeply appreciate her savvy, hard work, and friendship. Many thanks to another friend, Sarah Key, who stepped in and provided invaluable editorial assistance exactly when we needed it. Working with her again after so many years was a pleasure. Thanks to Miko McGinty, Rita Jules, and Eileen Moore, three additional perfectionists. Book designers do not come any better. I am grateful to the fabulous George Lang for generously supporting this endeavor. His knowledge and love of remembered dishes—as well as his enthusiasm and *joie de vivre*—are unparalleled. George, thank you once again.

I offer very special thank yous to my perfect daughters, Tess and Kate; to my aunt, Iva Hochstim; and to Engin Aiken, Steven M. Aronson, Julia Barreneche, Raul Barreneche, Michael and Ariane Batterberry, Vedat Besaran, Michael Boodro, Theresa Buongiorno, Daniel Cappello, Gray Foy, Alex Hitz, Joel Kaye, Mark and Nina Magowan, Janet Mavec, Athena McAlpine, Robert Pini, Karen Pritsker Puro, Susan Sheehan, Rosie Souza, and Jeremiah Tower.

The list of others to thank (for advice, consultation, support, a sense of perspective and humor, and just general hand-holding) is long—please forgive any omissions. Certainly to be included are: Randy Barone, George Beane, Eric Beesemyer, Pat Begley, Mary and Walter Chatham, Inigo de la Huerta, Brooke Hayward Duchin, Jim Dickson, Carol Fertig, Wendy Gray, Chris Hart, Virginia Hatley, Eleanor Jackson, Jennifer Josephy, Ray and Theo Marcus, James Marlas and Marie Nugent-Head Marlas, Adrian Nugent-Head, Tim Nugent-Head, Steve Pearlstein, Peter Schlesinger, David Smith at the New York Public Library, Sean Strub, Rose and David Thorne, Alan Wade, and Joan Witkowski. And I am grateful for the tasting done and feedback given by so many friends and students and by those who attended my long series of recipe-testing dinners.

Last, but in no way least, thank you to Naushab Ahmed of Allen Brothers and to Ben Robinson of Robinson's Prime Reserve for generously providing spectacular meat for the book's photography and recipe testing.

Bibliography

Acton, Eliza. *Modern Cookery for Private Families.* 1845. A facsimile of the first edition. East Sussex, England: Southover Press, 1993.

Artusi, Pellegrino. *The Art of Eating Well.* Toronto: University of Toronto Press, 2007.

Batterberry, Michael, and Ariane Batterberry. *On the Town in New York: The Landmark History of Eating, Drinking, and Entertainments from the American Revolution to the Food Revolution.* New York: Routledge, 1999. First published 1973 by Scribner's.

Beard, James. *Delights and Prejudices.* New York: Barnes & Noble, 1996.

———. *Love and Kisses and a Halo of Truffles: Letters to Helen Evans Brown.* New York: Arcade Publishing, 1994.

Boulestin, X. Marcel. *The Best of Boulestin: Choice Recipes of X. Marcel Boulestin; One of the World's Most Famous Chefs.* Surrey, England: The Windmill Press, 1952.

Boxer, Arabella. *A Second Slice: A Three-Tier Cookery Anthology.* London: Thomas Nelson & Sons, 1966.

Boxer, Arabella, and Jessica Gwynne. *Arabella Boxer's Book of English Food: The British Kitchen Between the Wars.* London: Hodder & Stoughton, 1991.

Brillat-Savarin, Jean Anthelme. *Real French Cooking with a Selection of Outstanding Recipes from Other Countries.* Translated by E. M. Hatt. Garden City, New York: Doubleday and Company, 1957.

The Brown Derby Cookbook, 50th Anniversary Edition, The Brown Derby International. Hollywood, California, 1976.

Carrier, Robert. *Great Dishes of the World.* New York: Random House, 1964.

Charleston Receipts. Memphis, Tennessee: Toof Cookbook Division, Starr-Toof, 1950.

Child, Julia. *Mastering the Art of French Cooking: Volume One.* New York: Alfred A. Knopf, 1961.

Choate, Judith, and James Canora. *Dining at Delmonico's.* New York: Stewart, Tabori & Chang, 2008.

Curnonsky. *Cuisine et Vins de France.* Paris: Librairie Larousse, 1987.

David, Elizabeth. *An Omelette and a Glass of Wine.* London: Robert Hale, 1984.

———. *French Provincial Cooking.* London: Michael Joseph, 1960.

de Rabaudy, Nicolas. *La Cuisine de chez Allard.* Paris: Editions Jean-Claude Lattès, 1982.

The Duchess of Windsor. *Some Favorite Southern Recipes of The Duchess of Windsor:* New York: Gramercy Publishing Co., 1942.

Edwards, John. *The Roman Cookery of Apicius:* London: Random House, 1988.

Escoffier, Auguste. *The Escoffier Cookbook.* New York: Crown Publishers, 1941.

———. *Ma Cuisine.* Translated by Vyvyan Holland. London: Hamlyn, 1965.

———. *Memories of My Life.* Translated by Laurence Escoffier. New York: Van Nostrand Reinhold, 1997.

Field, Michael. *Michael Field's Cooking School.* New York: Holt, Rinehart, and Winston, 1965.

Filippini, Alexander. *The International Cook Book.* Garden City, New York: Doubleday, Page & Company, 1911.

Fisher, M.F.K. *An Alphabet for Gourmets.* New York: North Point Press, Farrar, Straus, and Giroux, 1954.

Fizdale, Robert, and Arthur Gold. *The Gold and Fizdale Cookbook.* New York: Random House, 1984.

Fowler, Damon Lee. *Classical Southern Cooking: A Celebration of the Cuisine of the Old South.* New York: Crown Publishers, 1995.

Girardet, Fredy. *The Cuisine of Fredy Girardet.* Translated and annotated by Michael and Judith Hill. New York: William Morrow and Company, 1982.

———. *Emotions Gourmandes.* Paris: Favre, 2000.

Goodwin, Betty. *Chasen's: Where Hollywood Dined; Recipes and Memories.* Santa Monica, California: Angel City Press, 1996.

———. *Hollywood du Jour: Lost Recipes of Legendary Hollywood Haunts.* Santa Monica, California: Angel City Press, 1993.

Grigson, Jane. *Good Things.* London: Penguin Books, 1973.

———. *Jane Grigson's Fruit Book.* London: Penguin Books, 1982.

Hovis, Gene. *Gene Hovis' Uptown Down Home Cookbook:* New York: Rebus, 1993.

Jones, Judith. *The Tenth Muse: My Life in Food.* New York: Alfred A. Knopf, 2007.

Kaspar, Lynne Rossetto. *The Splendid Table.* New York: William Morrow and Company, 1992.

Kelly, Ian. *Cooking for Kings: The Life of Antonin Carême, the first Celebrity Chef.* London: Short Books, 2003.

Knopf, Mildred O. *The Perfect Hostess of Today.* New York: Alfred A. Knopf, 1950.

Lang, George. *Lang's Compendium of Culinary Nonsense and Trivia.* New York: Clarkson N. Potter, 1980.

Larousse Gastronomique: The World's Greatest Culinary Encyclopedia. New York: Clarkson Potter, 2001.

Liebling, A. J. *Between Meals: An Appetite for Paris.* 1959. A facsimile of the first edition. New York: North Point Press, 1986.

Margittai, Tom, Paul Kovi, and Josef Renggli. *The Four Seasons Cookbook.* New York: Simon and Schuster, 1980.

Médecin, Jacques. *Cuisine Niçoise: Recipes from a Mediterranean Kitchen.* Hardmondsworth, England: Peguin Books, 1983. Originally published as *La Cuisine du Comté de Nice* (Paris: Juilliard, 1972).

Menkes, Suzy. *The Windsor Style.* Topsfield, Massachusetts: Salem House Publishers, 1988.

Mitchell, Jan. *Luchow's German Cookbook.* Garden City, New York: Doubleday & Company, 1952.

Nignon, Edouard. *Éloges de la Cuisine Française.* Paris: Francois Bourin, 1992.

Norman, Barbara. *The Russian Cookbook.* New York: Bantam Books, 1970.

Oliver, Raymond. *La Cuisine.* Translated and edited by Nika Hazelton with Jack Van Bibber. New York: Tudor Publishing Company, 1969.

Olney, Richard. *The French Menu Cookbook.* Boston: David R. Godine, 1970.

———. *Ten Vineyard Lunches.* New York: Interlink Books, 1988.

Orsenna, Erik. *L'Atelier de Alain Senderens: Les Maîtres de la Gastronome.* Paris: Hachette Livre (Hachette Pratique), 1997.

Paddleford, Clementine. *How America Eats.* New York: Charles Scribner's, 1960.

Pellaprat, Henri-Paul. *Modern Culinary Art: French and Foreign Cookery.* Paris: Jacques Kramer, 1950.

Point, Fernand. *Ma Gastronomie.* Wilton, Connecticut: Lyceum Books, 1974.

Price, Mary, and Vincent Price. *A Treasury of Great Recipes: Famous Specialties of the World's Foremost Restaurants Adapted for the American Kitchen.* New York: Ampersand Press, 1965.

Ranhofer, Charles. *The Epicurean: Part One.* Whitefish, Montana: Kessinger Publishing, 2004.

———. *The Epicurean: Part Two.* Whitefish, Montana: Kessinger Publishing, 2004.

Ritz, Marie Louise. *César Ritz: Host to the World.* Philadelphia: J. B. Lippincott Company, 1938.

Rombauer, Irma, Marion Rombauer Becker, and Ethan Becker. *The All New, All Purpose Joy of Cooking.* Rev. ed. New York: Scribner, 1997. First published 1931 by Simon and Schuster.

Rouff, Marcel. *The Passionate Epicure.* New York: The Modern Library, 2002.

Roux, Michel. *Sauces: Sweet and Savory, Classic and New.* New York: Rizzoli International Publications, 1996.

Senderens, Alain. *The Table Reckons.* New York: Farrar, Straus, and Giroux, 1993.

Smith, Delia. *Delia Smith's Christmas.* New ed. London: BBC Books, 1994.

Stevens, Patricia Bunning. *Rare Bits: Unusual Origins of Popular Recipes.* Athens, Ohio: Ohio University Press, 1998.

Stewart-Gordon, Faith, and Nika Hazelton. *The Russian Tea Room Cookbook.* New York: Perigree Books, The Putnam Publishing Group, 1981.

Taylor, John Martin. *Hoppin' John's Lowcountry Cooking.* New York: Bantam Books, 1992.

Thomas, Lately. *Delmonico's: A Century of Splendor.* Boston: Houghton Mifflin Company, 1967.

Toklas, Alice B. *Aromas and Flavors of Past and Present.* New York: Lyons Press, 1996.

———. *The Alice B. Toklas Cookbook.* A facsimile of the first edition. New York: Harper and Row, 1954.

Volokh, Anne. *The Art of Russian Cuisine.* New York: Collier Books, Macmillan Publishing Company, 1983.

von Bremzen, Anya and John Welchman. *Please to the Table.* New York: Workman Publishing, 1990.

Wechsberg, Joseph. *Blue Trout and Black Truffles: The Peregrinations of an Epicure.* Chicago: Academy Chicago Publishers, 1985.

———. *Dining at the Pavillon.* Boston: Little, Brown and Company, 1962.

Willan, Anne: *Great Cooks and Their Recipes: From Taillevent to Escoffier.* London: Pavilion Books Limited, 1995.

Wolfert, Paula. *The Cooking of Southwest France.* Garden City, New York: The Dial Press, 1983.

Index

Conversion Chart *(All conversions are approximate.)*

LIQUID CONVERSIONS

U.S.	Metric
1 tsp	5 ml
1 tbs	15 ml
2 tbs	30 ml
3 tbs	45 ml
¼ cup	60 ml
⅓ cup	75 ml
⅓ cup + 1 tbs	90 ml
⅓ cup + 2 tbs	100 ml
½ cup	120 ml
⅔ cup	150 ml
¾ cup	180 ml
¾ cup + 2 tbs	200 ml
1 cup	240 ml
1 cup + 2tbs	275 ml
1¼ cups	300 ml
1⅓ cups	325 ml
1½ cups	350 ml
1⅔ cups	375 ml
1¾ cups	400 ml
1¾ cups + 2 tbs	450 ml
2 cups (1 pint)	475 ml
2½ cups	600 ml
3 cups	720 ml
4 cups (1 quart)	945 ml (1,000 ml is 1 liter)

WEIGHT CONVERSIONS

U.S./U.K.	Metric
½ oz	14 g
1 oz	28 g
1½ oz	43 g
2 oz	57 g
2½ oz	71 g
3 oz	85 g
3½ oz	100 g
4 oz	113 g
5 oz	142 g
6 oz	170 g
7 oz	200 g
8 oz	227 g
9 oz	255 g
10 oz	284 g
11 oz	312 g
12 oz	340 g
13 oz	368 g
14 oz	400 g
15 oz	425 g
1 lb	454 g

OVEN TEMPERATURES

°F	Gas Mark	°C
250	½	120
275	1	140
300	2	150
325	3	165
350	4	180
375	5	190
400	6	200
425	7	220
450	8	230
475	9	240
500	10	260
550	Broil	290

First published in the United States of America in 2010
by Rizzoli International Publications, Inc.
300 Park Avenue South
New York, New York 10010
www.rizzoliusa.com

©2010 Gail Monaghan

Photographs ©2010 Eric Boman

Project Editors: Sandra Gilbert and Sarah Key
Art Direction: Eric Boman
Designer: Miko McGinty, Inc.
Typesetting: Tina Henderson

2010 2011 2012 2013 / 10 9 8 7 6 5 4 3 2 1

Printed in Singapore

ISBN: 978-0-8478-3392-4

Library of Congress Control Number: 2010927319